REMBERT E. STOKES LEARNING RESOURCES CENTER
WILBERFORCE UNIVERSITY
WILBERFORCE, OHIO 45384

TECHNOLOGY AND HANDICAPPED PEOPLE

TECHNOLOGY AND HANDICAPPED PEOPLE

Office of Technology Assessment
Congress of the United States

Springer Publishing Company
New York

Published in 1983 by:

Springer Publishing Company, Inc.
200 Park Avenue South
New York, New York 10003

ISBN 0-8261-4510-8
Library of Congress Catalog Card Number 82-600546
Printed in the United States of America
All rights reserved.

> **OTA Reports** are the principal documentation of formal assessment projects. These projects are approved in advance by the Technology Assessment Board. At the conclusion of a project, the Board has the opportunity to review the report but its release does not necessarily imply endorsement of the results by the Board or its individual members.

Contents

OTA Project Staff and Publishing Staff..................vii
Foreword by John H. Gibbons......................ix

Chapter	Page
1. Introduction and Summary	3

Part One: Impairments, Disabilities, and Handicaps

2. Definitions and Demographics.....................	19
3. Assessing Disabilities and Planning Services	27
4. Conclusions From Part One.....................	43

Part Two: Technology

5. Technology and Its Appropriate Application	51
6. Research and Development	59
7. Evaluation of Technologies	75
8. Diffusion and Marketing of Technologies	87
9. Delivery, Use, and Financing of Technologies	101
10. Developing and Using Technologies: Conclusions From Part Two	129

Part Three: Resource Allocation

11. Resource Allocation: Issues and Conclusions	139

Part Four: Policy Options

12. Policy Options	161

Appendixes	Page
A. Method of the Study	185
B. Legislative Overview	187
C. Glossary of Acronyms, Glossary of Terms, Acknowledgments, Health Program Advisory Committee Members	190
D. Public Outreach Survey	196
References.....................	205

OTA Project Staff—Technology and Handicapped People

Joyce C. Lashof* and H. David Banta,** *Assistant Director,*
Health and Life Sciences Division, OTA

H. David Banta* and Clyde J. Behney,** *Health Program Manager*

Clyde J. Behney, *Project Director*
Anne Kesselman Burns, *Analyst*
Chester Strobel, *Analyst*
Arthur F. Kohrman, *Congressional Fellow*
Judith E. Randal, *Congressional Fellow*
Kerry Britten Kemp, *Editor*

Virginia Cwalina, *Administrative Assistant*
Nancy L. Kenney, *Secretary*†
Lorraine Gerbil Ferris, *Secretary*††
Michael P. Hughes, *Secretary*
Mary E. Harvey, *Secretary*

Special Consultants

Stephen Chitwood, *George Washington University*
Marvin Kornbluh, *Congressional Research Service*
Mark Ozer, *George Washington University School of Medicine*

Principal Contractors

Richard Beinecke, *Institute for New Challenges*
Nancy Carlson, *Michigan State University*
Candis Cousins, *Wright Institute*
Leonard Duhl, *University of California, Berkeley*
Kent Hull, *Michigan State University*
Tom Joe, *National Opinion Research Center, University of Chicago*
Sharon Lansing, *Management Instruction Resources*
Martha Ross Reddan, *American Association for the Advancement of Science*
Jeffrey Rubin, *Rutgers University*
Sally Shannon, *Washington News Associates*
Ellen Smith, *Georgetown University*
Virginia Stern, *American Association for the Advancement of Science*
Kenneth Warner, *University of Michigan*

OTA Publishing Staff

John C. Holmes, *Publishing Officer*

John Bergling   Kathie S. Boss   Debra M. Datcher   Joe Henson

---
*Until December 1981.
**From December 1981.
†Until September 1981.
††Until January 1982.

Foreword

Technology exerts a powerful influence over the lives of everyone, making life easier, more fulfilling, but sometimes more painful and frustrating. This statement is especially true for people with disabilities. The appropriate application of technologies to diminishing the limitations and extending the capabilities of disabled and handicapped persons is one of the prime social and economic goals of public policy.

The Federal Government is deeply involved in programs that affect the development and use of technologies for disabilities. Programs cover research and development, marketing, provision and financing of technologies, civil rights and their enforcement, employment, transportation, health care, income maintenance, and independent living, to name only a few categories.

Congress and other institutions have become increasingly interested in questions of how well programs that directly or indirectly develop technologies and support their use have been performing. Concerns have been raised about consistency of objectives, conflicting incentives, and lack of appropriate distribution of technologies.

The Senate Committee on Labor and Human Resources requested the Office of Technology Assessment (OTA) to conduct a study of technologies for handicapped individuals. OTA and the requesting Committee both recognized the extremely broad and complex range of issues that could be addressed in such a study. Therefore, OTA conducted a planning study. Using the results of that study, OTA prepared a proposal for a full assessment on technology and handicapped people, which was approved by the Technology Assessment Board in September 1980.

The study examined the specific factors that affect the research and development, evaluation, diffusion and marketing, delivery, use, and financing of technologies directly related to disabled people. The problems and processes of the development and use of technologies were analyzed in the context of societal allocation of resources and the setting of goals for public policy. The study concentrated on two critical matching processes: between technological needs and technological capabilities; and between allocation goals or intentions and resource capabilities.

As is the case for all OTA assessments, this study was guided by an advisory panel, chaired by Dr. Daisy Tagliacozzo. In addition, a large number of other consultants, contractors, and reviewers contributed significantly. We are grateful for their many contributions. As with all OTA reports, however, the content is the responsibility of the Office and does not constitute consensus or endorsement by the advisory panel or by the Technology Assessment Board.

JOHN H. GIBBONS
Director

1.
Introduction and Summary

...It is far more expensive to continue handicapping America than it would be to begin rehabilitating America. Keeping disabled people in dependency is costing us many times more than would helping them to independence.

—*Frank Bowe*

Contents

	Page
Study Boundaries	5
Organization of the Report	6
Summary	7
Technology	9
Resource Allocation	13
Policy Options	14

FIGURE

Figure No.	Page
1. Organization of the Report	6

1. Introduction and Summary

Many people have significant limitations in their ability to perform one or more important life functions. These limitations either are present from birth or result from injury, disease, or aging. They often result in disability and, less often but still commonly, in handicaps. Whether a disability becomes a handicap depends on the interaction of the disabled person with the physical and social environments surrounding that person, and many other factors. Technology is one of those other factors. This report is about technology, handicaps, and the ways in which technology may be used to keep impairments from becoming disabilities and disabilities from becoming handicaps. It is about the processes involved in developing and distributing technologies and about the governmental and social role in directing those technological processes to assure the appropriate distribution of technology. The report's major conclusion is that **despite the existence of numerous important problems related to developing technologies, the more serious questions are social**

Photo credit: Barry Corbet. Courtesy of North American Reinsurance Corp.

Sports and physical activity are an important part of the lives of all people. Technologies, such as special wheelchairs or sound-emitting baseballs, are often used to allow the fuller participation of disabled people. Mary Wilson, shown above, believes that sports builds self-esteem and confidence, and improves attitudes toward and among disabled people

ones—of financing, of conflicting and ill-defined goals, of hesitancy over the demands of distributive justice, and of isolated and uncoordinated programs.

The influence of technology is felt in nearly every dimension of the lives of disabled people and in policies relating to disabilities. In some cases, technology is the cause of impairments, disabilities, and handicaps. Industrial accidents, adverse drug reactions, and automobile injuries illustrate this. In other instances, technology, especially medical technology, can eliminate or reduce impairments and keep them from becoming disabilities. Knee implants and prescription eyeglasses are examples of medical technologies designed to do this. Furthermore, technology is used to facilitate "mainstreaming" in education, to prepare disabled people for employment or reemployment and to adapt the tasks and physical sites of jobs to the capabilities of disabled persons, and to create a controllable home environment. It is also used extensively to prevent disabilities from becoming handicaps—e.g., making transportation systems and accommodations accessible. Technology enters the lives of disabled people in ways that people without disabilities may consider mundane—e.g., in the form of special utensil attachments or uniformity of traffic light bulb placements. Yet even these types of technologies are far from mundane. They may fulfill important needs and, when applied appropriately, may make life easier, safer, and more fulfilling for disabled and nondisabled people alike.

The state of technological capability in part determines what legislation and regulations are possible. It very clearly affects their implementation. The Federal and State Governments have created dozens, perhaps hundreds, of programs that relate to the "needs" of disabled persons. At the Federal level, with which this report is most concerned, there are programs (and agencies) concerned with research, income maintenance, health care, education, transportation, housing, independent living . . . the list continues. An overview of much of the primary legislation for these programs is presented in appendix B. Many of the programs are described in the main body of this report, especially in chapter 9. It is important to understand the goals and operations of these programs, because not only are they affected by the state of technology, they in turn very much affect the development and use of technologies.

Increasingly, attention is being focused on how to effectively and efficiently implement the laws and programs that are already in place rather than on the passage of additional laws or establishment of new programs. The State and Federal involvement continues to lack a comprehensive, responsive, and coordinated mechanism to administer existing laws in the disability area. The volume, diversity, and often contradictory goals of many of the initiatives have tended to produce an administrative "gridlock," where movement of any kind, in any direction, is increasingly difficult. Other byproducts of this Federal-State blend of intervention and action are inconsistent definitions of "disability" in the laws and confusing payment or jurisdictional problems resulting from the definitional issues.

This report presents the results of a study requested by the Senate Committee on Labor and Human Resources. To support its broad responsibilities in the area of disabilities, the committee asked OTA to take a comprehensive look at the role played by technology in that area, identify technology-related problems, and suggest policy options for congressional consideration.

Congress and the executive agencies must create and implement policies that are of various natures: Some policies are concerned with broad questions of social goals, while others are directed at more narrowly defined objectives. Discussions with congressional staff, executive branch agency personnel, the advisory panel to this study, and other experts convinced OTA that in the area of disability-related technology, most of the focus has been on the latter. Accordingly, OTA decided that a study approach that first mapped the overall policy field, paying special attention to the connections between the individual parts, was necessary. Then, specific technology-related processes and problems were analyzed and broken down into manageable questions. Finally, and most important, the specific analytical information was synthesized in the context of broader social questions.

The study concentrated on specific problems by examining the development and use of technology as a lifecycle process—a complex flow of ideas and technologies from conception, through research and development (R&D), through diffusion (including marketing where appropriate), to delivery and use. For each of these areas, OTA examined the decisionmakers and the influences on them, the other relevant parties at interest, and the status of the area—including problems and missed opportunities. This flow was examined against a backdrop of appropriate development and use of technology. And this backdrop in turn was analyzed in relation to the demands of and influences on resource allocation processes. These last two steps were a process of synthesis—a combining of the more specific information gathered with information on broader goals and methods of decisionmaking. Policy options were generated from both the specific analyses of problems and from the more systems-oriented activities.

STUDY BOUNDARIES

OTA uses a broad definition of technology: the practical application of organized bodies of knowledge. Such a definition covers both hardware and process technology. The present study, however, limits the definition of technologies, so that the focus is on technologies that are intended for and applied to individuals. Broader technologies, such as transportation systems, are covered in this report only in the context of program and societal-level examination of costs and benefits—that is, the resource allocation and decisionmaking framework.

The study's involvement in certain disabilities and handicaps, as defined above and as expanded on in Part One, has been tempered by pragmatism. For example, chronic diseases often lead to major limitations in significant life functions; the study does not ignore issues related to chronic disease, but has tried to avoid becoming too involved with medical issues that are not substantially related to technology and the functional disabilities that stem *from* chronic illness. Similarly, the aging process often carries with it a gradual lessening of functional abilities in various areas; such disabilities are covered, but only as part of the central theme of handicaps. Admittedly, it is difficult and often impossible to separate issues related to aging from issues directly related to disabilities. Some aspects, however, are clearly outside of the study boundaries. Others will be of the same generic policy implications as more directly handicap-related issues and thus can be covered profitably. In effect, the staff has tried to exercise common sense and make boundary decisions as the study required.

Prevention of impairments, disabilities, and handicaps is covered only briefly. The issues involved in a full-scale inclusion of prevention technologies (e.g., highway safety technologies, prenatal screening and diagnosis, diet) are of such magnitude that they deserve attention on their own. Their importance should be recognized and they should occupy a high priority in policy research agendas. To illustrate some of the issues regarding prevention, a case study on passive restraint systems in automobiles is being issued as a separate background paper.

This report was prepared during a time of uncertainty regarding Federal block grants to the States for disability and other social programs.* Whether substantial numbers of these programs will become block grant programs in fiscal year 1983 is unclear, but the major conclusions and most of the options of this study will not be greatly affected because development and use of technologies will most likely still be guided by much the same forces as at present. The conclusions regarding the lifecycle of technology and assuring appropriate development and use should be affected very little by block granting. It is possible that there would be substantial positive effects if the States organize their use of the block grants around a comprehensive approach to delivering and financing technologies and services. The ma-

---

*The brief discussion concerning the possible effects of block granting refers to the use of block grants as opposed to the use of categorical grants or programs. It does not refer to the possibility of a 25 percent across-the-board cut in grant funds, which would certainly affect the *use* of technologies by disabled persons.

terial on resource allocation, of course, may have to be viewed in the context of a different set of decisionmakers, but the generic issues would remain essentially the same.

ORGANIZATION OF THE REPORT

The rest of this chapter presents a summary of the report and briefly lists the policy options. The body of the report is then organized into four parts. The relationship of the parts and the individual chapters to one another is shown in figure 1.

Figure 1.—Organization of the Report

Part I: Disabilities
- Ch 1: Introduction and Summary
- Ch 2: Definitions and Demographics
- Ch 3: Disability Identifying and Planning
- Ch 4: Conclusions

Part II: Technology
- Ch 5: Technology and Appropriate Application
- Ch 6: Research and Development
- Ch 7: Evaluation
- Ch 8: Marketing and Diffusion
- Ch 9: Delivery, Use, and Financing
- Ch 10: Conclusions

Part III: Allocating Resources
- Ch 11: Resource Allocation

Part IV: Policy Options
- Ch 12: Policy Options

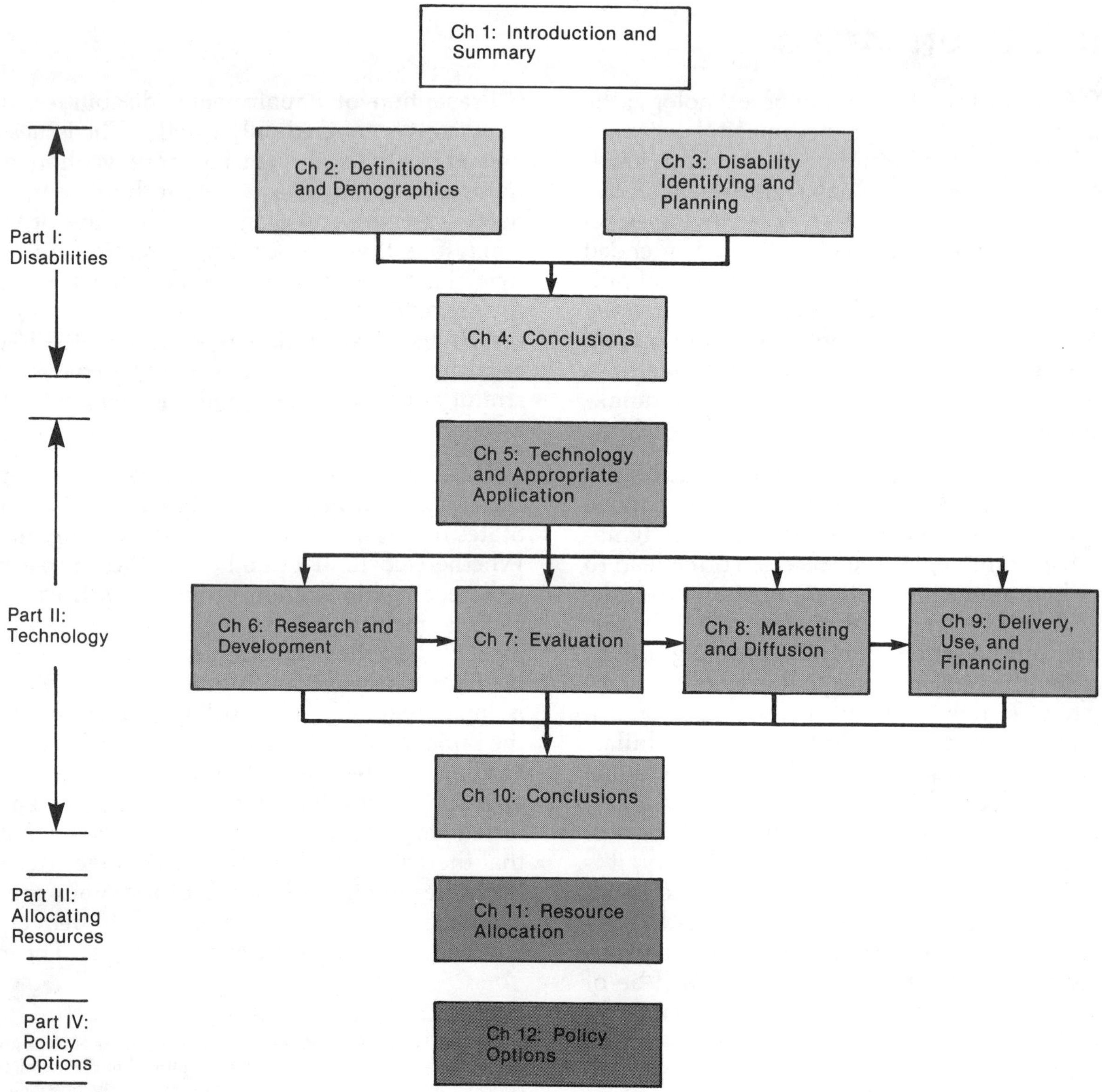

SOURCE: Office of Technology Assessment.

Part One provides information on impairments, disabilities, and handicaps. Chapter 2 provides definitions and a discussion of the implications of definitions. It also covers the problems of demographic information on disabilities and handicaps. The third chapter presents the processes of identifying impairments, disabilities, and handicaps, assessing those characteristics, and developing individual plans for reducing them. The goal of Part One is to provide background information for the examination of technology-related issues. Chapter 4 sets out conclusions from Part One.

Part Two presents chapters on the technology lifecycle and the concept of appropriate technology. Chapter 5 covers the elements that should be part of a framework for planning the appropriate development and use of technologies. Chapters 6 through 9, respectively, address R&D, evaluation, diffusion and marketing, and financing and use of technologies. The final chapter of Part Two contains conclusions on the development and use of technology.

Because many of the critical problems of the appropriate use of technology are financial and social ones, Part Three then moves to questions of resource allocation. Chapter 11 first presents a brief historical sketch of resource allocation in relation to disabilities. The main part of the chapter then discusses a series of critical issues of resource allocation, including conclusions regarding resource allocation and its relationship to technology development and use. It also discusses a number of elements of decisionmaking that might improve the process of allocating resources.

Part Four presents the policy options of the study.

Appendix A describes the method used by OTA to conduct the study and lists the background papers published as separate volumes. Appendix B is a brief overview of pertinent legislation. Appendix C contains the acknowledgments, the membership of the Health Program Advisory Committee, a glossary of acronyms, and a glossary of terms. Appendix D is a description of a public outreach survey used by OTA to identify problems and opportunities related to disability policy.

A series of case studies was used to provide specific examples of issues and problems. The report will make reference to the case studies throughout. The full cases themselves are printed in a separate volume of background papers.

In addition, a summary booklet is available. It contains information similar to the following two sections, summary and policy options.

SUMMARY

What constitutes an impairment, a disability, or a handicap? OTA's approach to definitional issues begins with the idea that society defines, implicitly, a population of people with "typical" functional ability. In contrast, society defines those who cannot perform one or more life functions within the broad range of typical as "disabled" or "handicapped."

There are many possible definitions of the terms "handicap" and "disability." Definitions are important because they affect the methods for identifying, and actual identification of, people in need of assistance. OTA found that it is most accurate to use the phrase "having a disability" in describing a person with some type of functional limitation, given no specific background information.

A "handicap" has to be specified within its environmental and personal contexts. Disabilities and handicaps arise from impairments, which are the physiological, anatomical, or mental losses or "abnormalities" resulting from accidents, diseases, or congenital conditions. Generally, an impairment results in a disability when a generic or basic human function such as eating, speaking, or walking is limited. It results in a handicap when the limitation is defined in a socially, environmentally, or personally specified context, such as the absence of accessible transportation to take the disabled people to work.

Technology for disabled people plays the role of improving the fit between individuals and their environments. By making a distinction between "disability" and "handicap," OTA recognizes the necessity of studying both individuals and the environments in which they function.

Another critical issue, closely related to definitions, is that of demographics—the numbers and distribution of disabled or handicapped people. In large part because impairments and disabilities are not as objectively measurable as is desirable and because handicaps may change depending on their context, there is no dependable count of the total number of disabled or handicapped persons. Nevertheless, considerable time is spent by researchers and various groups in making such estimates. Some of these estimates range as high as 45 million, including more than 10 million children. Typical lower range estimates are from 15 million to 25 million people. Higher numbers may reflect and attempt to count people with impairments; lower ones may be reflecting attempts to count people with disabilities or handicaps. For example, one study has estimated that approximately 12 percent of children have impairments but that only about 3.9 percent have a limitation of activity (see ch. 2).

Estimates of the number of people with disabilities are plagued by practical as well as conceptual problems. There is double counting of some people with more than one disability, underreporting of some disabilities (in part due to the stigma attached to being included on a list of disabled people), overcounting by organizations seeking to make a strong case for the extent of

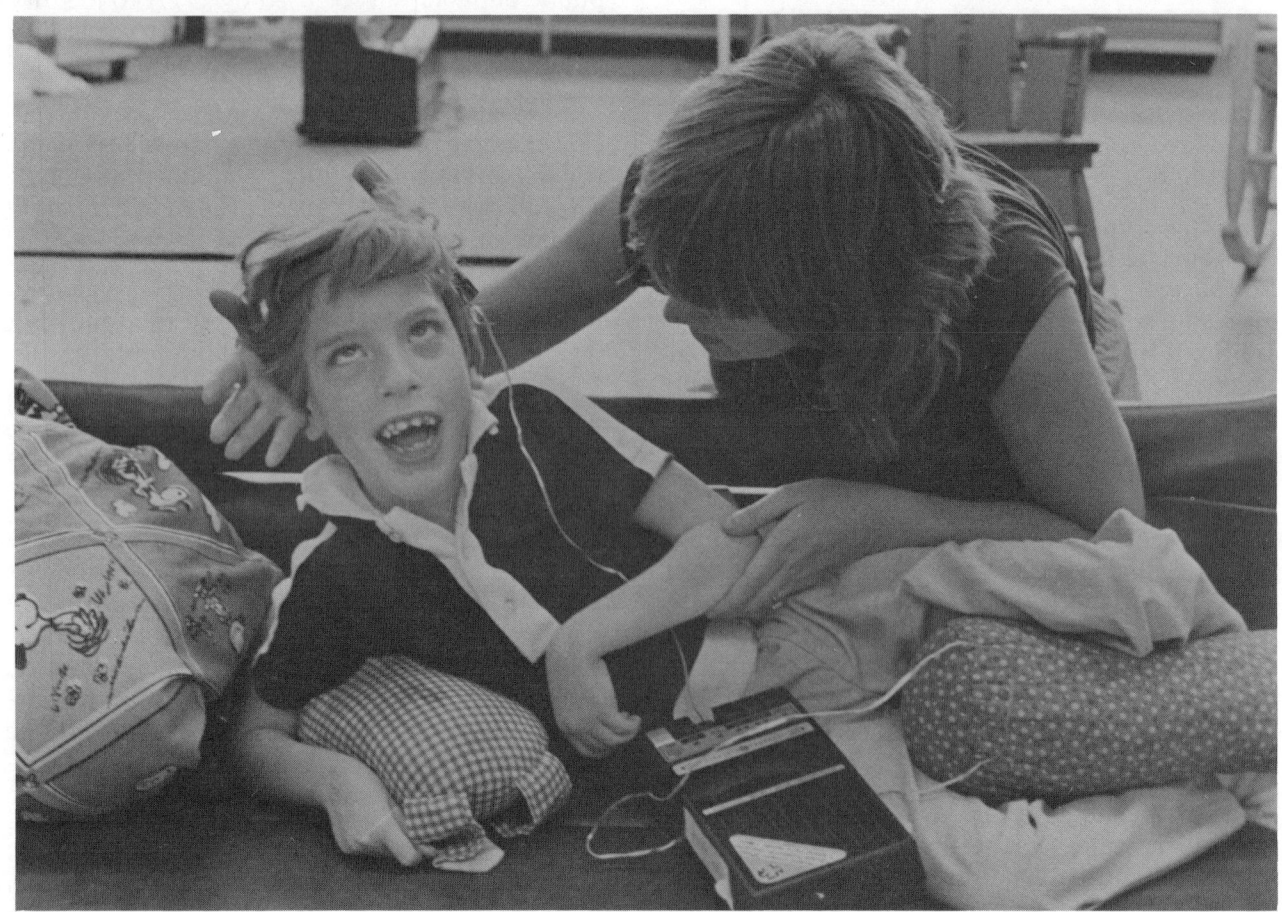

Photo credit: Provided to OTA by Pat Berilgen, Great Oaks Center, Silver Spring, Md.

This photograph shows Pat Berilgen assisting Danny Naylor in the use of a mercury head switch. The head switch activates the music on the tape recording when Danny holds his head in proper position. This training is used to give a person greater control over the use of muscles and nerves to position the head

a particular disability, and incomplete counting of some disabled people, particularly those in institutions. A perhaps more important problem with reported counts is that such counts usually do not take into account the severity of the functional impairment reported. Agencies and organizations who attempt to identify populations needing services should be very careful in designing surveys so as to take into account severity and functional status as well as type of disability and handicap.

Basic to the development and use of appropriate technology are the procedures by which disabilities and handicaps are identified, goals for their amelioration established, and resources to meet the goals expended. The planning and assessment methods used under three Federal programs—vocational rehabilitation services, services for developmentally disabled persons, and special education services—are examined in this report as a potential management information system in order to analyze their effectiveness and efficiency in aiding or determining the appropriate use of resources for modifying handicapping and disabling conditions.

To determine the effectiveness of planning and assessment methods, it is necessary to examine the degree to which data collected meet the needs of Congress and the Federal agencies concerned with the proper expenditure of public funds, and the needs of the actual participants in the assessment and planning process. Because the methods are costly, their efficiency (outcomes in relation to costs) must also be analyzed.

Technology

One of the necessary conceptual bases for an examination of policies related to technology and disabled people is a framework of "appropriate technology."*

A technology may be considered appropriate when its development and use: 1) are in reaction to or in anticipation of defined goals relating to problems or opportunities in the disability area, 2) are compatible with resource constraints and occur in an efficient manner, and 3) result in desirable outcomes with acceptable negative consequences or risks to parties at interest. A framework of appropriate technology and the attendant role of parties at interest in its definition serve to put policies regarding the development and use of technologies into perspective.

The key to appropriate development and use of technologies lies in finding a **compromise** fit between: 1) the needs, desires, and capabilities of users and other relevant parties; and 2) the costs, risks, and benefits of technologies. Analyzing such a compromise may be relatively straightforward when, for example, deciding to prescribe or wear eyeglasses. In a case in which the disability in question is of the type for which technologies such as an artificial, myoelectric limb are being considered, however, the compromise decision process becomes extremely complex, and a framework for analyzing alternatives becomes very important. Chapter 5 of this report presents several factors—e.g., explicitly stating the goals of the technology's use—that should be part of a policy approach to appropriate use. The factors presented are not intended to comprise a definitive analytical framework. Furthermore, no framework is a solution; at the most, it will be an organized method of structuring policy and technological problems.

The disability-related **research and development** system includes both public and private organizations: Federal, State, and local governments; individuals; companies; universities; special interest associations; and a number of other actors. The people that the system is intended to assist possess a broad range of handicaps and disabilities of varying severity. The technologies that the system produces cover an even broader range, both in type (including devices and process technologies or services), in sophistication, and in purpose.

The Federal role in disability-related R&D has been steadily increasing in scope and magnitude, although it remains small in comparison to the number of people affected and the complexity of the research problems involved. The organizations

---
*By "appropriate technology" OTA is not referring to the same concept as "intermediate technology" or "low-capital technology." Instead, the term refers to the appropriate development and, especially, *application* of technologies. See ch. 5 for a discussion of this idea.

expending the greatest effort, as measured by the size of their relevant R&D budgets, are the National Institute of Handicapped Research (NIHR), the Veterans Administration (VA), the National Institutes of Health (NIH), and the Office of Special Education. The National Aeronautics and Space Administration (NASA) is also involved in this area as a result of technology transfer efforts stemming from its primary mission. It collaborates with the above agencies to transfer new technologies evolving from its R&D base.

A recent survey conducted for NIHR found that the U.S. Government spends about $66 million a year on R&D related to technologies for disabilities. However, the U.S. Government also spends about $36 billion a year to support the income of disabled people. *Thus, its R&D expenditures in this area represent only 0.2 percent of its transfer payments.* By comparison, the Government's total health care R&D accounts for about 2 percent of its total health care costs.

Private sector involvement in R&D is difficult to characterize or quantify. The companies and organizations that conduct R&D range from multibillion dollar companies to small businesses to nonprofit organizations, associations, and disease-specific foundations. Often, these companies and organizations are the primary actors in the development, delivery, and purchase of new technologies for their constituent groups. The R&D funds used may come from the companies and organizations themselves or from the Federal Government. *Debate continues to surround the issues of how much R&D is enough, who should do it, and who should benefit financially from the complex interaction of private, public, and nonprofit-sponsored research efforts.*

Significant efforts have been made at the Federal level in recent years to systematically establish a comprehensive plan for identifying R&D needs so that efforts may be coordinated in attempting to meet them. The National Council on the Handicapped, which sets priorities for NIHR, and the Interagency Committee for Handicapped Research, which coordinates Federal efforts, are important contributors to this effort. Still at issue, however, is how the technical expertise of the various Federal agencies and the private sector can be combined within current resource constraints to continue to respond to the changing needs of disabled people.

Despite problems, disability-related R&D is characterized by innovation. Given sufficient funding and an effective organization of efforts, the predicted "explosion" in relevant technologies could become reality. Advances in solid-state electronics, other communications/information developments, new alloys, microcomputer-aided movement (e.g., of artificial limbs), and biomedical knowledge, including neurochemistry, are already producing dramatic new possibilities. The future may see an acceleration of technological developments. Some advances, such as writing aids for physically disabled children, may have great value; others may turn out to be useless. Most important, though, is planning for and identifying the appropriate ways to evaluate, distribute, and use the breakthroughs.

Evaluation of technologies involves a broad spectrum of activities and a number of criteria. Safety, efficacy, feasibility, and profitability are the criteria often used first in evaluation efforts. Criteria that follow include effectiveness, reliability, cost, repairability, convenience, affordability, esthetics, consumer satisfaction, patent protection, legal impacts, liability concerns, accessibility, economic impact, reimbursement status, social implications, cost-effectiveness determinations, and ethical concerns. However, these important criteria are rarely, if ever, applied consistently to new technologies for disabled people in the public or the private sectors.

There is, however, no shortage of agencies, organizations, and universities interested in the various issues surrounding the evaluation of technologies. The level of the Federal effort in terms of money spent on evaluation efforts is impossible to determine fully. The lead agency in evaluation of technologies for disabled people is NIHR. Evaluation research supported by NIHR is conducted along with basic research, applied research, and technology development at the various NIHR-funded research centers. In theory, evaluation research is an integral part of the R&D process. In reality, it is often done only in an oversimplified fashion or with inadequate funding.

NIHR does support some evaluation of devices produced outside of its research centers. However, the problem is that there are not enough of these activities. The Food and Drug Administration (FDA), the National Bureau of Standards (NBS), and NIH are three other agencies that focus on evaluation of technologies at the Federal level, but their efforts do not meet the evaluation needs in the area of technology for disabled or handicapped persons. FDA evaluates *medical* devices and drugs only; the NBS is short on time and money; and NIH, through its Consensus Development Program and its clinical trials, cannot be expected to maintain an adequate focus on relevant evaluative criteria (for the needs of this area) or on disability-related technologies. The private sector is also involved in the evaluation of technologies, particularly technologies that it develops or distributes.

OTA finds that the public-private sector partnership is inadequately designed to support fully useful evaluation efforts and that a coherent, adequately funded and focused program of evaluation is needed at all levels of diffusion and adoption of technology for disabilities.

Such a finding is particularly crucial in view of the possibility of an increase in the number of technological advances becoming available, such as communications devices and mobility aids.

Diffusion and marketing of technologies for disabled people require quite different methods, goals, and information than the R&D and evaluation efforts. The public-private sector interrelationship is particularly complex and close, and each sector brings with it attributes which assist as well as impede the process. In the disability field, models of diffusion and marketing in the general health care system and models of diffusion of innovations in the private sector—which are not necessarily complementary—are often at work simultaneously.

There are a number of successes in the diffusion and marketing of technologies that have been directly related to Federal efforts to bring a product developed under a Federal R&D program to private manufacturers for mass marketing and distribution. VA, NASA, and NIHR are lead agencies for these successes. However, such successes appear to be the exceptions. There are a number of reasons: The disability market population is ill-defined; the economic status of users is often far below the median; disability-related technologies often do not appear viable from a strictly "market" perspective, resulting in a lack of private interest in their production; product liability is often perceived by manufacturers to be a problem; and, especially, the systems for reimbursement of devices sometimes provide disincentives to the marketing of certain types of technologies. Two additional issues in this area are the problem of rapidly changing technology and the need to involve consumers to assure that diffusion and marketing efforts are appropriate and effective.

The **use of technologies** by disabled people appears to depend primarily, but certainly not entirely, on the public and nonpublic programs for which the individuals users are eligible. This is partly because many disabled people have lower than average earnings and partly because the variety of programs which exist are the primary source of information on available technologies. Through their affiliation with these programs and services, users either receive technologies directly, have them financed, or learn about them.

Although there are over 100 different Federal programs serving disabled people, the majority of public services are in the form of: 1) income maintenance, 2) health and medical care, 3) social services, 4) educational services, and 5) vocational rehabilitation and independent living. The greatest expenditures have been and continue to be for income maintenance, related transfer payments, and health and medical care.

The major income maintenance programs are Social Security Disability Insurance, Supplemental Security Income, VA pensions for nonservice-connected disabilities, and VA compensation for service-connected disabilities. Individual beneficiaries of these programs receive cash payments with no restrictions on their use. The programs influence the use of technologies not only because they provide the funds to purchase the technologies, but also because they establish eligibility for health, medical, and vocational-related services and technologies.

The major publicly financed health and medical care programs serving disabled people include Medicare, Medicaid, and VA medical services. The use of technologies is significantly affected by the amount of funds provided by these programs, either to individuals or providers, by the methods used to authorize payments, and by the organization of the provision of services. Policy issues that affect eligible Medicare and Medicaid recipients include: what technologies are covered and how are those decisions made, what types of professions and institutions are recognized as providers, what amount is reimbursed for the cost of covered services, what technologies are determined to be medically necessary, and what effects the Medicare and Medicaid programs have on the type and location of services to disabled beneficiaries.

The prime social services programs that serve disabled persons are those authorized under title XX of the Social Security Act and the developmental disabilities program authorized under the Developmental Disabilities Assistance and Bill of Rights Act. Under these programs, a wide range of technologies are directly provided to disabled people. Thus, the major issue affecting the delivery and use of technologies is the determination of eligibility for these programs.

The two largest education programs for disabled people are authorized under the Education for All Handicapped Children Act and the Vocational Education Act. If necessary for receipt of services under these programs, devices may be funded. The programs are more important, however, for preparing disabled people to use technologies and for providing information on what is available. The vocational rehabilitation and independent living programs authorized under the Rehabilitation Act directly provide technologies to eligible recipients for use in the workplace or to live outside of institutions (in the case of severely disabled individuals).

Although the availability of public funds in support of public policies has greatly shaped decisions in the private sector, nonprofit and for-profit private organizations are usually the actual providers of services under public programs. In addition, they provide services and funding not covered by the public programs. Private insurance companies provide income maintenance, although the total amount is much less than the public programs. Health and medical care is also provided; device technologies are funded using criteria similar to the public programs.

Several issues, related to the public programs in general, affect the use of technologies by disabled people. They include: 1) the degree to which services and funding are coordinated from program to program or are consistent from State (or region) to State (or region), 2) the effect, on coordination and consistency, of the methods for determining eligibility, 3) the extent of the gaps in eligibility for services under public and nonpublic programs, 4) the degree to which maintaining rehabilitative device technologies is difficult or costly, 5) the degree to which consumers are effectively involved in services delivery, and 6) the shortage of rehabilitation providers.

Photo credit: Courtesy of Phonic Ear, Inc., Mill Valley, Calif.

Aiding in preparing employment and carrying out job functions has always been one of the prime uses of technologies for disabilities. This photograph shows a woman using the Phonic Mirror Handivoice to communicate with her fellow workers. The Handivoice speaks the words which the person manually enters into it

OTA's examination of the current system of disability-related research, development, evaluation, diffusion, and use finds that the system suffers from a number of significant weaknesses. The system is, or could be, capable of a great deal more. *There is a critical lack of attention being paid to the concept of appropriate technology.* Analytical methods for determining and attaining appropriateness need to be developed and applied at each point in the lifecycle of technology development and use.

Information on available technologies is currently disseminated through publicly financed or publicly operated programs for disabled people. *Information is often fragmented,* since many of the programs cover discrete subject areas and are uncoordinated. *Strengthened information dissemination in a coordinated fashion is urgently needed.*

Providing disabled individuals with the advantages offered by technology requires the resolution of several policy issues. For example, what type of provider is needed to match a technology with a potential user? That is, who shall be responsible, in cooperation with the user, for identifying possible technologies, selecting a technology, fitting it to that specific user, and training the user in its use? Strategies for encouraging the use of appropriate types of providers need to be developed. Another issue concerns the criteria for selecting a particular technology once the type of technology and its purpose have been decided. Federal policies, including those involved with financing, should encourage the consideration of criteria such as rate of obsolescence, ease of maintenance, ease of actual procurement, and users' preferences. Selection of a manual wheelchair over a power wheelchair, for example, should be based in part on criteria such as these.

Resource Allocation

Clearly, the development and use of technologies for disabled persons are greatly affected by available resources and the ways in which they are allocated. In fact, all decisions about the development and application of such technologies are ones of resource allocation. Efforts to improve resource allocation must take into account the incentives and controls currently operating on the development, evaluation, diffusion, and use of technologies. They must also examine the "fit" between the intentions of policymakers to assist disabled people (create opportunities for disabled people to help themselves) and the actual assistance afforded by the available resources and the rules governing their allocation.

Effective resource allocation must take into account a number of current issues in the disability-related area. For example, to what degree should definitions of disability and handicap used in Federal programs focus on people's abilities as well as disabilities? An increased concentration on abilities could lead to the expenditure of a greater portion of resources to alter aspects of the environment that turn disabilities into handicaps. Another example of a current issue in resource allocation is the extent to which the Government should encourage and financially support independent living and the involvement of people with disabilities in pertinent actions, such as evaluation of technologies or the determination of the types of personnel who will prescribe or fit technologies.

Other issues have to do with the types of outcomes sought in allocating resources, the degree to which society and other decisionmakers support the development and application of technologies to prevent disability, the influence of an increasingly aged population has on resource allocation, and the proper role and use of analytical techniques in allocation decisionmaking.

Since the quality of analysis directly affects the resource allocation process, more attention needs to be given to the development and use of analytical techniques. This report presents a series of suggestions for helping to inform and *structure the decision process* in order to: 1) clarify and make explicit why a decision is being made and what problem is being addressed, 2) assure that all assumptions being made are explicitly stated and subject to examination, and 3) force the orderly examination of all relevant potential consequences of any decisions. The goal is not to produce perfect decisions, but rather to make the allocation of resources more sensitive to uncertainty and to a broader range of interests and possibilities.

POLICY OPTIONS

The final chapter of this report presents policy options for congressional consideration. Rather than recommending specific actions, OTA's policy is to provide Congress with a series of alternative actions and discussions of the possible consequences of implementing them. The options are organized by issue area. In chapter 12, each issue is described, findings related to that issue are discussed, and a series of options is presented for each issue. The issue areas for which policy options are provided are:

- How can the production, marketing, and distribution of technologies for disabilities be encouraged and improved?
- How can the involvement of disabled persons and other pertinent consumer be increased and made more effective?
- How can the process of research, development, and evaluation of technologies related to disabilities be made more responsive to the needs of disabled people?
- How can financial barriers to the use of technologies by disabled people be reduced?
- How can Federal policies assure a well-trained and adequate supply of personnel in disability-related disciplines and services?

Part One:
Impairments, Disabilities, and Handicaps

2.
Definitions and Demographics

I hate definitions.
—*Benjamin Disraeli*

Round numbers are always false.
—*Samuel Johnson*

Contents

	Page
Introduction	19
Definitions	19
Demographics: The Problem of Numbers	20

2.
Definitions and Demographics

INTRODUCTION

Data on impairments, disabilities, and handicaps are not only important as background information but are also critical to the creation and carrying out of policy. There is considerable confusion among analysts, the public, and disability workers concerning a number of definitional and "counting" issues. What is a handicap? A disability? Impairment? How is severity classified? What is the difference between functional and categorical (disease- or condition-specific) classification?

How many people have what types of handicaps or handicapping conditions? Or, how many people have what types of functional limitations? What is the distribution of severity, whichever approach is taken? Who is entitled to which programs?

DEFINITIONS

OTA's operational approach to definitional and classification issues starts with the simple idea that society defines, implicitly, a population of "normal" people; that is, people tend to think of the "standard human model" as able-bodied, having what are considered typical functional abilities. Despite the fact that the range of what is considered typical is extremely broad, this concept of normality or typical functional ability still has great power to affect the way people think about other people. In opposition to this concept of able-bodiedness, society defines those individuals who cannot perform one or more of the typical life functions within the accepted range as "disabled" or "handicapped." The philosophical implications and causes of categorizing people in this way are beyond the boundaries of this study. Still, it is important for policymakers to remember that the type of functional limitations that come to be included in programs for disabled people are based in part on this background concept and are in many cases the result of arbitrary decisions.

For the purposes of this study, an exact definition of a "disability" is less important than the idea that disabilities can be identified and can often be eliminated, ameliorated, or bypassed through technological intervention. For this purpose, a classification scheme based on the idea of functional limitations will usually be more useful to policy formulation than will one based on disease- or condition-specific diagnosis. For example, policies might be more rationally developed and implemented in relation to the need to provide aids for certain types of mobility rather than in relation to the fact that people have cerebral palsy or some other specific condition. And, in fact, the legislation enacted in the last few years seems to recognize this advantage.

OTA finds that the most accurate general term to use in describing a person with some type of functional limitation, given no specific background (contextual) information, is "disabled." A "handicap" has to be specified within its environmental and personal contexts.

Impairment is the basic condition. An impairment is, in the ideal, an identifiable, objectively measurable or diagnosable condition. An impairment is the expression of a physiological, anatomical, or mental loss or "abnormality." It may or may not be the result of a pathological process. An impairment is the physical or mental, and causal, base of a disability and can be the result of accident, disease, or congenital condition. Impairment implies an "impaired" functional ability of some sort and can be described in terms of cause, severity, population distribution, etc. Impairments can lead directly to disabilities or to a

19

nondisabled state. Loss of an arm through accident is an impairment. If no prosthesis is used or if a prosthesis does not adequately compensate, then the accident victim has a disability, a "dis" (lack of) "ability" to perform certain functions because he or she does not have use of two arms. Disabilities apply to generic or basic human functions: walking, speaking, grasping, hearing, excreting, and so on. It is a much simpler concept and a more objectively measured one than is "handicap." The concept of a functional limitation can be placed in clearer perspective when it is divided into the basic or generic function being limited by the disability versus a socially, environmentally, and personally specified limitation, which then becomes a *handicap.*

Aspirations or life goals must be taken into account when defining or identifying a handicap. But the approach to taking these into account must be one based on pragmatism. A person's life goals and self concept are a legitimate part of the context of a handicap. Society doesn't tell people that they cannot be computer programers; the choice of career is for the most part considered a valid personal decision. This view may change when society is asked to pay for the cost of special training, the cost of civil rights or incentives programs to make it easier for a disabled person to be hired, the cost of adapting the computer console, the cost of allowing accessibility to a worksite, and so on. But within a relatively small range, there is little difference in such costs across a large number of career choices. So, if a disabled person *aspires* to an occupation that will present no handicap or a minor one, there may be no problem beyond the ordinary one of preparing for and being hired for that position. If the disabled person *aspires* to one that presents a more severe—or more difficult to reduce, eliminate, or bypass—handicap, that should not be excluded from consideration, because the success of rehabilitation may be increased by personal factors such as being in, or training for, a desired job. The point is that aspirations should not be automatically excluded from the conditions differentiating a disability from a handicap.

Finkelstein gives an example (88):

> A man has had a leg amputated. He therefore is impaired, and since he would have a reduction of his locomotive ability, he is disabled. If, however, he has a satisfactory prosthesis . . . and a car adjusted to hand controls . . . he might well not be restricted in activity and therefore not handicapped.

Technology thus can be used to increase the fit between the individual and his environment. With the use of this formulation of the distinction between "disability" and "handicap," it becomes necessary to view not only the individual but the context in which he or she operates. A person, therefore, may be handicapped under certain circumstances and at certain times. The disability remains, but the handicapping environment varies. Personal factors, such as poor self concept or a defeatist attitude, may also turn a disability into a handicap.

Although the concept of "typical" abilities can be offensive to disabled and able-bodied people alike, it is an important aspect of the definition process. Without it, such ideas as functional "aspirations" may make identification of the disabled or handicapped population even more difficult. A test of reason must be applied. Playing symphony-quality flute is not a typical level of functioning. People who cannot do so may regard themselves as handicapped, *but that is not likely to be a matter that society or its agents consider to be worthy of public intervention.*

DEMOGRAPHICS: THE PROBLEM OF NUMBERS

Another critical issue, closely related to definitions, is that of numbers: the demographics of the numbers and distribution of impaired, disabled, or handicapped people. For example, as described in chapter 11, the allocation of resources is intricately dependent on valid and usable census data of numerous types. These data are also vital for planning and implementing actual projects and programs at all stages of the lifecycle of technology development and use.

There is no dependable count of the *total* number of disabled or handicapped persons. Indeed, such a measure is conceptually ambiguous and methodologically unsound, despite the visibility it may have in public policy considerations. Still, various groups and researchers do spend considerable time in attempting to establish such a count. Estimates range as high as 45 million, including more than 10 million children. Typical lower range estimates are from 15 to 25 million people. Generally, the higher range estimates represent attempts to measure the number of impaired Americans, while the lower ranges represent attempts to count the number with disabilities or handicaps. For example, Butler, et al., report that while approximately 12 percent of all children are affected by some physical or mental impairment, only 3.9 percent have a limitation on daily activities (26).

The Butler study also addresses another issue related to "counts." Is the number of disabled people increasing or decreasing? Despite advances in technology and the growth of such movements as independent living, it may be that the number is on the rise. As chapter 11 will cover, the percentage of the population that is 65 years and older is rising, and this trend is expected to continue, with resultant increases in impairment and disability. This fact does not have to mean that "handicaps" will increase, but if the current situation with elderly people and the reaction of society to them and their roles and abilities persists, an increase in the number of elderly people might very well mean an increase in the number of handicapped people.

Similarly, there has been a substantial reported increase in the proportion of children with limitations of activity in the past decade. Between 1967 and 1979, the percent of children with some degree of limitation nearly doubled, from 2.1 percent to 3.9 percent. Those seriously limited in function showed a similar increase, from 1.1 percent to 2.1 percent. The reasons for such increases are not clear (and readers should keep in mind the caveats regarding statistics given in this chapter). It is likely that the increased numbers reflect a heightening of public awareness resulting in increased use of services, an increase in the number of children with serious diseases living longer, and artifacts caused by reporting procedures. If the number of children with activity limitations is actually increasing significantly, then the cost of services is also likely to increase (26).

Although the overall trend in the numbers of disabled people in the population is difficult to establish, it appears that the numbers are increasing. The challenge, in any event, remains a dual one—to decrease future disabilities while providing the appropriate climate and support for minimizing the effects of existing disabilities (i.e., keeping them from becoming handicaps).

Apart from exhibiting conceptual problems, estimates of the numbers of people with disabilities are plagued by a number of practical deficiencies. Many individuals have more than one disability and thus may be counted more than once. Counts may also be inflated when reported by advocates of people with particular disabilities or impairments—these advocates may select the highest number in a possible range in order to help assure that enough money is allocated to assist all those who *might* need assistance.

Conversely, many people in institutions are sometimes missed in "counts" of disabled people. There are several other reasons why reported counts are sometimes deflated. First, many of the data on disabilities are self-reported. This method has an unknown potential for misrepresentation and bias, but it is generally believed that it leads to underreporting. (In the case of certain impairments and illnesses, such as arthritis and influenza, this method may lead to overreporting.) A related reason is that some people desire to exclude themselves or their children from lists of disabled people to avoid the stigma that is still often attached to being disabled. This may be the primary reason for particular gaps in data pertaining to mental health and to those under 17 years old. Finally, some of the data are collected from places that work with disabled people; thus, individuals who are not being worked with or who move are often excluded.

Problems in definition and classification are manifested in attempts to collect demographic information. Given the range used in defining "impairment," "disability," and "handicap," it is not surprising that there are many different definitions for words used in describing different *types* of impairments, disabilities, or handicaps. Furthermore, in counting those with a particular disabling condition, it is often difficult to define when the condition is definitely present. For example, epilepsy may cause substantial disability for those affected. Yet it is not always active—epileptics may be cured, or they may be free of seizures owing to treatment. Conversely, the presence of an epilepsy-like seizure does not always indicate the presence of the disease. Different surveyors, however, use different definitions to establish the presence or absence of the disease (81).

Perhaps more important than problems in definition, however, are problems in classification. At their simplest, these problems result from the use of different categories by different authors, so comparability is reduced. Yet the problem is actually more complex, because the *types* of categories differ widely. The primary difference is whether the disabilities or impairments reported are classified by functional categories or by diagnostic (etiology-specific) categories. Examples of the former include communication and mobility disabilities; examples of the latter include retinitis pigmentosa and spina bifida. Essentially, functional categories provide a context for an impairment by explicitly stating the disability that results. Although functional categories are more descriptive of effects than diagnostic categories, they are equally difficult to standardize.

By focusing on categories of impairments, diagnostic categories often do not provide information on the severity of disabilities. In addition, they obscure the interaction of the environment with the disability and do not distinguish between impairments, disabilities, and handicaps. On the other hand, diagnostic categories do convey some information on whether an impairment is static or progressive and whether it reduces life expectancy—information which is often as critical to policymakers as information on functional ability. Furthermore, these categories are reasonably accurate and have commonly accepted meanings.

It is unlikely that there will be any agreed-upon choice between the two methods of classification. It is important, however, that the type of classification used suits the purpose for which the information was collected.

Surveys of the number of disabled individuals can be deceptive in another way: They often do not distinguish between: 1) mildly disabled individuals, who function at very nearly "typical" levels; and 2) severely disabled or handicapped people, who may be institutionalized, homebound, or critically dependent on a complex of devices and services. Thus, reports that cite very large numbers of disabled people may be diluting the attention devoted to certain segments of the severely disabled population. Therefore, agencies and organizations that attempt to identify populations needing services should be careful in designing surveys so as to take into account severity and functional status as well as type of disability and handicap.

The preceding problems having been noted, some data on the numbers and impairments of disabled people are presented below. These data are provided primarily as examples to place other problems relating to the development and use of technologies in perspective.

Estimates developed from the 1977 Health Interview Survey provided the following numbers on persons with selected impairments (64): 11,415,000 blind and (at least moderately) visually impaired people; 16,219,000 deaf and hearing-impaired people; 1,995,000 speech-impaired people; 1,532,000 people affected by paralysis; 2,500,000 people with upper extremity impairments (not including paralysis); 7,147,000 people with lower extremity impairments (not including paralysis); and 358,000 people with the absense of major extremities. The total is 41,166,000, and there are definitely overlaps. Overall, 67 percent of the impairments are found in the categories of blind and visually impaired and deaf and hearing impaired. And, except among those over 65, there are slightly more impaired males (52 percent) than females (48 percent).

An examination of the working-age population is useful, because an inability to work because of disability results, in our society, in income subsidization or in technological assistance to allow employment. According to the Department of Health and Human Services (70), in 1978, of 127.1 million noninstitutionalized working-age Americans, 17 percent, or 21 million, were limited in their ability to work due to a chronic health condition or impairment. While similar proportions of men and women reported some degree of disability, a greater proportion of women were characterized as severely disabled. The prevalence of disability increased with age—adults between the ages of 55 and 64 were 10 times more likely to be severely disabled than adults aged 18 to 34. Severe disability was almost twice as prevalent among the black population as among members of other races. This higher prevalence among the black population is apparent only when all disabilities are considered. If a particular condition is viewed separately, cerebral palsy, for example, the prevalence may be higher among the white population (197). Cerebral palsy also appears to affect people in all economic, social, or geographic categories equally (197), but that is not the situation for *all* disabilities (70). Generally, disabled people are much poorer and less educated than the nondisabled, and this is particularly true in the case of those who are severely disabled. As pointed out elsewhere, however, statistics on average earnings and levels of education can be deceptive, based as they often are on people in or known to public and private sector programs. Thus, those people who are less educated and who earn less are those most likely to be counted. This does not mean that there is no problem of low disposable income or of educational level among disabled people; it merely implies that the most successful disabled people may be counted less, with implications not only for resource allocation and statistical bases but also for the development and maintenance of stereotypes and attendant attitudes.

3.
Assessing Disabilities and Planning Services

Do not do unto others as you would they should do unto you. Their tastes may not be the same.

—*George Bernard Shaw*

Contents

	Page
Introduction	27
Measures of Effectiveness	28
Determination of Eligibility	28
Determination of Services Required	29
Determination of the Effectiveness of Services Provided	30
Determination of Client Participation	31
Summary of the Effectiveness of the Assessment and Planning System	32
Methodological Issues in Assessment and Planning	33
Determination of Eligibility	33
Determination of Services Required	35
Determination of the Effectiveness of Services Provided	37
Technical Addendum to Chapter 3	39
Individualized Written Rehabilitation Program	39
Individualized Habilitation Plan or Habilitation Plan	40
Individualized Educational Program	40

3.
Assessing Disabilities and Planning Services*

INTRODUCTION

Basic to the development and use of technology are the procedures by which disabilities and handicaps are identified, goals are established for their elimination or reduction, and resources are expended. This chapter addresses: 1) the methods for accomplishing the first two of these three functions, 2) the extent to which these methods are effective in providing information to aid the third function of allocating resources for the lessening of handicapping and disabling conditions, and 3) the extent to which these methods may be used efficiently, since they are themselves costly.

The assessment and planning methods (or procedures) in the disability area can be considered parts of a systems technology. The effectiveness of this system should be measured by criteria that are important to and determined by the users of the system. The primary users of the assessment and planning system, from the perspective of this study, are Congress and the Federal agencies concerned with the allocation of public funds. This chapter, therefore, examines the degree to which data provided by the assessment and planning system are useful to or effective in public policy decisions. After focusing on the effectiveness of the systems in generating such data, the chapter presents a methodological discussion of the techniques for identifying and assessing impairments, disabilities, and handicaps. The chapter also discusses the degree to which the data collection procedures are or might be useful to the individual participants in the assessment and planning process.

The major laws dealing with the treatment of disabled persons in three areas will be reviewed:

1. the portion of Public Law 95-602 (the Rehabilitation, Comprehensive Services, and Developmental Disabilities Amendments of 1978) dealing with vocational training and rehabilitation,
2. the portion of Public Law 95-602 dealing with developmental disabilities, and
3. Public Law 94-142 (the Education of the Handicapped Act), dealing with the education of disabled children.**

The objectives of the assessment and planning system are to provide data for the following: 1) determination of eligibility for services, 2) determination of services required, and 3) evaluation of the effectiveness of services provided. The next section of this chapter examines these three goals, from the perspective of the assessment and planning system's actual or potential effectiveness in providing data for policy decisions. The section following that examines them from a methodological perspective.

---

*This chapter is based on a paper presented for OTA by Dr. Mark Ozer of the George Washington University School of Medicine.

**An overview of legislation in this area is presented in app. B. Also, a note on terminology: Many of the statutes in this area use the term "handicapped" instead of "disabled" in places where the latter term would be more appropriate, according to OTA's definition scheme. OTA uses the terms of the legislation only in quotes from those laws.

MEASURES OF EFFECTIVENESS

The measures of the assessment and planning system's effectiveness are based on the objectives of the data collection system as determined by the laws relating to disabilities.

Determination of Eligibility

The first objective of the assessment and planning system is the collection of data to determine eligibility for services. Each law addressing disabilities has required that services be provided to the appropriate persons. Although definitions of which individuals are entitled to services vary, in every instance some determination must be made of the presence of disability.

Eligibility for vocational training and rehabilitation under Public Law 95-602 (Rehabilitation Act of 1978) is defined as follows [sec. 7(7)(A)]:

> The term "handicapped individual" means any individual who (i) has a physical or mental disability which for such individual constitutes or results in a substantial handicap to employment and (ii) can reasonably be expected to benefit in terms of employability from vocational rehabilitation services.

There is a requirement under this law to deal with the needs of "severely handicapped" people, and "severe handicap" has been given the following definition [sec. 7(13)]:

> The term "severe handicap" means a disability which requires multiple services over an extended period of time and results from amputation, blindness, cancer, cerebral palsy, cystic fibrosis, deafness, heart disease, hemiplegia, mental retardation, mental illness, multiple sclerosis, muscular dystrophy, neurological disorders (including stroke and epilepsy), paraplegia, quadraplegia, and other spinal cord conditions, renal failure, respiratory and pulmonary dysfunction, and any other disability specified by the Secretary.

Eligibility for services for developmentally disabled persons under Public Law 95-602 shares the basic requirement of an impairment of a physical or mental nature but defines more functionally the areas of disability that may occur as a result of such an impairment [sec. 102(7)]:

> The term "developmental disability" means a severe, chronic disability of a person which (A) is attributable to a mental or physical impairment or a combination of physical and mental impairments; (B) is manifested before the person attains age twenty-two; (C) is likely to continue indefinitely; (D) results in substantial functional limitations in three or more of the following areas of major life activity: (i) self-care, (ii) receptive and expressive language, (iii) learning, (iv) mobility, (v) self-direction, (vi) capacity for independent living, and (vii) economic self-sufficiency; and (E) reflects the person's need for a combination and sequence of special, interdisciplinary or generic care, treatment, or other services which are of lifelong or extended duration and are individually planned or coordinated.

This definition also extends to the severity of the problem in that it is long lasting and starts prior to adulthood.

The eligibility criteria in Public Law 94-142 (Education of the Handicapped Act) establish the need for special educational services on the basis of multiple evaluations in several functional areas by multidisciplinary teams as follows [sec. 12a5] (*Federal Register*, Aug. 23, 1977):

> The term "handicapped children" means those children evaluated . . . as being mentally retarded, hard of hearing, deaf, speech impaired, visually handicapped, seriously emotionally disturbed, orthopedically impaired, other health-impaired, deaf-blind, multi-handicapped, or as having specific learning disabilities, who because of these impairments need special education and related services.

At first glance, this definition is the least functional of those presented so far, but it is amplified in the regulations, which further define each category, so that it is at least equal to the others in its functional orientation.

In all three laws, there is a requirement for documentation of impairment and functional limitations resulting from such impairments. An administrative decision must be made regarding the presence of "disease." The data from such disability determinations can be used in individual cases to justify the expenditure of public funds for disability-related services. These data are a prerequisite for accountability, but they have only limited value for the determination of appropriate services for individuals or for any specific category of persons.

The prime function of such determinations is to document the presence of impairments. One measure of the effectiveness of the assessment and planning system, therefore, is the degree to which data might be generated on the incidence of such impairments in the population. Such data would presumably be valuable to States and Federal agencies for more rational planning with respect to the amount of resources necessary for various categories of impairment.

The State plans required from each State to establish eligibility for Federal funds under Public Law 95-602 do require reports that include estimates of the disabled individuals requiring services, with particular emphasis on those with most severe disabilities. The law also requires estimates of service costs for such categories. Furthermore, it requires "continuing statewide studies of the needs of handicapped individuals and how these needs may be most effectively met . . . with a view toward the relative need for services to significant segments of the population of handicapped individuals and the need for expansion of services to those individuals with most severe handicap" [sec. 101(15)].

The requirements for identification of disabled children under the provisions of Public Law 94-142, in order to assure accountability in Federal reimbursement, are very specific. The State education agency is required to report data on the numbers of disabled children within each category of disability and their age distribution [sec. 121a.751]. However, the data are frequently inaccurate, and the estimates of the numbers and types of disabilities are considered to be highly unsatisfactory. Many children are incorrectly classified as disabled; others possess undetected disabilities. There is wide variation in the criteria used to assess the severity of a disability. Children, particularly those from minority groups, are often falsely identified as having impairments (109).

In fulfillment of Public Law 95-602, a component of each State's evaluation system for developmental disabilities specifies a requirement for "client identification and demographic data" [sec. 110]. This includes age and sex, ethnic group and income level, as well as whether the person is living in an urban or a rural setting. Data are to be collected on the type and degree of impairment based on various assessment scales (145). Unlike data collected under the requirements of Public Law 94-142, such data are collected in a variety of functional areas, reflective of the definition of developmental disabilities in the law. The definition in Public Law 95-602 does not mention categories in terms of "disease" entities as does Public Law 94-142. Furthermore, the data collected under the former law, in contrast to the latter data, are not primarily to be used for determination of eligibility for programs or for reimbursement of service costs, but rather for purpose of evaluating comparable effectiveness in terms of "case mix."

Determination of Services Required

The second major objective of the planning and assessment system is the collection of data for the planning of appropriate services to persons who are deemed eligible. The evaluation process designed to determine eligibility has been expanded to deal with determining the specific problems of individuals and establishing plans for services.

In the area of vocational rehabilitation, Public Law 95-602 specifies that the evaluation to determine "rehabilitation potential" should be not only a component of the determination of eligibility but also a part of an individualized written rehabilitation program (IWRP). The IWRP specifies the services and technologies to be provided to the individual and also the goals for the use of those interventions (see the technical addendum to this chapter for those specifications).

The law relating to developmental disabilities as amended most recently (Public Law 95-602) has comparable requirements for the development of a habilitation plan for each developmentally disabled person (see the technical addendum to this chapter).

Like the requirements for vocational rehabilitation, but unlike the requirements for developmentally disabled individuals, Public Law 94-142 deals with the character of the evaluation procedure in some detail. It also deals with the character of the individualized educational programs (IEPs) to be developed for each disabled child. Comparable requirements for parental participation are highly specified (see the technical addendum to this chapter for the law's language relating to IEPs).

In these three laws, the procedures required for data collection have moved beyond the categorization of impairments alone. The evaluation process is now concerned with sampling functional capabilities in a variety of areas so as to lead to a rehabilitation program plan for each individual disabled person.

Despite the focus on the assessment of function rather than impairments, each such assessment is usually carried out in a framework of expected "norms" or standards. That is, the determination of the existence of a problem is generally derived from tests and other evaluation instruments that have been standardized in "normal" populations. Thus, data are collected on the areas of function in which the person is to be considered "deviant." These findings are translated into a set of "remedial" objectives and can be used to justify why any particular set of objectives has been chosen.

Even though such procedures may be a prerequisite for accountability of the objectives, they have limited value for the determination of the actual objectives that should be established for any individual. The data derived from the behaviors sampled on standardized tests frequently lack specificity as to the day-to-day problems that should affect the objectives set for individuals.

Because the prime function of such problem identification is to establish a rehabilitation program plan, one measure of the effectiveness of the assessment and planning system is the degree to which data have been generated for use in determining and planning *appropriate* services. The decision regarding which services to use and to what degree is a crucial one; assuring the appropriate use of technologies—both services and devices—for each individual is one of the critical goals of any effective assessment and planning procedure.

Although data could potentially be generated on needs for technology and other services, an analysis of the various laws and the regulations to implement them indicates that the generation of such data remains highly unlikely at the present time. Only in the case of the portion of Public Law 95-602 dealing with developmental disabilities is the evaluation system to be implemented directly linked to data derived from the habilitation plans. One of the components of each State's reporting system is to include "service characteristics." Included in this category are data on each service received in terms of hours of service, frequency, type of provider and professional level of provider. In addition, each service planned for (or required) but not rendered is to be categorized as to its being scheduled (awaiting an opening or some other reason) or not available (due to "lack of funding" or "no appropriate service"). In this highly developed system, clear potential exists for the collection of information on the needs, both met and unmet, for services and other technologies (145). The developmental disabilities evaluation system is not yet in place throughout the country and has met with considerable resistance by a number of the States.

Determination of the Effectiveness of Services Provided

The third major objective for the assessment and planning system is the collection of data that could be used to evaluate whether services and other resources expended have been effectively used. This objective has been reflected, at least in part, in the ongoing evaluation provision within each of the laws discussed in this chapter. Some measure of outcome is required in each instance.

For persons enrolled in vocational rehabilitation programs, reassessment goes on at two different stages. During an extended evaluation period to determine vocational rehabilitation potential, the focus is on data that would support the decision to maintain eligibility. The IWRP developed following this evaluation period must include "a procedure and schedule for periodic review and evaluation of progress toward achieving rehabilitation objectives based on objective criteria and a record of those reviews and evaluations" ([361.41(a)(5)] (*Federal Register*, Jan. 19, 1981). The State plan for vocational rehabilitation services must also include "an evaluation of the effectiveness of the State's vocational rehabilitation program in achieving service goals . . . as established in [its] plan" [361.17(c)] (*Federal Register*, Jan. 19, 1981). There is no specific provision for the use of data derived from the IWRPs as to the degree of accomplishment of objectives. There is merely a requirement that there be documentation of the existence of these data in case records.

The existing reporting system based on the evaluation standards issued in 1975 moves in its Standard No. 6 toward the assessment of client outcomes. It seeks "to insure that the clients rehabilitated retain the benefits obtained from the rehabilitation process." To determine the degree to which this standard is met it is necessary to collect data on the percent of rehabilitated clients still employed at 1 year, 2 years, or 3 years after closure of the case; their earnings; and the percent of time unemployed (86). A more comprehensive information system has been designed by the Rehabilitation Services Administration (RSA) but is not yet in place. This projected system is described later in this chapter as providing the potential for assessment of the effectiveness of services provided.

In the education of disabled children, the IEP has as one component a reassessment, on at least an annual basis, to determine whether short-term instructional objectives are being achieved. However, failure to achieve the stated objectives is not necessarily tied to the services provided (84):

> Each public agency must provide special education and related services to a handicapped child in accordance with an individualized education program. However . . . the Act does not require that any agency, teacher, or other person be held accountable if a child does not achieve the growth projected in the annual goals and objectives.

Unlike the vocational rehabilitation data collection system, there is provision of the collection of data derived from IEPs at a State level [sec. 121a232] (*Federal Register*, Aug. 23, 1977).

Most far-reaching is the commitment to evaluation of effectiveness of services for people with developmental disabilities. The portion of Public Law 95-602 dealing with such disabilities mandates an evaluation system and ties it directly to data derived from the habilitation plans. State plans are required, under this section of the law, to phase in such an evaluation system as a condition of receipt of Federal funds with implementation of each State's system of October 2, 1982.

Program effectiveness is to be judged, with data from habilitation plans, on the results of services provided to clients. The primary measure is that of changes in developmental status from entry into service to completion. Functional assessment scales are to be used, employing tests meeting specified criteria of reliability and validity appropriate to the areas of concern. There is an opportunity, therefore, for service providers to choose their own measures that will take into account the variability of clients and the need to use different scales. Data are to be collected on the numbers of clients by level of developmental status at entry and at the end of the reporting period. Thus, the percentage of clients making progress (or regressing) can be calculated (145).

Still another measure projected by this system is the proportion of client objectives achieved to the number of planned objectives. An analysis of costs and effectiveness can then be done using data on the cost of the services provided. In both these measures, further breakdown of effects can be determined by data concerning age, sex, type of disability, and area of primary functional limitation (e.g., self help, communication). Particularly noteworthy is the opportunity in this evaluation system to report data from the States as to the comparable effectiveness of similar programs.

Determination of Client Participation

In addition to the three major objectives of the assessment and planning system, a fourth objective is the participation of individuals in planning for their own needs. The evaluation process leading to individualized plans for treatment has been expanded in principle from one carried out *for* disabled persons to one potentially carried out *with* disabled persons, with their parents or guardians, or with both.

Each of the laws discussed in this chapter has stated a commitment toward such participation. This provision recognizes that the underlying goal of treatment is independent functioning on the part of disabled persons; the very process by which plans are made may be seen as contributing to such a goal. More directly relevant to the emphasis of this study, the appropriateness of the technology recommended, whether training or devices, may be expected to increase if the user(s) are participants in the planning decision.

In the area of vocational rehabilitation, client participation in IWRP development is one aspect of the case record to be monitored in State plans. The regulations implementing Public Law 95-602 describe such participation as follows (85):

> The individualized written rehabilitation program must be developed jointly by the . . . staff member and the handicapped individual, or as appropriate, his or her parent, guardian or other representative . . . A copy of the written program [must be provided] and each handicapped individual [must be advised] of . . . procedures and requirements affecting the development and review of individualized written rehabilitation programs . . . The State must assure that the individualized written rehabilitation program will be reviewed . . . at least on an annual basis. Each handicapped individual . . . must be given an opportunity to review the program and, if necessary, jointly redevelop and agree to its terms.

Documentation within the record of the IWRP is to include "the views of the handicapped individual, or, as appropriate, his or her parent, guardian or other representative, concerning his or her goals and objectives and the vocational rehabilitation service being provided" (85).

In the case of developmental disabilities, the habilitation plan is similarly required to be developed jointly with the person and, where appropriate, such person's parents or guardian or other representative. Further, at the time of the at least annual review of such a plan, "in the course of review, such person . . . shall be given an opportunity to review such a plan and participate in its revision" (214). Documentation of such participation would presumably be included in the requirement for assurances from the States in their State plans that habilitation plans are being adequately implemented. However, there is no provision within the design specifications of the new comprehensive developmental disabilities evaluation system for direct incorporation of such data as parental participation. It is unlikely, therefore, that data on participation would be readily available for policy review on an easily accessible basis.

There are extensive provisions within the regulations implementing Public Law 94-142 for the disabled child's (parents') participation in the entire assessment and planning process. At present, however, there is no management information system that collects data on actual parental participation. Such data would ordinarily be collected in the course of sampling IEPs in field reviews.

Summary of the Effectiveness of the Assessment and Planning System

The collection of data from individualized program plans could be particularly crucial to planning for technological needs. However, the existing vocational rehabilitation information system does not incorporate data derived from IWRPs as to the services required. The projected developmental disabilities evaluation system does attempt to incorporate data on specific service requirements. There is no expectation that such information will be collected on the education of disabled children.

Measurements of the effectiveness of the services actually provided are also potentially available from the individualized program plans. Again, however, the existing vocational rehabilitation information system does not collect data directly from IWRPs. The projected developmental disabilities evaluation system does have that potential. Although existing regulations make provision for the collection of data on the education of disabled children, there is no plan for the direct collection of data as to effectiveness of services from IEP review.

Measurement of the degree of participation of disabled persons in the planning process is generally carried out as a component of administrative reviews but not part of any projected management information systems.

The next portion of this chapter examines the technical and other difficulties in the assessment and planning approaches being used in individual cases.

METHODOLOGICAL ISSUES IN ASSESSMENT AND PLANNING

This section, as the previous one, is organized by the three major objectives of the assessment and planning system: 1) determination of eligibility, 2) development of an individualized plan for rehabilitation ("determining need for services"), and 3) evaluation of the individualized plans' ability to contribute to assessment of the effectiveness of services.

Technical and methodological issues arise with each of these objectives. Each of the program areas being surveyed—vocational rehabilitation, developmental disabilities, education of disabled children—share these issues. For purposes of the analysis in this section, however, the methods in use for the determination of eligibility will be explored in the area of education of disabled children; the development of functional plans will be explored primarily in the area of developmental disabilities; and evaluation of the effectiveness of services will be explored primarily in the area of vocational rehabilitation.

Determination of Eligibility

There is a distinction between the methods appropriate for the determination of eligibility and the methods that may be required for the generation of individualized plans. This distinction is tied to the identification of impairments, as required by each of the existing laws, versus the identification of actual functional disabilities that may result from such impairments. In the following discussions, it is important to remember that although the various laws use the term "handicapped" interchangeably with "disabled," OTA reserves the term "handicapped" to mean the result of the interaction of a person with a disability and the environment, as set forth in chapter 2.

Several of the methodological issues concerning the determination of eligibility lie in the medical framework from which many of the methods arose. In Nagi's formulation (148), various etiologies (or causes) such as infection, trauma, or metabolic imbalances interrupt the normal processes of the body. The body responds to such interruptions by mobilizing its defensive and coping mechanisms in an attempt to restore a normal state of existence. These responses are then observed as a state of pathology. Modern scientific medicine is concerned with the relationship of pathological findings to underlying causes. Treatment in the medical framework is intended to help the organism regain equilibrium by providing medical or surgical intervention.

Medically, impairments are findings of loss or deviation from the "norm" which may be a result of active pathological processes but may also remain even after the underlying causes are no longer operative. For example, impairments such as congenital deformities may be thought to have occurred as a result of infection or some other harm prior to birth. These impairments are described in terms of the organs affected. Their prognosis, such as prospects for recovery and stabilization, is also described. The medical questions to be answered by the history and physical examination are: 1) the nature of the disorder or disease process; 2) the activity of the process (acute exacerbation, remission, or exhaustion of active disease; 3) the specific structure and site affected; 4) what medical treatment is appropriate and its possible complications.

Some of the data collected by the medical approach are relevant to the treatment of persons who also have disabilities, but it is important to recognize the limitations of this model of data collection, derived as it is from acute illness. For persistent conditions, the determination of impairment tends to place "undue emphasis on morphological diagnosis with . . . subordination of function to form, and . . . pathological phenomena are considered as though they are unrelated to the individual in whom they become manifest" (229). For the affected individual, it is not so much the underlying disorder and its resultant impairments that are of greatest concern but the manner in which they impinge on everyday life (87). Further, an impairment does not necessarily indicate that disease is present or that the individual should be regarded as sick. One basic methodological issue, therefore, is the use of experience and models based on acute illness to establish methods for the analysis of long-term problems.

Even less appropriate is the extension of this set of medical questions to intellectual and mental impairments in fields such as mental health or education. Except for certain organic diseases, there is an absence of any ability to differentiate indicators of pathology, impairment, and disability. The manifestations are behavioral. There is an absence of well-established criteria for classification relevant to decisions as to treatment. Different sets of criteria may result in differing reported patterns of disability (148).

Despite such incongruities, however, the same methods in use for the determination of disease are used in education. Diagnosticians in this field are concerned whether "disease" in the guise of developmental differences is present. Categories of "problems" have been established by tests based on "norms." For example, the diagnosis of "learning disabilities" has, at least historically, been established in large part by a child's scoring lower on the performance subtests and higher on the verbal portion of the widely used Wechsler test. Considerable effort is devoted to relating patterns of "deviance" to some causal event(s) in the life of the child. Thus, children with developmental problems are categorized as "brain injured," "emotionally disturbed," or "culturally deprived." Other categories in use are designated on the basis of some functional problem, presumed abnormality in some specific site in the nervous system, and presumed cause. Dyslexia, for example, is the diagnosis for a functional problem in reading associated with a presumed abnormality in the visual cortex of the brain and a strongly positive family history of similar difficulties.

One of the difficulties with this approach is that the criteria by which children are assigned to a specific category are elusive and ill defined. Such categorization is almost always arbitrary and subject to disagreement.

The present system of categorizing "deviant children" has come under recent attack as being culturally biased. Opponents maintain that the taken-for-granted value framework in which professionals operate (using tests based on the total population) limits the opportunities of children with minority backgrounds. The central issues here are both technical and, even more important, conceptual and ethical (142).

The problems of the existing classification system are summarized in the report of the Project on the Classification of Exceptional Children (109):

> To call a child retarded, disturbed or delinquent reduces our attentiveness to changes in development. To say he is visually impaired makes us unappreciative of how well he can see and how he may be helped to see better . . . competent authorities agree that categories impede program planning for individual children by erecting artificial boundaries, obscuring individual differences, inhibiting decision-making by people closest to the problem, discouraging early return of children to the regular classroom, harming children directly by labeling and stigmatizing, and denying service to children with multiple handicaps and to other children who do not fall into neat categories.

The methods for determining the existence of impairments, and thus eligibility for services, in the various program areas are derived from a medical framework, which is often applied inappropriately. The methods often depend on categorizations that are frequently incorrect—and when presumed correct, are frequently harmful to the individuals involved.

The methodological limitations of the data actually collected using the medical framework-based process are even more germane to the issue of the appropriateness of services provided. To a considerable degree, a small number of standardized tests are given to determine a child's educational program. Keogh (120) pointed out the potential inappropriateness of data derived from psychological testing. The normative (based on "norms") framework provides quantification that may be excessively generalized, such as the intelligence quotient (I.Q.) used for placement for mentally retarded people. Qualitative data on the functional characteristics of persons (e.g., how they organize, the kinds of cues they select to guide their actions, their speed of decision, and their persistence) are not collected by the standardized measures currently in use, despite the documented relevance of such traits (38).

The methods in use to determine eligibility have been ineffective in providing useful data even for the purpose of appropriate placement of the child. The operation of Public Law 94-142 has, in addition, increased the use of these determinations of eligibility. That law has placed a premium on the identification of disabled children in order to receive Federal reimbursement for each child identified. Support has been given for finding larger numbers of disabled children despite considerable question as to the figures projected (99).

Under Public Law 94-142, the goal of parental involvement in the process of determining eligibility has led to the provision of due process hearings and a full system of legal recourse. The existence of legal remedies has been cited as one cause of what appears to be excessively comprehensive testing (99). Such testing may be done as a precautionary defense against possible legal action. Yet the data derived from standardized tests are frequently inadequate to deal with disputes as to eligibility. The actual tasks of a classroom are not sampled; data are not collected about the conditions under which the child functions most effectively. The methodological limitations of the procedures in use to determine eligibility may contribute to perhaps unnecessary litigation rather than to problem resolution.

In summary, the eligibility determination methods may be ineffective in aiding decisions about appropriate educational placement, particularly in the face of cultural diversity and the need for flexibility to create or use "least restrictive environments." The methods are often inefficient, perhaps because they are burdened with substantial demands for evaluations of questionable utility. They yield insufficient specificity on the characteristics of identified problems in a child. Rather than contributing to effective parental involvement, they frequently limit and obscure potential areas for collaboration between parents and schools.

Determination of Services Required

The development of individualized program plans is the second stage of the assessment process. These are relatively new requirements, and there is a less highly developed methodology to deal with the identification of problems in functional terms, the identification of the appropriate means by which problems may be solved, and ultimately the making of the plan to do so.

The focus in planning is shifting from the delineation of *impairments* inherent in the determination of eligibility to the delineation of *disabilities*. However, the distinction is sometimes difficult to apply, because the medical model so prevalent in the area is oriented to the identification of patient problems in terms of impairments. The "medically based" concept of *disability* is derived from the concept of loss of function or "deviation from the norm" used to establish the existence of disease in the first place. Thus, this merging of the concepts of impairment and disability permeates the methods for problem identification and for planning rehabilitation.

The notion of (re)habilitation used by the World Health Organization indicates some of the limitations of the standard concept. It has been defined as "the combined and coordinated use of medical, social, educational, and vocational measures for training and retraining the individual to the highest level of functional ability" (229). This specification puts little emphasis on the individual autonomy of the client in the rehabilitation process and concentrates on professional actions—doing something to and for somebody. Wood advocates a definition such as "restoration of patients to their fullest physical, mental and social capabilities, within the limits of a disability" (229). The inference is that the person has been placed at a disadvantage in failing to fulfill what has been expected of him or her because of the presence of illness or other disorder. Wood feels that it is then possible to begin to formulate objectives such as maximizing performance and promoting expectations commensurate with altered capabilities. The ultimate goal, again according to Wood, is restoration of the patient's good name, which involves exploration of new roles that are acceptable both to the individual and to society (229).

A different approach has been advocated by some disabled persons and eloquently expressed by Finkelstein (88). He suggests that "disability" be viewed as a special class of social relations between persons with impairments and their social and physical environment. As chapter 2 indicates, OTA prefers this approach, but uses the term "handicap." The traditional analysis, inherent in the concepts expressed by Wood, has been that the person with impairments has failed to meet the socially imposed nondisabled standards of typical functionings. Finkelstein suggests that the focus should shift to the social context in which the problem exists. The example is given of the wheelchair user as being unable to get through the doorway. The focus is on the architectual barrier. It is an architectural problem and it can be studied, analyzed, and solved independently of the individual disabled person. Focus may then shift from the disabled person(s) to the environment, which may be modified.

The methodological issues in the making of an individualized program plan may be analyzed in light of this background. The step of problem identification is crucial to the making of an appropriate plan. To a considerable degree, the framework of expected behavior or "norms" has been retained from the medical approach, which focuses on the areas of loss. The assessment procedures identify areas of deviations from a "norm." To an even greater degree, the focus has been on the disabilities residing in the person, and not on those in the environment nor on the inappropriate interaction between person and environment.

The procedures in use with persons with developmental disabilities will be analyzed as an example.

The characteristics of developmentally disabled people, more specifically those who are defined as mentally retarded, require considerable precision in designing rehabilitation programs. Progress may be expected to be slow, but it may be enhanced to the degree that training program objectives are clearly defined. Assessment instruments (tests) leading to a more precise identification of functional problems have therefore proliferated (75). These behavioral rating scales are used for prescriptive purposes rather than the diagnostic purposes of the general intelligence tests. They are applied directly to the design of individualized program plans and are thus useful at the time of re-test as a measure of progress in meeting objectives. If used on a wide scale, they may also be used for overall program evaluation.

At their best, these behavioral scales describe the levels of function an individual has reached and is able to reach rather than simply what the individual is unable to do. They also describe the criteria to be met rather than attempting to relate those criteria to standardized "norms." The selection of the particular functional content areas to be sampled, still reflect the cultural bias of the test developers.

Far less highly developed are rating scales which sample the environment in which the individual is required to function. An individual's developmental progress may also come about by changes in the environment. Many of the existing "environmental" assessment laws require a focus on the "least restrictive environment" (75). As such, categories examined in environmental assessment tend to include such things as the degree of autonomy permitted and the exercise of individual rights, as well as the amount of activity available in programs. Particularly noteworthy is the Community Adjustment Scale, which directly samples both the individual's ability to perform tasks and the opportunities afforded by various sites available to the individual to perform those skills (75).

Despite the wide range of rating scales available, many important areas of function are apparently not ordinarily surveyed in relation to developmentally disabled people. These include functions related to work habits and work adjustment, as well as emotional development.

All the instruments surveyed are concerned with the measurement of status. That is, data are collected concerning what the person is able or unable to do. Data are not collected concerning the conditions under which the person has been able to accomplish whatever has been accomplished. Data are not collected regarding the process by which development has come about and might come about in the future. The failure to collect such data is inherent to the testing model that underlies assessment.

Nevertheless, data on *process* could be very useful to the making of an individual program plan, where it is necessary to identify not only problems and possible objectives but also the most appropriate means by which the objectives might be met.

The traditional commitment to the collection of replicable quantitative data has generally limited data to that collected by professionals and not usually from those people most directly and frequently involved with the disabled person. The search has been for objective data uncontaminated by interaction between the person with disabilities and the examiner. This goal has limited the value placed on data derived from more natural settings and has limited the participation of parents and disabled persons themselves in the assessment process (75).

A recent, large-scale study, focusing on a range of disabilities including developmental disabilities, described the degree to which individualized planning procedures have been implemented in education (188). In a survey of 208 school districts in 46 States, the study reviewed the individualized plans of about 2,500 students receiving special education and related services in public schools and an additional 550 students in special facilities. Parents were found to have provided inputs to the planning process in about one-half, and students in about 10 percent of the cases (188). Only 20 percent of the parents were thoroughly familiar with the contents of the plan. Although there was awareness of the child's placement and the general services being provided, parents were less familiar with the goals and the short term objectives (188).

This low level of parental awareness of the *objectives* of the plans made for their own children suggests that there may be considerable limits on the degree to which parents can effectively participate in the *implementation* of the plans. A major resource in terms of parental support and cooperation may therefore be lost. Such cooperation is particularly crucial in the treatment of children who are severely disabled.

The survey indicates that a more generic problem may exist in the entire planning process. The relationship between identified problems and the goals and objectives set was not well documented. Such relationships were documented in respect to language programs in a majority of cases. However, many of the plans did not have goal statements and objectives specified for identified needs. Plans concerned with speech and mathematics were complete in about one-half the cases. Areas such as social adaptation, self-help skills, motor skills, and vocational/prevocational skills, where parental input and participation in implementation of programs might be most helpful, were complete in less than 25 percent of the cases (188). Although almost all plans surveyed contained information as to the services to be provided, the lack of connection made between the service objectives and identified need brings into question the effectiveness of the entire planning process in determining appropriate services.

Determination of the Effectiveness of Services Provided

The review of individualized program plans at specified intervals is the third stage of the assessment process. In each of the areas being examined in this chapter—vocational rehabilitation, developmental disabilities, and education—there is a provision that, after the plan is made, the degree of accomplishment of the objectives originally set must be evaluated and the plan accordingly revised for the next interim. The principle of a cyclical procedure in which evaluation of the effectiveness of services is an integral part of the rehabilitation process has thus been established. The provision for client involvement in the planning stage also extends to this evaluation stage. This review and revision is a relatively new requirement for human service programs, and both technical and conceptual issues arise in its implementation.

The vocational rehabilitation program will be used as an example for the purposes of this analysis.

Measurement of client outcome in terms of "case closure" by the attainment of employment has been well established in vocational rehabilitation. The largely public source of funds for vocational rehabilitation has mandated a commitment to accountablity and statistical reports (86). The use of outcome data from the IWRP is a more recent phenomenon. A management information system incorporating data from the IWRP is being developed (as of early 1982). The need for the collection of data on a large scale for the evaluation of rehabilitation programs and rehabilitation counselors has been one of the major incentives behind the development of methods in this area. However, the focus for discussion in this analysis will be on the implications of evaluation methods in respect to services provided for the individual client.

Many of the methodological issues described earlier concerning the identification of problem areas and objectives for rehabilitation are also directly applicable to the evaluation stage. Rating scales descriptive of functional behaviors are used as a posttest to measure changes in the client. These rating scales must also meet the need for a system of relatively specific indicators that reflect the wide range of possible settings for rehabilitation and the possible sequence of outcomes within any one setting. They must permit agreement between observers as to outcome achieved. The measurement of outcomes must also address the issues inherent in the collection of data in standardized test settings versus more naturalistic ones and in the collection of data by professionals versus those who are more directly consumers of services. Just as in the determination of the initial plan, there must be awareness of the process by which data are collected and the source of such data (114).

Recent changes in the vocational rehabilitation programs have mandated a commitment to dealing with "more severely disabled" people, and outcomes to be sought now include not only the ability to function within the work force but also to live more independently. The "independent living" provisions of the Rehabilitation Act mark a fundamental change in the character of the goals of rehabilitation. A significantly different approach is required, because the principle of independent living does not necessarily imply that one is free of the need for services, but rather that those services are under the control of the disabled person (45).

An expanded management information system for vocational rehabilitation has been in the process of development over the past several years (7,45). Within the past year, the character of this projected system has been extensively modified to incorporate scales measuring functional aspects of clients. It is also planned that the system will use life status indicators for measures of IWRP goals and client changes. Plans to test this new system, which was developed in close collaboration between RSA and State vocational rehabilitation agencies, are now underway. This section will focus on this developing system as the expression of present thinking on evaluation.

The movement away from the identification of client problems in medical or psychiatric diagnostic categories of impairment has been well established in vocational rehabilitation. A number of functional assessment measures have been developed, and two have gained particular acceptance —the "functional assessment inventory" (FAI) developed by a group at the University of Minnesota (43) and "rehabilitation indicators" (RI) developed by a group at the Rehabilitation Institute at New York University (71,72). The goal of both these measures has been to provide behavioral statements that are readily observable and reliably measured by different observers. Both measures, but particularly the RI, can be used to provide descriptors of a range of goals and problems to be corrected and may then be used in the evaluation of client changes. The focus in the FAI is mainly on the characteristics of the client, rather than the environment. Out of the 30 categories of problems, only two have their locus outside the individual. A new scale, not yet being used, will describe "elements of the person's physical, social, cultural, and political environment that may hinder or support goal attainment" (72).

The availability of these functional assessment measures has led to the incorporation of items from both in the projected management information system for vocational rehabilitation on a national basis. "Life Status Indicators" from the RI scale are to be used to reflect client characteristics at entry into the rehabilitation process and at the completion of the service to assess change. For example, one such status indicator relates to self-care: a four-item scale ranges from "needs substantial assistance" through "occasional assistance" and "minimal assistance" to "needs no assistance."

Other measures of effectiveness of service relate to the more traditional aspects of rehabilitation, focusing on ability of clients to function in the work force. These include increased economic independence in terms of employment at or above the minimum wage, removal from public assistance rolls, and percentage competitively employed.

The potential use of the IWRP as the primary planning mechanism is recognized only to a limited degree. Measures that would evaluate the contribution of the services actually provided in accordance with the IWRP to any of the outcomes are apparently not contemplated. Moreover, there is no measure of the degree to which the client has taken active part in the planning and evaluation process mandated by IWRP procedures.

The evaluation system for vocational rehabilitation has addressed the implications of the independent living movement only in part. There has been attention given to measures other than traditional ones related to employment, in recognition of the movement toward working with people with more severe disabilities. However, there have not been substantial changes in how rehabilitation problems are viewed: The problems are not yet widely seen as centered in the environment as well as in the disabled person. Even more crucial to the independent living movement has been the issue of the rehabilitation process itself and active client involvement in decisionmaking. This has not been addressed directly either in the functional assessment scales or any of the other data collection sources.

There is a critical need at this stage of the process for data not only on *status* but also as to the *means* by which successful outcomes were achieved:

Evaluation has traditionally been perceived as an end point activity. The principle of assessment-planning-evaluation incorporated in the IWRP process could more effectively be considered as an ongoing, cyclical process. Plans should be revised in light of experience.

Evaluation has been traditionally perceived as dealing with the measurement of outcomes alone. The potential clearly exists, although rarely realized, to collect data as to what means were most useful in bringing about whatever successful outcomes occurred.

Evaluation has traditionally been perceived as separate from treatment. However, the assessment-planning-evaluation process may in itself be a major and ongoing therapeutic activity, especially if focused on the means by which problems have been solved.

If a major goal of rehabilitation is to encourage the development of disabled persons to take control of their own lives, one skill to be engendered and fostered is the ability of disabled persons to plan for themselves. Thus, the abilities of disabled persons to answer pertinent questions for themselves—about successes and the strategies for achieving them, about problems to be encountered, and about goals and the means for realizing them—should be exploited and enhanced (172).

TECHNICAL ADDENDUM TO CHAPTER 3

Individualized Written Rehabilitation Program (Public Law 95-602)

[An] individualized written rehabilitation program . . . in the case of each handicapped individual is developed jointly by the vocational rehabilitation counselor . . . and the handicapped individual (or in appropriate cases his parents or guardians) . . . Such written program shall set forth the terms and conditions, as well as the rights and remedies, under which goods and services will be provided to the individual . . . Such program shall include . . . (1) a statement of long-range rehabilitation goals for the individual and intermediate rehabilitation objectives related to the attainment of such goals, (2) a statement of the specific vocational rehabilitation services to be provided, (3) the projected data for the initiation and the anticipated duration of each such service, (4) objective criteria and an evaluation procedure and schedule for determining whether such objectives and goals are being achieved . . . [Public Law 95-602: sec. 7(5), sec. 102(a)].

Individualized Habilitation Plan or Habilitation Plan (Public Law 95-602)

(1) The plan shall be in writing.

(2) The plan shall be developed jointly by (A) a representative or representatives of the program primarily responsible for delivering or established, (B) such person, and, (C) where appropriate, such person's parents or guardian or other representative.

(3) The plan shall contain a statement of long-term habilitation goals for the person and the intermediate habilitation objectives relating to the attainment of such goals. Such objectives shall be stated specifically and in sequence and of progress. The plan shall (A) describe how the objectives will be achieved and the barriers that might interfere with the achievement of them, (B) state objective criteria and an evaluation program and schedule for determining whether such objectives and goals are being achieved . . .

(4) The plan shall contain a statement (in readily understandable form) of specific habilitation services to be provided, shall identify such agency which will deliver such services, shall describe the personnel (and their qualifications) necessary for the provision of such services, and shall specify the date of the initiation of each service to be provided and the anticipated duration of each such service . . . (C) Each habilitation plan shall be reviewed at least annually . . . In the course of the review, each person and the person's parent or guardian or other representative shall be given an opportunity to review such plan and to participate in its revision . . . [Public Law 95-602: sec. 112(b)].

Individualized Educational Program (Public Law 94-142)

The individualized educational program for each child must include: (a) A statement of the child's present levels of educational performance (b) A statement of annual goals, including short term instructional objectives; (c) A statement of the specific special education and related services to be provided to the child, and the extent to which the child will be able to participate in regular educational programs; (d) The projected dates for initiation of services and the anticipated duration of the services; and (e) Appropriate objective criteria and evaluation procedures and schedules for determining, on at least an annual basis, whether the short term instructional objectives are being achieved . . . [sec. 121a.346 of the regulations implementing Public Law 94-142].

4. Conclusions From Part One

It is not the hand but the understanding of a man that may be said to write.
—*Miguel de Cervantes*

Contents

	Page
Definitions	43
Numbers	44
Planning and Evaluating Rehabilitation Services	45

4.
Conclusions From Part One

The purpose of Part One is to provide background information on disabilities and handicaps that places later material on technologies and on resource allocation in perspective. The need for technology and for the allocation of resources to develop and distribute them is, after all, derived directly from the existence of disabilities and handicaps. The numbers and specific types of limitations on people's functioning are, or should be, a principal source of guidance for Federal and other programs that develop and diffuse technologies and that expend funds for the use of technologies.

DEFINITIONS

The three-tiered definition in chapter 2 of impairments, disabilities, and handicaps has significant implications for rehabilitation approaches based on the application of technology. Because it is the most objectively diagnosable condition of the three, and because it is based on a physical or mental loss or deficiency, an impairment is the condition for which medical care is the most crucial and appropriate. Medical or surgical intervention is usually the first form of intervention applied in order to eliminate or reduce the impairment, to keep it from becoming a disability or to keep the disability to a minimum.

As long as the impairment exists and is not fully compensated for, however, a disability will also exist. *With disabilities, the role of medical care is still important, but it will normally be supplemented by other interventions.* Some of these will be quite closely related to medical care, such as training in the use of braces. Examples of other types of services that become important include attendant care, special education services, modified automobiles, environmental control systems, and communications devices.

The objective of any technological application is to eliminate, reduce, or bypass functional limitations of the individual. When limitations cannot be eliminated, a disability remains but it may be prevented from handicapping the individual. A handicap, as defined in chapter 2, is the result of interaction between a disability and the social and physical environments of the disabled person. *A disability may change the way one accomplishes a task or reduce one's ability to do it at a certain level, but a handicap may prevent the person from doing the task at all or at an acceptable level* (to the person). For example, a person who uses a communication device that produces artificial speech will speak in a different way from nondisabled people, and that person may not be able to speak as quickly or as expressively as is "typical." The person may become handicapped by that disability in combination with social expectations for conversational style and rate.

A person's disability may change over time. For example, physical and mental conditions improve and deteriorate. The aging process carries with it a gradual lessening of some functional abilities, such as sight and hearing. New technologies are developed or are acquired by the disabled person, and these may change or influence abilities and disabilities. Handicaps, too, can change. In fact, *the nature of handicaps implies that they can change daily or even hourly, depending on changes in the disability-environmental interaction.* When a wheelchair fits through a doorway and into an elevator, the disabled person has access and is not handicapped in relation to that functional ability. An hour later, in the next building, a doorway may create a handicap.

Having noted these properties of disabilities and handicaps, OTA finds that accurate terminology would involve using the phrases "a person with a limitation on the ability to perform one or more functional tasks because of an underlying condition," or "a person with a disability in one or more functions who is, in a particular situation, limited in the ability to accomplish certain tasks." However, the terms "disabled person" and "handicapped person" are useful as a shorthand. In this report, therefore, the terms disabled or handicapped person or individual should be read as implying the longer phrases.

The properties of disabilities and handicaps also lead to several conclusions relating to Federal policies. *Even though the role of medical care and medical specialists may lessen in the progression from impairments to disabilities to handicaps, Federal policies are still primarily oriented to medical solutions.* As will be covered in chapter 9, a physician's prescription is required for many devices and services not of a strictly medical nature. Reimbursement under Federal health insurance programs is not permitted to rehabilitation engineers. The criterion for inclusion in reimbursement appears to be less concerned with effect on health or functioning than it does with affiliation with a medical field.

Similarly, the properties of disabilities and handicaps as defined here imply that the person with those conditions could play a substantial role in identifying needs for technologies, deciding to acquire or use technologies, applying them, and assessing their worth. This is not to say that the disabled individual is the best judge of all aspects of technology use. However, OTA finds that *often, more attention has been paid to the disability than to the person with the disability.* Thus, many opportunities for more informed and appropriate use of technologies may have been missed. A source of expertise has been substantially overlooked. It may be that many researchers are more interested in what they can do for disabled people than in what ways they can assist disabled people in doing things for themselves, or that many program administrators are more interested in what their programs can do directly than in what disabled people can do on their own, given opportunity and some level of resources. These possibilities cannot be investigated and resolved fully, but the evidence available to OTA indicates that they have some basis in fact.

Although the situation is changing somewhat, many Federal policies and programs are oriented to thinking of disability in terms of categories of disease or diagnosis. This orientation of programs is reinforced by the categorical organization of most advocacy groups and other consumer groups. *One partial result of viewing disability in categorical instead of broader functional terms is the narrow focus and lack of coordination that characterizes Federal efforts.*

The categorical orientation may also result in less than an adequate share of attention and resources being devoted to changing the environment within which disabled people function, or to changing the way in which the disabled person interacts with the social and physical environments.

NUMBERS

OTA finds that "numbers" are a critical problem area. Aside from their use in debates about the national costs or missed opportunities due to disability, counts of the *total* number of disabled people in the country are deceptive, ambiguous, and, for most policy purposes, unnecessary. *The biggest need for the appropriate use of technology and for the planning of governmental programs is valid, reliable data on the numbers of people with specific forms of functional limitations and on the demographic characteristics of the people.* Such data do not exist in sufficient amounts to greatly improve policymaking and the use of technologies. Methodological weaknesses contribute to the poor state of information, *but increased attention and funds for the collection of data relevant to decisionmakers could be of tremendous help. A concerted effort to improve data collection methods and systems is needed before large sums of money should be spent on actual collection. This effort must include substantial participation by people with disabilities.*

The above discussion should be seen in light of the fact that existing statistics, especially those on impairments or categorical conditions, usually were not designed to meet the now apparent needs of policymakers and others. In addition, data on impairments and other categorical information may still be needed for certain purposes (e.g., planning the allocation of specific prevention services).

The goal of most public and private nonprofit organizations should be to make their efforts less and less necessary over time. They should work toward the reduction of handicapping forces—e.g., physical and attitudinal barriers to mobility, transportation, employment, education, and training. This perspective on the part of organizations should then lead them to *identify, generate, and disseminate data not only for their own immediate, program-related uses but also for the purposes of reducing barriers and involving others in the effort, such as private firms.* This implies, for example, that the Social Security Administration may want to identify areas, and collect data about them, where the need for income maintenance and health care resources could be reduced due to the lessening of handicapping elements. Similarly, the National Institute of Handicapped Research could decide to include, to a much greater extent than at present, the data needs of manufacturers and marketers of disability-related products in the agency's own designing of data collection efforts.

PLANNING AND EVALUATING REHABILITATION SERVICES

Before technologies to eliminate or reduce disabilities and handicaps can be appropriately applied to an individual, that individual must be identified and an assessment made of the nature and extent of the individual's abilities and disabilities. Only then can services be planned, and only in the context of that information can later evaluation of outcome take place. Similarly, only when the service and other technological needs of a population have been assessed can informed planning of resources be accomplished.

The processes in place to do this identifying, planning, and evaluating, as discussed in chapter 3, suffer from various shortcomings. Their substantial, though not complete, reliance on categorical definitions of disabilities has been mentioned above. As the chapters of Part Two will cover, *the "need" for technology is most often based on needs of disabled persons as perceived by professionals or program administrators instead of on a blend of the disabled person's needs, desires, and capabilities, as identified with the full participation of the disabled person or a representative.* This situation not only detracts from the process of applying individual technologies but also makes it more difficult to allocate resources at individual, programmatic, and societal levels.

There is great potential for improving this situation through the use of the individualized plans required under programs for education, developmental disability, and vocational rehabilitation. Techniques for creating and carrying out such plans do not, however, appear to be well developed. Nor does adequate *effective* effort seem to be devoted to making those planning opportunities work.

At the Federal level, OTA finds an apparent lack of attention, and a definite lack of significant funding, given to the use of management information systems based on data from individualized plans. Such information systems could be used to generate data that could be used in planning, evaluating, and modifying programs.

Part Two:
Technology

5.
Technology and Its Appropriate Application

Man is a tool-using animal . . . Without tools he is nothing, with tools he is all.

—*Thomas Carlyle*

Contents

	Page
Introduction	51
Technologies and Disabled People	51
Appropriate Application of Technology	52
Some Suggested Elements To Structure a Framework	54
Specifying the Decision Perspective	54
Specifying the Range of Relevant Decisionmakers	54
Explicitly Stating the Goals for the Use of Technology	55
Specifying Needs, Desires, and Capabilities	55
Identifying the Full Range of Possible Technological Options	55
Identifying and Analyzing Characteristics of Technologies	55

5.
Technology and Its Appropriate Application

INTRODUCTION

Policies in the disability area must take into account large numbers of technological possibilities, organizational factors, resource allocation demands, and competing levels of decisionmaking. OTA finds that an approach that helps to structure analysis and decisionmaking is needed to fulfill the goal of matching the technology needs of disabled people with the ability to develop and deliver the needed technology. The idea of matching technologies to users and to delivery capabilities is one of the two principles that guided the OTA study. A concept of "appropriate technology"* is one of the necessary conceptual bases for an examination of policies related to technology and disabled people.

The second principle is one of matching decisionmakers' resource capabilities to their allocation goals. Despite the many problems associated with the processes of developing technologies for disabled persons, a perhaps more critical problem lies in the reaction of society and its institutions to existing technological capabilities. This country's ability, imperfect as it is, to deliver technologies is running ahead of decisions about what ends society seeks through technology, about who shall receive technologies that already exist, and about how those technologies will be provided and financed.

---

*It is important to remember that, as the text of this chapter points out, OTA uses the term "appropriate technology" to refer to technology that is developed or adapted in response to the needs, desires, and capabilities of disabled people and *applied appropriately*. This concept should not be confused with the "small is beautiful" intermediate technology movement, although there are important similarities. "Appropriate technology," to OTA, may be complex or simple, expensive or inexpensive, fascinating or mundane appearing. The key is whether it matches the situation of use.

TECHNOLOGIES AND DISABLED PEOPLE

Technology in its broadest sense is the application of an organized body of knowledge to practical purposes. This definition encompasses physical objects, such as wheelchairs or subway elevators, and also processes, such as vocational rehabilitation or reimbursement systems—in short, a tremendously varied and complex collection of society's tools. A full study of "technology and disabled people" would in effect be a study covering nearly all issues related to disabilities and handicaps, an impossible task. For the purposes of this study, OTA accepts the broad definition of technology as valid, but primarily will focus on technologies designed for and used by individuals with the intent of eliminating, ameliorating, or compensating for (bypassing) one or more functional limitations of individuals as opposed to populations. Elevators in subway systems, for example, are not designed to address the needs of specific individuals but instead are oriented to "populations." Thus, this study focuses on what are sometimes called personal assist (or assistive) devices and services.

Drugs and medical devices are clearly within this study's boundaries. So, too, are Autocom communications devices, modifications of automobiles and vans, employment technologies (including training and skills counseling), and special typewriters. The working definition, however, eliminates or reduces in emphasis technologies designed to address population-oriented needs.

51

Examples of such technologies are transbuses, transportation systems, education systems as a whole, or systems of providing rehabilitative therapy.

This leaves a set of technologies in the middle—those that are established and operated for groups of disabled people and yet are oriented to individuals. An example of this form of technology is "sheltered employment." Other examples are education programs designed to provide appropriate educations to individuals (as opposed to entire systems of education, as noted above), vocational counseling programs, and centers for independent living. There was no clear-cut way to decide whether to include such technologies. Therefore, technologies of this sort were considered individually and in most cases were included in at least the research phases of this study.

The three classes of technologies for disabled individuals presented above form one possible taxonomy or method of classifying technologies. Others, however, are also necessary. One method is to classify technologies by their broad goals. OTA used the following scheme:

- communication
- sensory input
- mobility
- manipulation (of objects)
- education
- security (physical, psychological)
- health (medical care)
- employment (for activity, satisfaction, livelihood)
- social interaction, recreation
- daily living (e.g., shelter)

The items on the left are more basic goals; those on the right are broader goals. One way to view technology is as a method of enhancing the ability goals on the left in order to accomplish goals on the right.

The usefulness of a taxonomy lies in its ability to guide the development of further sets of goals for the development and evaluation of technologies. If one knows the human need that a technology is designed to address, one has identified the broad goal of the technology. The subsequent process is one of refining the statements of functional goals of the technology to arrive at outcome measures that can be used for development and evaluation. Wheelchairs are obviously intended to fulfill the primary need for mobility. An evaluation of wheelchairs, however, should be based on criteria that take into account the secondary functions for which mobility is necessary. For example, reliability of wheelchairs and ease of service are important evaluation criteria when travel to and use in employment is viewed as one of that technology's functions.

APPROPRIATE APPLICATION OF TECHNOLOGY

By using the terms "appropriate technology" or "appropriate application of technology," OTA is not necessarily referring to the "intermediate technology" or "light capital technology" movements, although the background of those movements has many elements in common with the OTA use of the term. Appropriate application does not require that a technology be simple or that it be inexpensive, only that it be suitable for the intended effects and that it take into account any constraints, such as the resources available.

Appropriate technological use for even a single individual may span the full range of cost and complexity possibilities. For example, one person might need a complex, $3,000 microcomputer-based, voice-synthesizing communications device; a $300 manual wheelchair; attendant care for certain periods of the day; and relatively simple and inexpensive aids such as special eating utensils and a pole with a "velcro" attachment for retrieving fallen keys from the floor.

Appropriateness cannot be defined until and unless its context is specified. That context will always involve *value*, as well as *technical*, considerations. Thus, a technology may be considered appropriate when its application is: 1) in reaction to or in anticipation of defined goals relating to problems or opportunities, 2) compatible with constraints, including resource constraints, and 3) results in desirable and sufficient outcomes with acceptable negative consequences or risks to parties at interest.

There are, logically enough, degrees of appropriateness. The most appropriate technology in a given situation is one that provides the greatest ratio of desirable outcomes to negative effects and resources consumed, providing that outcomes and consequences have been defined and are of sufficient value as judged by appropriate parties at interest.

"Appropriate parties at interest" introduces an involved concept, one that is extremely sensitive as well. An "appropriate party at interest" is one who has a stake in the development and use (especially as regards outcomes) of technologies for people with disabilities. The primary party is the disabled individual or population. But the relevant set of parties will vary from situation to situation. Disabled individuals affect or define the appropriateness of technology not only by their judgments of outcomes, but also by their judgments on the worth of those outcomes in relation to resources required (especially when they will personally allocate those resources).

Other parties at interest include parents and family members; physicians and other health professionals, vocational counselors, biomedical researchers, electronics scientists, and other R&D people; the public at large; governmental and private policymakers; voluntary health and social organizations; industry; school systems; insurance companies; and many other groups. All these people and groups provide definitions of "appropriate" from their perspectives. It is their values and goals that give meaning to the appropriate application of technology.

Attention to the concept of appropriate technology and the attendant role of parties at interest serves to put policies regarding the development, evaluation, diffusion, and use of technologies into perspective. One line of reasoning, for example, is that a technology should not be developed simply because a researcher finds it a fascinating challenge. Although this argument is a strong one, it ignores the many substantial contributions made by research that was seen as unrelated to its eventual uses. Thus, the difficult but necessary approach is placing policy decisions into perspective —trying to find an appropriate balance between practical directed research and research with a less visible connection to near-term applications. Nor, for example, should society expect disabled persons to use a technology that is not compatible with their needs, desires, and capabilities.

The expansion of an appropriate technology approach from a concept to a framework that can be used to analyze questions of legislative and regulatory policy, resource allocation, and general decisionmaking will be a difficult and frustrating task. Such an approach, however, holds great promise for the goal of developing a more coherent and efficient set of policies, especially in an era of increasingly constrained resources.

It is possible to state some of the critical elements that will have to be taken into account. That is, some of the elements that can be used to structure decisionmaking or analysis can be suggested. Paramount among these is the forced, explicit identification of parties at interest, positive and negative outcomes relevant to each such party, resources needed or consumed, conflicts among parties at interest in terms of desirability of various outcomes, methods of compromise or reconciliation between the various parties, and the differing motives and goals of the parties.

The development of methods for assuring appropriate development and use of technologies implies the importance of a coordinated and coherent system for:

- involving the potential users and their associates in all the steps possible—from identification of needs, to design of the technology, to evaluation of the resulting technology;
- identifying functional limitations of potential users;
- identifying individuals with limitations;
- identifying the need for technological aids to eliminate or reduce limitations;
- specifying the goals sought for technology before design begins;
- identifying existing technologies that may provide such aid;
- conceiving, designing, and developing new

technologies or modifications in existing technologies to provide such aid;
- conceiving, designing, and developing the necessary training programs, support services, financial services, and information dissemination services to allow the appropriate use of any such technologies;
- being aware of attitudes and values that facilitate or hinder the application of technologies;
- being aware of statutes or regulations, or needed changes in statutes or regulations, that will affect the success of the application of the technologies;
- eliminating or reducing marketing, especially financial, hindrances to successful application of the technologies;
- evaluating, prospectively to the maximum extent feasible, the safety, efficacy, sufficiency, quality, costs and other implications of the technologies;
- considering the application of any such technologies in relation to the many other types of technologies to be used by the individuals and the range of life functions to be performed;
- conducting followup evaluations to determine: 1) actual v. predicted performance and benefit of the technologies, and 2) whether any modifications or adjustments are needed to better match the goals; and
- sharing successful efforts with other potential users of the technologies.

If such a framework can be developed (and it need not be a quantitative one; identification of critical factors and subsequent qualitative analysis may be sufficient for many aspects of decisions), then analysis of costs and benefits can be better accomplished at the varying levels of the individual, program, and society.

SOME SUGGESTED ELEMENTS TO STRUCTURE A FRAMEWORK

The key to appropriate application of technologies lies in finding a fit, which will always involve tradeoffs, between: 1) the needs, desires, and capabilities of users and other relevant parties, and 2) the costs, risks, and benefits of technologies. Based on the conceptual and system factors presented above, this section lists factors that might be part of a policy approach to increasing the appropriateness of technologies. The information to be presented is not intended to be a definitive analytical framework. Instead, it is intended to provide examples of the types of considerations that would have to be used in the structuring of any such analytical approach. Also, it is important to remember that no framework is a solution; it will at the most be an organized method of structuring policy and technological problems and decision processes.

Specifying the Decision Perspective

Analysts, those supporting or funding the analysis, and decisionmakers must decide clearly the perspective from which the analysis is to be done —i.e., the decision to be made might be an individual one, a program-oriented one (e.g., Medicare), a geographic or regional one, or a societal one. If the decision and analytical perspectives are societal but not concerned with specific technological applications, a resource allocation framework, as discussed in chapter 11, would also be very important. Specifying the decision perspective is necessary before decisions can be made about the range of costs, risks, and benefits to be considered in the analysis. It also affects the relative weight to be given to the various parties at interest.

Specifying the Range of Relevant Decisionmakers

This step also influences the analytical focus. It is particularly critical when a societal perspective is to be used. Even when an individual perspective is relevant, however, the task is difficult. Besides the individual directly involved, there may be other important decisionmakers: parents, counselors, physicians, insurance companies, teachers, social workers, and so on. The following steps should be examined from the viewpoint of each of the relevant decisionmakers.

Explicitly Stating the Goals for the Use of Technology

What are the goals and objectives of each of the parties affected by these decisions? These must be stated explicitly because they will very often be different, usually competing, depending on the relevant party. Successful tradeoffs can only be made when there is an open admission and examination of conflicting desires with regard to the technology's application. For each goal: How was it set? Based on what information or data? What is the quality of such information? When goals are based on different data about the problem to be addressed, the desired objectives to move toward, and the interventions that will bring about such movement—and when goals of various relevant parties are in conflict—what is the relative quality of the different data? And how can differences in data be reduced or eliminated? When information gaps are present, how can the needed information be collected or acquired? Who will do so, in what ways, and with what support or funding? Are goals and progress toward them measurable? Will the evaluation information be in a form that will allow modifications in the interventions being used? Who will monitor progress and be responsible for reporting it to relevant parties?

Specifying Needs, Desires, and Capabilities

This step primarily applies to the direct party at interest—the disabled individual or discrete population. The need for a technological intervention must be assessed. The disabled person must either specify the need or be extensively consulted in its specification. Need should be expressed in terms of minimal functional levels required to perform tasks—the "threshold" standard. In addition, however, the desires (goals, aspirations) of the parties must be taken into account, as should the capabilities of the parties to effectively and efficiently use the intervention. Whereas it is most common to specify the need for a technology based on a problem definition, this step assumes that a blend of needs, desires, and capabilities must be explicitly identified. The needs, desires, and capabilities of other relevant parties besides the disabled individual or population must also be considered. (An example is the case of teachers who must implement provisions of the Education for All Handicapped Children Act.)

Identifying the Full Range of Possible Technological Options

An attempt should be made in this step—at least at first—to identify as broad a range of technological options as feasible. Information on possible technological applications should be combined with information based on goals and on needs, desires, and capabilities. This step involves consulting with other disabled individuals, identifying technologies used in the past, and obtaining information from professional sources, data banks (ABLEDATA, etc.), advocacy groups, Government agencies, trade journals and newsletters, manufacturers, etc.

Identifying and Analyzing Characteristics of Technologies

For each of the technologies considered to be potential interventions, the following types of information should be analyzed.

- its availability;
- its simplicity of operation;
- its initial cost, including installation if applicable;
- its reimbursement or financing status;
- its future adaptability (add-ons, cost, flexibility);
- its repair record (including ease and time);
- the extent and quality of performance or evaluation data;
- its cost of operation, if any; and
- its ability to provide desired functions to the necessary level.

These are examples of characteristics; others certainly can be added to the list. For each technology, the traits above should be compared to the following characteristics of the potential users and their needs, desires, and capabilities. Again the list is illustrative, not exhaustive.

- the functional limitations of the user.
- the physical and mental capabilities of the user to apply the technology;
- the user's affinity or preference for the various types of technology (e.g., computers, or power assists);
- the user's desire for independence;
- age, sex, and other demographic characteristics of the user;
- the physical location of the user—geographic and environmental;
- type of transportation services available;
- the occupation or potential occupations of the user;
- the vocational and avocational aspirations of the user;
- income or other funds available;
- any ways in which the above characteristics might change over time; and
- the specific performance level requirements of the activity/environment in which the individual will be involved.

The discussion above has focused on the individual. No matter what the decision and analytical perspectives are, the need for the information above will still usually apply. If the decision perspective is other than the individual's, however, the information outlined above may have to be supplemented by similar information on the characteristics of the new decisionmaker. Information on desires and resources available will be especially critical.

Selection of the technological intervention to be applied can then be based, *in part*, on completing the above steps for each technological possibility. "In part" is highlighted because decisions will rarely if ever be based entirely on the results of analysis, no matter how informed or structured the process of analysis and decisionmaking has been. Structure *informs*, and ideally improves, the decision; it does not and should not *make* the decision.

6.
Research and Development

Indeed, what is there that does not appear marvelous when it comes to our knowledge for the first time? How many things, too, are looked upon as quite impossible until they have been actually effected?
—*Pliny the Elder*

Contents

	Page
Introduction	59
Current Activities and Programs	59
The Federal Role in R&D	59
Funding Levels of Disability-Related R&D	59
The Federal Government's Involvement in Disability-Related R&D	60
National Institute of Handicapped Research	62
Veterans Administration	64
Other Federal Agencies	65
The Private Sector Role in Disability-Related Research	68
Discussion	70

LIST OF TABLES

Table No.	Page
1. Science Information Exchange Grants Awarded for Disability-Related Research by Federal Agencies, Fiscal Year 1979	60
2. National Funding for Health R&D, 1980	61
3. Veterans Administration RER&D Budget Distribution	65
4. Veterans Administration R&D Budget Overview	65
5. National Health Agencies	68

LIST OF FIGURES

Figure No.	Page
2. A Comparison of Public and Private Expenditures for Health Care, Transfer Payments to Disabled People, Health Care Research, and Disability-Related Research, Fiscal Year 1979	61
3. NIHR Grant Allocations by Program, Fiscal Year 1979	63
4. NASA's Technology Transfer Process	67

6. Research and Development

INTRODUCTION

"Research, development, and diffusion" is a shorthand phrase for a diverse and complex process of creating, producing, and delivering technologies. The research and development (R&D) system is an intricate arrangement of public and private organizations. These include Federal, State, and local governments; individuals; companies; universities; and a host of other participants.

The research, development, and diffusion of technologies for disabled people covers an extremely broad range of conditions. The National Institute of Handicapped Research (NIHR), for example, includes the following in its research plan: mental retardation, mental illness, and physical disabilities—i.e., paraplegia, arthritis, sensory deficits (blind, deaf, deaf-blind), epilepsy, heart disease, cancer, stroke, amputations, multiple sclerosis, cerebral palsy, muscular dystrophy, osteogenesis imperfecta, spina bifida, cystic fibrosis, chronic respiratory dysfunction, specific learning disabilities, and many other categories (52).

Each of these conditions alone could easily consume a major part of the research attention of the agencies involved in this area. The research task is further complicated by the varying severity of disabilities present in the population. Between the individuals of near "typical" functioning and those with extremely severe disabilities are the majority who require widely varying amounts of assistance, either social or technological, to perform various life functions.

Furthermore, there are thousands of specialized technologies to assist disabled individuals. Such technologies range in complexity from $25,000 computerized reading machines for blind people to $3 specially designed utensils for easier gripping. In addition to devices for the individual, technologies include "system" technologies that make public transportation, buildings, and communication networks more easily accessible. "Service" or process technologies are equally diverse. Programs to assist disabled people include rehabilitation therapy provided by health care organizations, job counseling, sheltered workshops, independent living centers, traditional medical care, income assistance, and a number of other services. Disability-related research encompasses all of these diverse and interlocking technologies.

CURRENT ACTIVITIES AND PROGRAMS

The Federal Role in R&D

Funding Levels of Disability-Related R&D

The amount of funds devoted to R&D in the disability area is quite small in comparison to the number of people affected, the complexity of the research problems involved, and the total health care R&D budget. A recent White House study estimated that approximately $40 million to $50 million was spent annually by Government agencies responsible for various forms of disability-related research (181). A more current survey conducted by Richard LeClair of NIHR estimates the amount spent in fiscal year 1979 to be about $66 million (126). A breakdown of the survey and the agencies involved is presented in table 1.

An important addition to the research more traditionally thought of as disability related is the general research of the National Institutes of Health (NIH). Much of NIH's research aims at preventing, treating, or diagnosing the diseases and conditions that directly or indirectly contribute to disabilities. The expenditures and resource allocations of NIH—especially those of the Na-

Table 1.—Science Information Exchange Grants Awarded for Disability-Related Research by Federal Agencies, Fiscal Year 1979

	Vocational/ educational	Management/ service delivery	Physical restoration (medical)	Behavioral/ social	Rehabilitation engineering	Total
Office of Special Education...	$4,265,550	$ 1,949,207	$ 2,551,993	$1,071,609	$ 781,372	$10,619,731
Veterans Administration......	—	400,000	1,550,000	750,000	3,886,011	6,586,011
National Institutes of Health..	50,000	321,404	7,660,022	3,024,373	1,039,165	12,094,964
Department of Commerce....	—	—	—	—	160,000	160,000
National Institute of Handicapped Research..........	1,532,358	9,346,536	7,976,239	3,879,114	9,465,753	31,700,000
National Science Foundation .	—	59,000	—	—	1,941,000	2,000,000
Department of Defense.......	—	—	—	—	183,331	183,331
Department of Agriculture	50,000	50,000	—	—	—	100,000
Bureau of Occupational and Adult Education............	540,049	—	—	—	—	540,049
Department of Labor.........	50,000	100,000	50,000	—	—	200,000
Social Security Administration............	—	100,000	—	—	—	100,000
Health Care and Financing Administration............	—	—	—	37,436	38,000	75,436
Department of Transportation.	—	300,000	—	—	238,037	538,037
Smithsonian Institution......	—	50,000	—	—	—	50,000
Department of Justice.......	—	246,580	—	—	—	246,580
Department of Housing and Urban Development........	—	—	—	—	500,000	500,000
Totals.................	$6,487,957	$12,922,727	$19,288,254	$8,762,532	$18,232,669	$65,694,139

NOTE: These figures are within 10 to 20 percent of the actual expenditure levels. Differences in definitions, accounting procedures, etc., all contribute to variations in estimates.

SOURCE: Richard LeClair, National Institute of Handicapped Research.

tional Institute of Arthritis, Diabetes, and Digestive and Kidney Diseases; the National Eye Institute; the National Institute of Neurological and Communicative Disorders and Stroke (NINCDS); the National Institute of Child Health and Human Development; and the National Institute on Aging —and of the Alcohol, Drug Abuse, and Mental Health Administration within the Department of Health and Human Services (DHHS) all play a role in research aimed at lessening the incidence and severity of physical and mental conditions present in the population as a whole and in the population of disabled individuals specifically. Even if a more inclusive definition of disability-related research is used, *the total Federal level of involvement is still rather small compared to health care expenditures in general, health care research efforts, and money spent on transfer programs for disabled people.* Figure 2 and table 2 illustrate these comparisons. Note that if figure 2 were drawn to scale, the amount for disability-related research could not even be seen.

The Federal Government is responsible for an estimated 66 percent of all health research in this country (163). As a result, the Federal Government is the major force in setting research priorities for health care research in general and also for disability-related research. The figure and tables mentioned above help provide an overview of the Federal R&D effort and the complex network in which biomedical, health care, and disability-related research exist. They also provide an indication of the general direction the Federal Government has established for the national research effort.

The Federal Government's Involvement in Disability-Related R&D

The official role of the Federal Government in vocational rehabilitation, prosthesis research, and other disability-related research dates back to the 1930's and 1940's. The presence of the Federal Government as a purchaser of devices to aid disabled people reaches back even further to the years following the Civil War (210). Much of the groundwork for the current system of rehabilitation research was laid in the 1940's by the National Academy of Sciences and the armed services in

Figure 2.—A Comparison of Public and Private Expenditures for Health Care, Transfer Payments to Disabled People, Health Care Research, and Disability-Related Research, Fiscal Year 1979

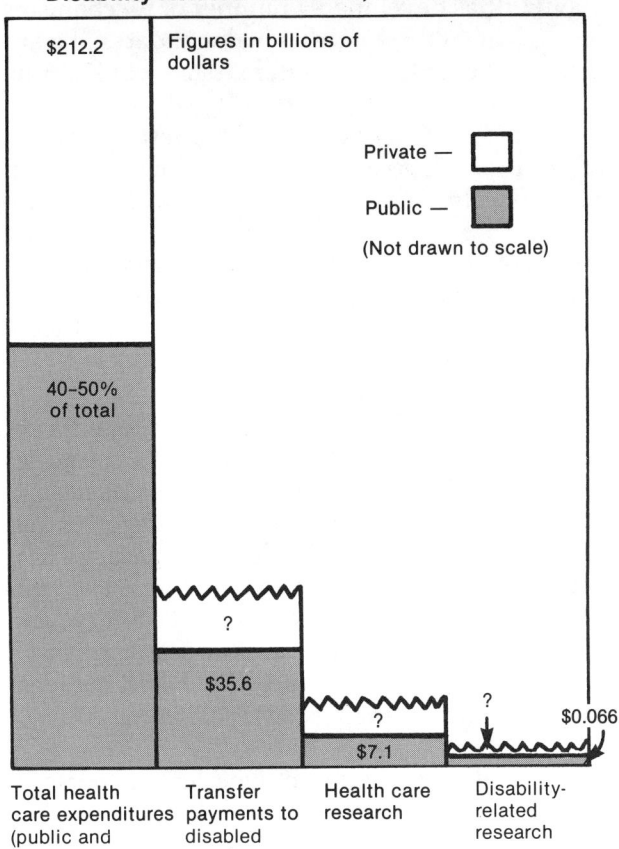

- Total health care expenditures (public and private): $212.2 billion (40–50% of total public)
- Transfer payments to disabled people: $35.6 billion
- Health care research: $7.1 billion
- Disability-related research: $0.066 billion

(Not drawn to scale)

SOURCE: Office of Technology Assessment.

Table 2.—National Funding for Health R&D, 1980
(millions of dollars)

Total funding	$7,891[a]
Government:	
Federal	4,723
State and local	455
Industry	2,391[b]
Nonprofit organizations	322[b]

[a] Includes expenditures for drug research.
[b] Estimates.

SOURCE: Office of Program Planning and Evaluation, National Institutes of Health.

mensity of the problems involved. The private and nonprofit sectors of our society have also become increasingly involved in disability-related products and services. These two areas are examined more closely later in this chapter.

Earlier, in table 1, Federal spending levels were used to illustrate the level of Government involvement in disability-related research.* Naturally enough, levels of spending correlate very closely with levels of involvement and commitment to research. With research budgets as the measuring stick, four organizations stand out prominently: the Office of Special Education (OSE), VA, NIH, and NIHR. The National Aeronautics and Space Administration (NASA) is also involved in this area as a result of technology transfer efforts stemming from its primary aeronautical and space mission.

The Interagency Committee for Handicapped Research is responsible for reviewing proposed research projects and for identifying areas that overlap with ongoing projects. The committee must include the Director of NIHR and representatives from RSA, NASA, NIH, the Department

response to the postwar needs of veterans. A large share of the initial research was conducted by the Department of Defense (DOD) and the Veterans Administration (VA) on prosthetic devices. Prosthetics research, along with an expanded focus on other areas of disability-related research, still continues in the VA system. The present day Rehabilitation Services Administration (RSA) had its beginning as the Office of Vocational Rehabilitation within the then Department of Health, Education, and Welfare (DHEW) in the early 1950's (210). Since these early efforts, the range and depth of the Federal initiative have expanded markedly. In addition, this area of R&D has steadily gained increased attention and recognition by the Federal Government over the years, though it remains small in comparison to the im-

---

*There is a lack of consistent definitions for the terms rehabilitation research, handicap-related research, biomedical research applied to the disabled, and similar terms. Each term means something different to different people, and they carry different connotations and emotional undertones. Often, definitions of research in this area primarily include the rehabilitation engineering efforts (hardware-oriented) efforts of the VA, NIHR, NASA, and NSF. Other definitions expand the hardware orientation and include the services and methods efforts of various organizations; for example, OSE or NIHR's research training centers. Still others include the biomedically focused efforts of NIH, or the "systems" research of the DOT and so on. A large number of agencies and organizations do some amount of research, most of which is narrowly focused in rather specialized areas. These efforts are included in some definitions and excluded from other.

of Transportation (DOT), the National Science Foundation (NSF), VA, and the Department of Education (DOE). A member of the National Council on the Handicapped also sits on the committee. Representatives from the nonprofit and private sectors are also included.

Another mechanism that NIHR and other Federal agencies involved in this area use is the Interagency Committee on Rehabilitation Engineering. This working group, composed of representatives from NSF, the National Council, the National Bureau of Standards (NBS), NASA, VA, NIHR, the Department of Housing and Urban Development, DHHS, DOT, NINCDS, and the Senate Committee on Labor and Human Resources, has been meeting for the last 5 years. It was instrumental in the development of NIHR's Long-Range Plan.

National Institute of Handicapped Research.— NIHR, a major source of disability-related research funds, is an "old" program with a new name and a new location. The Rehabilitation, Comprehensive Services, and Developmental Disabilities Amendments of 1978 (Public Law 95-602) removed the engineering and training programs previously administrated by RSA in DHEW and placed them, as NIHR, in the newly reorganized DOE under the Office of Special Education and Rehabilitative Services, along with the restructured RSA.

NIHR was a response to a need for a centralized and more visible focus on rehabilitation research and engineering. The agency was given the mandate to establish a comprehensive and coordinated approach to the development of a rehabilitation research program. It was also charged with facilitating the dissemination of information concerning developments in rehabilitation procedures and devices to professionals and disabled individuals. In addition, NIHR was directed to help improve the development and distribution of technologies to disabled people and to increase the scientific and technical base currently existing in the area (10).

NIHR has an extensive mandate considering its size and funding levels. Its fiscal year 1981 budget is $35 million. Its closest competitors for research funding are NIH, OSE, and VA, all of which have smaller research budgets directed toward disability-related research.

NIHR has developed a number of mechanisms to implement its congressional mandates. To approach the critical research issues confronting disabled people, it has developed a three-step process (52): 1) identification and establishment of priorities for research programs for the application of technology to the needs of disabled individuals; 2) development of the technologies that have been identified; and 3) evaluation, verification, and demonstration of the research results and the dissemination of information and technology to the rehabilitation practitioners.

From this process, NIHR has developed a research plan that it has stated in terms of categories of "needs." Each of the general areas of need is further subdivided by functional categories and then once again divided by disability group. These categories are also examined and divided according to age categories, severity of disability, and so on. The general functional areas of research needs, with specific examples, that NIHR has identified are the following (52):

- Mobility: locomotion, wheelchairs, personal licensed vehicles, and public transit.
- Housing: accessibility (architectural barrier removal), and appropriate fixtures and furniture.
- Communication: reception and expression of information (interpersonal communications in person and through telecommunication and access to stored information).
- Function/physical restoration: orthotics, prosthetics, functional electrical stimulation, tissue mechanisms (e.g., pressure on tissue), biomechanics (joint replacement), surgical procedures and equipment (therapeutic), sensory stimulation substitutes, and diagnostics.
- Education: specialized equipment (equipment for delivery of services for diagnostics, and for therapeutics).
- Employment: job station adaption, job modification, specialized equipment, and physical adaption for work.
- Recreation/physical education: specialized equipment.

- Activities of daily living: environmental control systems, medical self-care (monitoring of one's condition and progress), feeding and hygiene devices.

NIHR translates these research goals and needs into practice via: 1) rehabilitation research and training centers (RTCs), 2) rehabilitation engineering centers (RECs), 3) spinal cord injury rehabilitation centers, 4) centers for deaf-blind youths, and 5) coordination with the international rehabilitation research centers (55). A breakdown of the budget levels and grant allocations that NIHR devotes to these various areas is shown in figure 3.

The RECs grew out of the major research and training programs in prosthetics and orthotics at RSA and its predecessor agencies. The REC approach was initiated in the early 1970's and was designed to encourage the application of technology to improve the quality of life of physically disabled people. This goal was to be reached by combining medicine, engineering, and related sciences to form a coherent and total rehabilitation effort (51). Since 1971, 12 RECs have been established in the United States, with three additional collaborating centers overseas. Each center has its own research agenda, developed within the general context of NIHR's long-range research plan.

NIHR also funds a number of other centers that address a range of disability-related issues. Among these are 21 RTCs: 11 medical RTCs, three mental retardation rehabilitation RTCs, three vocational rehabilitation RTCs, two deafness rehabilitation RTCs, a blindness rehabilitation RTC, and a mental health rehabilitation RTC. These centers pursue research that deals with problems pertaining to employment, living skills, rehabilitation personnel training programs, discrimination, service delivery models, consumer involvement, etc. In addition to supporting research on the topics just mentioned, RTCs have responsibility for conducting training programs for rehabilitation and health care professionals.

The legislation that created NIHR also established a formal mechanism for setting research priorities and for coordinating activities among the various agencies that support disability-related research. The 15-member National Council on the Handicapped, for example, is to perform the following tasks (10):

- establish general policies for, and review the operation of, NIHR;
- provide advice to the Commissioner with respect to the policies and conduct of RSA;
- advise the Commissioner, the appropriate Assistant Secretary, and the Director of NIHR on development of programs to be carried out under the Rehabilitation Act, as amended;
- review and evaluate on a continuing basis all policies, programs, and activities concerning disabled individuals and persons with developmental disabilities conducted or assisted by Federal departments and agencies in order to assess their effectiveness in meeting needs;
- make recommendations to the Secretary, the Commissioner, and the Director of NIHR respecting ways to improve research

Figure 3.—NIHR Grant Allocations by Program, Fiscal Year 1979

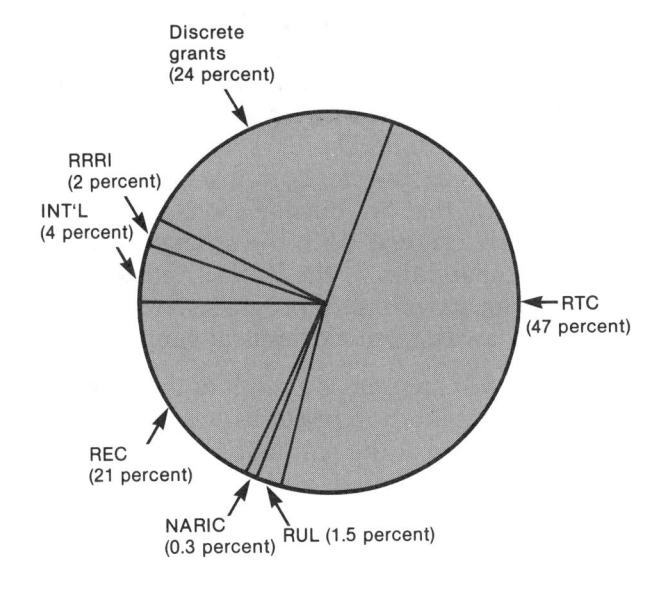

- Discrete grants (24 percent)
- RRRI (2 percent)
- INT'L (4 percent)
- RTC (47 percent)
- REC (21 percent)
- NARIC (0.3 percent)
- RUL (1.5 percent)

Key:
INT'L — International centers and programs
NARIC — National Rehabilitation Information Center
REC — Research engineering centers
RRRI — Regional rehabilitation research institutes
RTC — Research and training centers
RUL — Research utilization laboratories

SOURCE: NIHR research and demonstration grants awarded in fiscal year 1979.

concerning disabled individuals, and the methods of collecting and disseminating the findings of such research and to make recommendations for facilitating the implementation of programs based on such findings; and
- submit annually a report to the Secretary, Congress, and the President containing: a) a statement of the current status of research concerning disabilities in the United States; b) a review of the activities of RSA and NIHR; and c) such recommendations concerning (a) and (b) as the council considers appropriate.

Since the National Council was not appointed and confirmed until September 1980, it has only begun its work. Its first task was a review and revision of NIHR's 5-year plan.

Veterans Administration.—As mentioned earlier, VA has been involved in disability-related research since the late 1940's. For many years, VA was the primary supporter of federally sponsored research in this area, especially in the field of prosthetics research. Since 1947, VA has spent over $25.5 million on prosthetics research alone, not including the money devoted to the support of the VA Prosthetics Center on the VA Research Center for Prosthetics in New York City (152). In the last few years, VA has expanded its disability-related research focus to include a broader range of areas. The establishment of the Rehabilitation Engineering Research and Development (RER&D) program is the VA's response to the increased research and service needs of the veteran population and of disabled people in general.

The VA health care system is the largest health care delivery organization in the Nation. It encompasses 172 medical centers, 100 nursing homes, 16 domiciliaries, and 229 outpatient clinics. VA employs the full-time equivalent of approximately 181,440 physicians, dentists, nurses, and administrative and support personnel (218). Further, there are an estimated 28 million veterans over age 40 who are eligible for health care services should the need arise (151). VA presents a unique example of a system that includes the continuum of clients, needs, facilities, money, personnel, and the mandate to develop, deliver, evaluate, and support a full range of technologies and services to disabled individuals. It also provides an excellent setting for the evaluation of medical technologies. Neither VA, the private sector, nor any of the other Federal agencies has made much use of this system for such evaluation. The service aspects of the VA system are discussed in greater detail later in chapter 9.

VA has three centers that perform or support varying types of rehabilitation R&D. One, the VA Prosthetics Research Center in New York City, is organizationally separate from the RER&D program. The two other centers are directly tied to the VA RER&D program: one located in the Palo Alto VA Medical Center in California, and one in the Hines VA Medical Center in Chicago. The RER&D program is also establishing university-affiliated research engineering programs to help support qualified engineering graduate students and faculty who undertake rehabilitation engineering projects (37). The thrust of this program is twofold: 1) to interest engineering students in rehabilitation engineering (a critical shortage of trained rehabilitation engineering professionals exists in this country*); and 2) to infuse new ideas and concepts into the VA RER&D program by having a flow of information on program needs and possible solutions between academia and VA. In addition, the RER&D program supports investigator-initiated projects, both intramurally and extramurally, that are outside the efforts of the two RER&D centers. With the strengthening of in-house capabilities at the RER&D centers and in the university-affiliated programs, however, it is moving away from extramural support.

The RER&D program is a result of the increased focus on rehabilitation research and engineering needs at VA and at the national level in general. In 1973, this program was separated from the general R&D efforts of VA and given the mandate

---

*In 1976, a workshop held at the University of Tennessee recommended that a master's degree in rehabilitation engineering be established for qualified engineers and that it include training in computer science, anatomy, clinical medicine, and appropriate engineering disciplines. These recommendations were made with the following factors in mind: 1) there are currently (in 1976) only 50 individuals designated and functioning as rehabilitation engineers; 2) the current estimated need is for 250 rehabilitation engineers; and 3) the projected need for rehabilitation engineers is 1,000 in 5 years and 2,000 in 10 years (123).

to improve the quality of life and facilitate greater independence for physically disabled veterans. The program is to do this through research, development, and evaluation of new devices, techniques, and concepts in rehabilitation. In addition, the RER&D program is required to coordinate and cooperate with NIHR and to support RECs. (This does not mean that VA is obligated to assist these centers financially. Rather, support takes the form of information exchange and consultation regarding ongoing efforts at both agencies.) The RER&D program is primarily a hardware—sophisticated technology—oriented effort that has as its major goal the development of usable devices that assist individuals, have an impact on the delivery of clinical services, or assist in increasing the availability of new devices on the open market. The RER&D budget was $8.1 million in fiscal year 1980 and is estimated to be $8.8 million in fiscal year 1981. The personnel ceiling is 143—including centers, university programs, and RER&D staff. Table 3 summarizes the budget distribution and the priorities and research goals established by VA. Table 4 provides an overview of the RER&D budget in relation to the VA's overall medical and health services research effort (37).

Other Federal Agencies.—NASA and NSF are also involved in hardware-oriented research in this area. NSF's authorizing legislation (Public Law 95-434) for fiscal year 1979 included $2 million for disability-related research programs in the Applied Sciences Research Applications Directorate. NSF has supported grant requests dealing with various aspects of disability-related research. Two examples are: 1) the Johns Hopkins University project on personal computing to aid disabled people—a project in conjunction with the Tandy Corp. to develop computer-based programs and ideas to aid disabled individuals; and 2) a project to develop a graphic computer display that blind and visually impaired people can use to create, edit, interpret, store, and retrieve full page braille and tactile programs. Other projects include "Micro-Processor-Based Prosthetic Controls" and a "Needs and Design Concepts for Voice-Output Communications Aids" grant (157). Given the current budget situation and research goals of NSF, however, it is unlikely that this program and NSF's interest and involvement in disability-related research will thrive.

In the late 1970's, Congress formally expanded the mandate of NASA by adding bioengineering for disabled people to its functions (Public Law 95-401). Congress felt that (211):

> The general welfare of the United States requires that the unique competence of NASA in science and engineering systems be directed to

Table 3.—Veterans Administration RER&D Budget Distribution (thousands of dollars)

	Fiscal year 1980	Estimated fiscal year 1981
RER&D centers and affiliations	$2,425	$2,450
Amputation/surgical procedures	1,483	1,547
Prosthetics/orthotics	910	1,045
Blindness and visual impairment	749	823
Hearing and speech impairment	729	804
Kinesiology (Gait analysis)	543	682
Mobility	524	576
Spinal cord injury	269	297
Maxillofacial restoration	212	230
Robotics	165	196
Functional electrical stimulation or neural control	119	134
Total	$8,085	$8,784

SOURCE: Veterans Administration.

Table 4.—Veterans Administration R&D Budget Overview (thousands of dollars)

	Fiscal year 1977	1978	1979	1980	1981
Medical research program	$101,567	$108,153	$118,016	$122,745	$129,943
Staffing	4,220	4,367	4,217	4,171	4,171
RER&D program	4,419	5,502	7,191	8,085	8,784
Staffing	69	90	112	143	143
Health services R&D program	3,604	2,996	3,004	3,153	3,083
Staffing	45	90	105	104	104

SOURCE: Veterans Administration.

assisting in bioengineering research, development, and demonstration programs designed to alleviate and minimize the effects of disability.

NASA has been involved in transferring technology and information gained from its bioengineering efforts, as well as its general research efforts, to the health care sector since the late 1960's. Biomedical applications teams attempt to: 1) identify and interpret national trends in medicine as well as technology-related problems in health care delivery, and 2) develop potential solutions to these problems through the use of aerospace technology (227). NASA tries to pursue technology transfer opportunities when it finds that: 1) a problem is recognized as significant by medical agencies; 2) a solution in the form of a commercially available product is not available or anticipated; 3) a solution would make a significant contribution to medical research or to clinical practice; 4) the problem can be defined in terms that indicate the applicability of aerospace technology; 5) the solution requires application engineering rather than basic research; and 6) the application has a high probability of success in the marketplace (227). Figure 4 illustrates the process that NASA employs to implement these guidelines. It also provides a model that might be useful as a general guide to the technology transfer process of other Federal agencies involved in disability-related research, development, and diffusion.

NASA has attempted three types of bioengineering applications projects—commercial, institutional, and demonstration. Commercial projects are those that directly involve a manufacturer; institutional projects are those developed by a Federal agency; and demonstration projects are ones for which NASA develops the prototype on its own (227). An example of a commercial project is the fully implantable, programmable, rechargeable human tissue stimulator that was developed in conjunction with the Johns Hopkins Applied Physics Laboratory. An example of an institutional project is the Autocuer, an automated speech analyzer developed as a joint venture between NASA and VA, on the basis of initial work sponsored by NINCDS, with the involvement of NSF, the Research Triangle Institute, RSA, Bureau of Education for the Handicapped, and a Gallaudet College scientist. The liquid-cooled garment used for temperature control is an example of a demonstration project that NASA pursued as a result of its research that had potential in the biomedical/disability area. Other examples of NASA's technology development and transfer efforts are the rechargeable cardiac pacemaker battery, heat activated switches, a hand-finger flexor, and biocompatible pure carbon that has proven very useful in prosthesis attachment materials (226). Obviously, research in the area of disabilities is not NASA's primary focus; rather, it is a lower level priority to be pursued as part of NASA's overall research and technology transfer efforts. NASA devotes about $600,000 to $750,000 to projects related to disabilities, and less than $2.5 million to its entire bioengineering applications programs.

Other Federal agencies that fund R&D programs in the disability-related area are DOT, the Department of Labor, NBS, the Department of Commerce, the Food and Drug Administration, the Health Care Financing Administration, the Social Security Administration, and DOD. These and other agencies have varying degrees of involvement in research on disability-related issues. Recent legislation and the increasing militancy of advocacy groups have forced many Federal and State agencies to examine a wide variety of issues in this area.

RSA is primarily oriented towards the delivery of services at the State and local level via its matching grants programs, which include a small percentage of funds for innovative programs to improve the quality and delivery of services. Most of its research programs were shifted to NIHR when that agency was created in 1978.

OSE still retains a significant research budget that is geared mostly toward the "soft" research areas (i.e., nonhardware directed areas of research). OSE is the third largest Federal supporter of disability-related research and the largest in the area of educationally related efforts. OSE's research priorities include programs for deaf-blind, severely disabled, and gifted and talented persons, for early childhood educational programs, for media and research uses, and for special education personnel development projects.

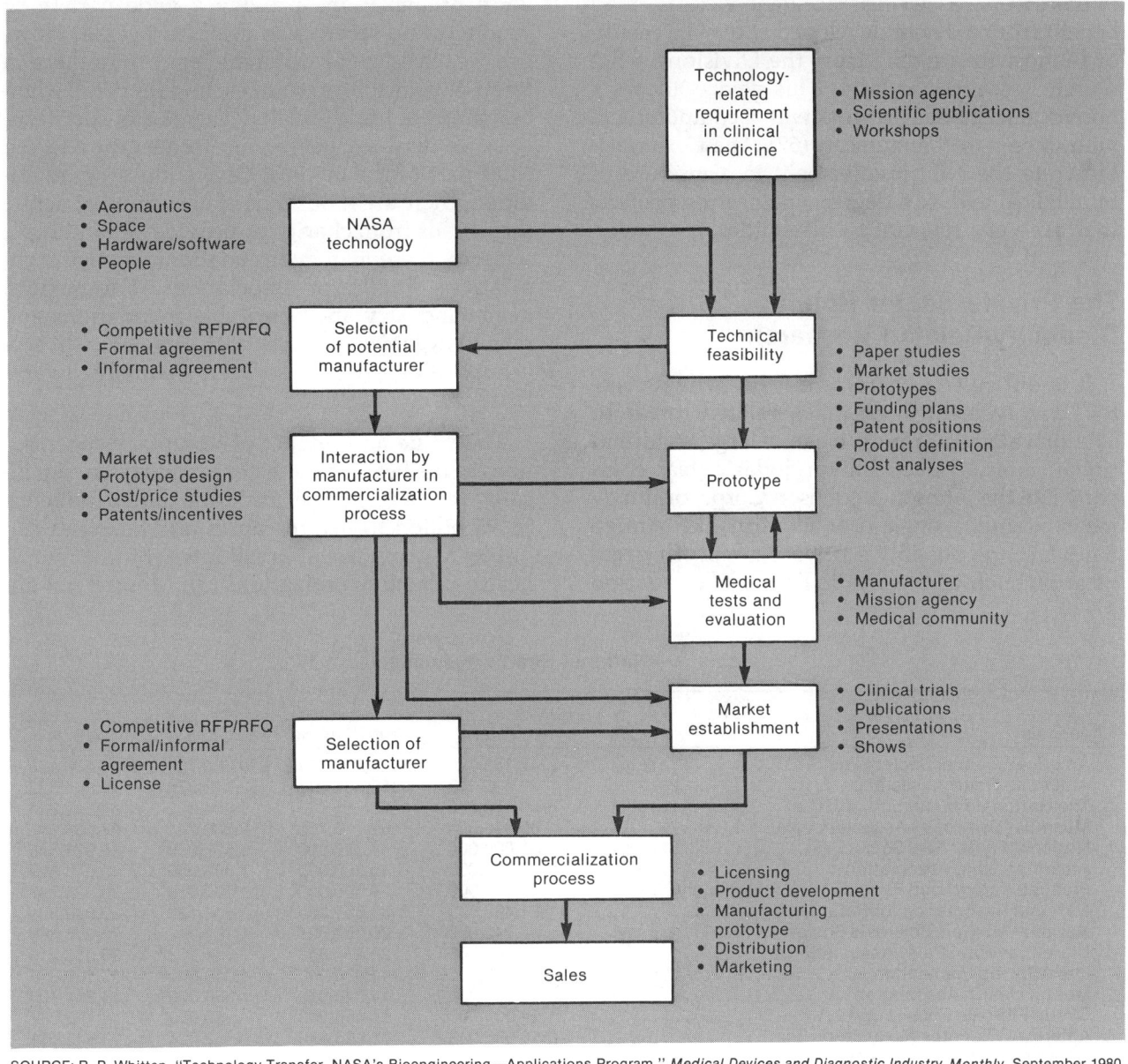

Figure 4.—NASA's Technology Transfer Process

```
                                    Technology-
                                    related              • Mission agency
                                    requirement          • Scientific publications
                                    in clinical          • Workshops
                                    medicine

• Aeronautics        NASA
• Space              technology
• Hardware/software
• People
                                                         • Paper studies
• Competitive RFP/RFQ   Selection        Technical       • Market studies
• Formal agreement      of potential     feasibility     • Prototypes
• Informal agreement    manufacturer                     • Funding plans
                                                         • Patent positions
                                                         • Product definition
• Market studies        Interaction by                   • Cost analyses
• Prototype design      manufacturer in   Prototype
• Cost/price studies    commercialization
• Patents/incentives    process
                                          Medical        • Manufacturer
                                          tests and      • Mission agency
                                          evaluation     • Medical community

                                                         • Clinical trials
• Competitive RFP/RFQ                     Market         • Publications
• Formal/informal       Selection of      establishment  • Presentations
  agreement             manufacturer                     • Shows
• License

                                    Commercialization   • Licensing
                                    process             • Product development
                                                        • Manufacturing
                                                          prototype
                                                        • Distribution
                                    Sales               • Marketing
```

SOURCE: R. P. Whitten, "Technology Transfer, NASA's Bioengineering—Applications Program," *Medical Devices and Diagnostic Industry Monthly*, September 1980.

NIH presents an interesting definitional problem. A very good argument could be made that most of its basic and applied biomedical research directly or indirectly affects currently or potentially disabled people. NIH then becomes the runaway leader in the disability-related research area. Using a more restricted set of criteria still puts NIH near or at the top in terms of resources devoted to research in this area.

NINCDS is currently supporting research on regeneration of spinal cord, or the central nervous system (CNS) nerve tissue. Such research is potentially of great value to the population with spinal cord injuries (103). NINCDS also has a Neural Prosthesis Program that is currently working on a project involving artificial control of the bladder through electrical stimulation (103). Persons with muscular dystrophy, multiple sclerosis, cerebral palsy, speech, and other communication impairments, as well as accident victims, may benefit from a device developed at the University of Idaho with funding from the Division of Research Resources at NIH. This device allows a nonvocal individual to work with a computer and video screen to communicate (67). These examples illustrate the NIH involvement in a mixture of biomedical and, to a degree, engineering projects that are very relevant to disabilities.

The Private Sector Role in Disability-Related Research

It is difficult to characterize the "private sector" involvement in disability-related research. The private sector may mean a large, multinational, multiproduct, billion-dollar-a-year company like the Johnson & Johnson Corp., or it may mean a small, single-product firm like Amigo Sales Co., or possibly a private nonprofit organization such as the Cystic Fibrosis Foundation or Muscular Dystrophy Association. These diverse organizations provide a wide variety of products and services to disabled people. However, each is quite different from the others in terms of priorities, resources, and function. Manufacturers of health-related devices that specifically serve disabled people are frequently referred to as part of the medical device industry. In addition, there are thousands of agencies that derive their funds from charity or provide philanthropic services; these may be foundations, service organizations, funds, or associations. The medical device industry and charitable foundations and related organizations are both extremely diverse groups that exist to serve an equally diverse "market."

The value and impact of voluntary contributions to the health care sector of society are significant. In 1980, Americans contributed a record $5.95 billion to health causes and hospitals (3). Table 5 provides a breakdown of the major health-related organizations (3). Most, if not all,

Table 5.—National Health Agencies

Agencies	1979 Total	1979 Contributions	1979 Bequests	1978
American Cancer Society, Inc.	$142,138,732	$102,778,011	$39,360,721	$126,106,570
American Heart Association	82,938,148	59,594,573	23,343,575	73,801,722
The National Foundation	65,170,640	63,765,738	1,404,902	64,692,941
Muscular Dystrophy Association, Inc.	65,016,996	62,736,755	2,280,241	57,635,996
National Easter Seal Society	52,000,000[a]	46,323,000[a]	5,677,000[a]	46,921,946[c]
American Lung Association	47,000,000[a]	45,500,000[a]	1,500,000[a]	45,548,629[c]
Planned Parenthood Federation of America, Inc.	35,000,000[a]	34,500,000[a]	500,000[a]	29,334,747[c]
National Association for Retarded Citizens	34,465,963[a]	33,851,235[a]	614,728[a]	30,605,321[c]
National Multiple Sclerosis Society	27,242,099	26,052,827	1,189,272	25,206,469
United Cerebral Palsy Association, Inc.	24,888,956[a]	24,274,853[a]	614,103[a]	20,010,219[c]
The Arthritis Foundation	18,000,000[a]	14,000,000[a]	4,000,000[a]	17,109,399[c]
Mental Health Association	15,000,000[a]	14,640,000[a]	360,000[a]	14,811,703[c]
Cystic Fibrosis Foundation	14,500,000[a]	14,450,000[a]	50,000[a]	12,723,617[c]
American Diabetes Association, Inc.	11,996,043	11,433,379	562,664	10,945,701[c]
Leukemia Society of America, Inc.	11,314,627	10,850,156	464,471	10,757,023
National Kidney Foundation	9,306,368	9,088,429	217,939	7,739,719
National Society to Prevent Blindness	5,600,000[a]	3,600,000[a]	2,000,000[a]	4,799,622[c]
Epilepsy Foundation of America	4,800,000[a]	4,500,000[a]	300,000[a]	4,755,719[c]
Recording for the Blind[b]	3,642,594	2,928,619	713,975	3,384,646
Juvenile Diabetes Foundation	3,261,061	3,261,061	—	2,498,083
The National Hemophilia Foundation	3,100,000[a]	3,100,000[a]	—	3,500,000
American Foundation for the Blind, Inc.	2,459,967	1,131,515	1,328,452	3,875,444
Damon Runyon-Walter Winchell Cancer Fund	1,009,225	140,452	868,772	2,498,083
National Council on Alcoholism	845,582	783,272	62,311	966,425
Total	$680,697,001	$593,283,875	$87,413,126	$622,229,744

[a] Estimate.
[b] Educational organization.
[c] Revised.

SOURCE: American Association of Fund Raising Council, Inc., *Giving U.S.A.: 1980 Annual Report*, 1980.

of the top 24 health-related agencies deal directly, or certainly indirectly, with a range of disabling and handicapping conditions. Many of these organizations support ongoing R&D efforts in their areas of interest. Often, these organizations are primary actors in the development, delivery, and purchase of new technologies for their constituent groups. With yearly budgets in total exceeding $680 million, these organizations are powerful forces in the disability-related R&D system and are significant contributors to the service delivery system as well.

The general medical technology industry is a collection of over 3,000 firms responsible for over 12,000 products at an annual sales level of over $9 billion (34,221). In terms of firm size, 80 percent of the medical technology companies have annual sales of *less than* $20 million; the remaining 20 percent are much larger and, in almost all instances, are multiproduct companies (221)—e.g., Johnson & Johnson had total sales in 1975 of $2.25 billion, American Hospital Supply Corp. claims to distribute over 57,000 different products, and Everest & Jennings had gross revenues of $51 million in 1975 (34). One study, by Wenchel, found that there are essentially two types of companies in this industry: large, multinational and multidivisional companies with a variety of products; and smaller, single- or several-product firms (221).

Several studies have indicated that the industry is somewhat noncompetitive (34,221). Yet, Wenchel points out that in the realm of technical innovation (rather than in the cost of products), there does seem to be some competition (221). She further states that the market is highly responsive to new products, with a high entry and exit rate among new firms, especially among the smaller firms. The small, single- or several-product firms are often the ones introducing innovative technologies into the marketplace; this is their ticket into the arena (221):

> The measures of R&D and patent activity reflect a higher level of innovation than can be found in most industries in the U.S. economy . . . The medical technology industry appears to have maintained its levels of R&D by providing funding that the Federal Government had previously provided. Further, the level of patent activity is twice that existing in other industries throughout the U.S. economy.

A great deal of debate surrounds the issues of how much R&D is enough, who should do it (e.g., should Everett & Jenning support more R&D on wheelchair design, or just wait for and use the results of the numerous federally sponsored studies in this area?), and who should benefit financially from the complex interaction of private/public/nonprofit sponsored research efforts.

It is difficult and perhaps deceptive at times to use an industrywide description—medical devices industry—to characterize the efforts of a single firm or a specialized group of firms. The industry is too diverse, even if one can narrow the category to disability-related firms. Perhaps one good indicator of what and how much activity is going on is the visibility and frequency of articles in general circulation publications. When innovations or trends reach this level of the business community's or the public's awareness, especially in a specialized area such as this, then there may be a significant level of activity below the visible surface.

Articles in *Business Week* (24,25), *Medical World News* (139,140), *The New York Times* (160), *Discover* (220), and the *Wall Street Journal* (190) are representative of the "general circulation" accounts of the increase in corporate interest, investment, product development, and marketing of technologies for disabled people. Most of the activity that has reached this level of recognition, though, has been in the area of fairly sophisticated technology. It is almost a certainty that by far the largest share of corporate interest is geared toward the application of emerging technologies that are hardware based. Examples of the types of technologies that have received media attention are the Kurzweil Reading Machines, electronic communication devices, voice-command control systems, new types of wheelchairs, (the Amigo, the Levo chair, and battery-powered chairs), the Lifeline Emergency Alarm and Response System, the Autocom, environmental control systems, bionic prostheses, robotics, television captioning systems, microcomputer controlled implants, the Optacon, and artificial organs. Obviously, these technologies are the "gee-whiz" offerings that are in, or coming into, the marketplace. This observation does not mean to say that there is no activity in the more mundane, yet critical, areas of disability-related R&D—but the latter type of activity is not as evident or glamorous, and possibly not as rewarding (intellectually, scientifically, or financially) to many scientists and investors.

DISCUSSION

The research goals and priorities in the disability-related R&D process are, to state it mildly, diverse and challenging. The Federal agencies working in this area have extremely broad mandates to address very complex and difficult problems. The research agenda of NIHR alone is overwhelming. The agencies will not be able to do it alone. Private and nonprofit organizations are key components in the R&D process. To date, Congress has recognized great potential in R&D related to disabilities, but the organization of the R&D effort has been inadequate for substantial results. The Federal Government devotes approximately 0.7 percent of the total amount of healthcare related research funds to research directly related to disabilities. The annual expenditure for direct disability-related R&D has been estimated to be between $1.00 and $2.92 per disabled person (210). The private sector's contribution is very difficult to determine, but it, too, appears to be less than the amount that could profitably be used. The purpose, though, is not to arrive at precise figures, but rather to obtain and provide a general sense of the level of public and private commitment to the needs of disabled people. The R&D activity is a very important component of the effort to meet those needs. The current research needs are extensive. The ability of the Federal Government to reach those goals, given current outcomes of R&D, is limited.

It is possible that the combined efforts of NIHR, VA, NASA, RSA, DOD, the many other agencies that are involved in this process, and the private sector will be able to make a significant contribution to the population of disabled people. There is reason for some optimism. The focus of R&D, while still firmly entrenched in the "hardware" approach to solving problems, is slowly changing to incorporate and value the work in services, delivery systems, appropriate technology solutions to problems, evaluation of R&D efforts, and the other inputs that are necessary to the "total" rehabilitation of the individual. The research network is being formed to combine these varied fields of investigation. The challenge is to fit the parts together to make a coordinated, comprehensive, and effective research effort that will respond to the changing needs of increasingly active and independent disabled people.

The use of the peer review and advisory council system to assess the value and performance of research products and the likelihood of success of research proposals, deserves attention. Various agencies have different approaches to making use of committees of experts and in-house professionals to judge the quality of the programs and research proposals being funded and the resulting research products.

VA uses a combination of in-house professionals, the directors of its various departments and programs, in conjunction with a panel of non-VA experts drawn from a range of disciplines. This two-level process is used to help set research priorities and to conduct reviews of research proposals and results. The NIH dual advisory/peer review system is well known and does not need elaboration here. The existing peer review systems in other agencies are usually variations on the NIH system.

The RSA peer review system has been an "on-again, off-again" system over the last decade. Currently, it is an "on-again" system that uses the "project announcement in the Federal Register" system as the first step in the process. From there, proposals submitted are routed to internal RSA staff and, if appropriate, to relevant regional rehabilitation officials. There is also a peer review process for research proposals that is conducted by non-RSA, non-Federal Government experts (97).

NIHR also goes through the program announcement process in the Federal Register. In the past, this process was followed with a weak, infrequently applied peer review process. The agency is now in the process of implementing a formal peer review process in its project/program selection and evaluation process. The VA system is much better established and has been more effective than NIHR's. NIHR, prior to the recent changes, concentrated most of its priority-setting efforts in the long-range plan development process.

It should also be noted at this point that announcing project proposals in the Federal Register may satisfy public notification requirements, but it does not guarantee quality research. Often these announcements can be so vague and all-inclusive that the agency discretion retained in the selection process is almost unbounded. Peer review systems are workable and effective only if the spirit of the process is honored rather than just the letter of the law.

An idea suggested to OTA is the removal of much of the peer review process in favor of much stronger program and project manager systems. To a large degree, this idea follows the administrative model used by NASA—i.e., a very goal-oriented, results-directed approach where the various program and project directors are given significant leeway within the general goals of the project being conducted. The effectiveness of the personnel involved and the quality of work being conducted are measured in terms of the performance and success of the program and project. The advantage of a system such as this, especially in an applied research setting, is that once the program or project goals are established (possibly the most difficult part of this approach), the various administrators and scientific personnel are left to reach their goals in the most effective and efficient means at their disposal. There are many obstacles to using this approach, but it is worth noting and perhaps considering (at least on a pilot or demonstration basis) for certain projects. This system seems less appropriate for the setting of research priorities or the awarding of initial R&D contracts and grants.

The disability-related R&D system at present is primarily operating on a basic research model—i.e., one where the funding agencies react rather than act. This approach seems appropriate for basic-research-oriented programs and projects. However, a large part of this R&D area is geared to applied research goals and needs. OTA was frequently told that there are numerous, potentially useful devices in existence: "We are overwhelmed by available technology; we just need to get it to the consumers so they can adopt it to their uses at a price they can afford."* Having Federal agencies or researchers attack these "applied research" problems a piecemeal and basic research approach only exacerbates the view that little of value has resulted from the money, time, and efforts of the myriad research centers and programs supported by the Federal Government.

The alternative to the "goal-oriented" approach is a system of rigorous peer review. The NIH dual review system has served the biomedical and health care systems well. By adopting a similar, though modified, system in this area, the resulting information and products that come out of the federally supported disability-related R&D process may be of a higher quality and thus useful to a wider range of consumers, researchers, manufacturers, and others. On the basis of its research and the results of its public outreach survey, OTA finds that there is a common perception, though certainly not a unanimous one, on the part of consumers and the scientific and professional communities that much of the research conducted in this federally supported system is of poor quality. Strengthening the formal peer review systems of this process could help to alleviate some of these problems. However, effective evaluation mechanisms are very much dependent on the "state-of-mind" in an organization and should be more than a pro forma attempt at satisfying a legislative or agency requirement.

---
*Other people, however, believe that "overwhelmed" is a deceptive term. They believe that there are some technologies ready for diffusion but that other existing technologies need to be better developed prior to widespread use.

7.
Evaluation of Technologies

Be not swept off your feet by the vividness of the impression, but say, "Impression, wait for me a little. Let me see what you are and what you represent. Let me try you."

—*Epicetus*

Contents

	Page
Introduction	75
Current Activities and Programs	76
Discussion	81

LIST OF TABLES

Table No.	Page
6. DHHS Technology Coordinating Committee	76
7. Non-DHHS Agencies Involved in Evaluation of Health Technology	77

7.
Evaluation of Technologies

INTRODUCTION

Evaluation covers a broad spectrum of activities. Depending on the importance and nature of a given innovation, public agencies, nonprofit organizations, and private sector firms will rely on a number of criteria to evaluate a given technology. The historically most common, and perhaps most important, criteria used in the initial stages of evaluation and development of health-related research products are safety, efficacy, technical feasibility, and technical performance. For commercial products (or potentially commercial products, even if developed with public or nonprofit funds), another basic criterion is potential profitability.

Other criteria will then follow. Depending on the use or intended market for the innovation, evaluation efforts might include such "tests" as: effectiveness, suitability for the goals of its use, reliability, cost, repairability, convenience, affordability, esthetics, consumer satisfaction, patent protection, legal impacts, liability concerns, accessibility, reimbursement status or potential, social implications, cost-effectiveness determinations, ethical concerns, and so on.

The periodic efforts of the National Institutes of Health (NIH), the Veterans Administration (VA), and other health-related agencies tend to rely on and support safety and efficacy more often than any of the other criteria. The Food and Drug Administration (FDA) requires drug and device manufacturers to focus on safety and efficacy criteria if they produce items that fall within FDA's jurisdiction. If VA and the National Institute of Handicapped Research (NIHR) develop devices that fall within FDA's guidelines, they too must submit them for clearance. The private sector manufacturers, as well as NIHR, VA in its rehabilitation research role, and the National Aeronautics and Space Administration (NASA), also rely on many of the evaluation criteria cited above to help guide their decisionmaking.

The major issue, though, remains: Are the evaluation efforts of the public and private sectors sufficient to adequately inform the many levels of decisionmaking related to technology for use by disabled people? Current analysis and informed opinion indicates to OTA that the answer is an emphatic "No."

If one examines the literature on the adequacy of evaluation efforts concerning safety and efficacy in the health care system in general, it is clear that there are noticeable weaknesses in the process. A recent OTA study assessed the state of evaluating the safety and efficacy of medical technologies and identified several shortcomings in the evaluation process (164):

- There is no formal or well-coordinated overall system.
- Identification of technologies to be studied remains an underdeveloped, usually agency-specific, process.
- Existing technologies are identified much less frequently for study than are new and developing technologies; thus, they are studied much less frequently.
- Medical drugs and devices are subject to a more rigorous process of assessment than medical procedures.
- Preventive technologies receive far less attention than therapeutic ones.
- Serious questions have been raised concerning the adequacy of funding for clinical trials and other types of evaluations.
- Synthesis activities are still at a modest level despite their recent expansion.
- The quality and appropriateness of medical literature, the primary source of synthesized information, has been criticized.
- Synthesis activities cannot be adequate when there is a critical lack of information regarding efficacy and safety.
- Federal agencies have not assigned a high priority to disseminating information.

In the disability technologies area, OTA found similar weaknesses. In fact, shortcomings in this area are more pronounced than in the medical technology area. The reasons for this are difficult to know with much certainty. It appears, though, that there is less of a tradition of formal and scientific evaluation in the rehabilitation area, that the diversity of disabilities makes evaluation extremely complex, that the technologies in this area are sometimes seen as less "medically necessary" and thus less in need of careful evaluation, that few funds are devoted to evaluation, and that emotionalism is very strong in this area, making evaluation a difficult undertaking.

Actual or potential improvements in many of the areas listed above for medical technology evaluation can be in part attributed to the (now ended) existence of the National Center for Health Care Technology (NCHCT).* For example, over half of the items on NCHCT's list of emerging technologies that might need assessment were existing ones (this does not mean that they would have been assessed). To the extent, which might have become considerable, that NCHCT would have been involved with disability-related technologies, there was distinct potential for significant improvements in the evaluation process. However, NCHCT received no funds for fiscal year 1982 and stopped functioning in December of 1981.

---

*NCHCT was established by statute in 1978 in response to the feeling of Congress that not enough careful and scientific evaluation of medical technologies was being done to assure its appropriate use. Further, there was no focus for coordinating the numerous related activities taking place.

CURRENT ACTIVITIES AND PROGRAMS

Oddly enough, there is no shortage of agencies, organizations, and academics interested in the various issues surrounding the evaluation of technologies. If, for example, one examines the list of Department of Health and Human Services (DHHS) representatives to the Department's Technology Coordinating Committee, it is, if not surprising, then disappointing that such a disparity between interest and information exists. Table 6 shows those representatives. A similar breadth of potential involvement in evaluation is shown by the list in table 7 of non-DHHS agencies that are involved, to some degree, in health-related technology issues.

The level of Federal effort—money being spent on evaluation efforts—is impossible to fully determine. It is fairly accurate to say that no one really knows how much is being spent, either Government-wide or at specific agencies. The reason for this is easy enough to understand—it is difficult to define what activities, projects, or programs should or should not be counted when tallying up what the various agencies or programs consider "evaluation" activities. At best, agencies can provide rough estimates of these activities and spending levels. OTA has estimated that about

Table 6.—DHHS Technology Coordinating Committee

Representatives of
Alcohol, Drug Abuse, and Mental Health Administration
Centers for Disease Control
Food and Drug Administration
Health Care Financing Administration
Health Resources Administration
Health Services Administration
National Center for Health Statistics
National Center for Health Services Research
National Institutes of Health

Liaison representatives:
Office of Health Research, Statistics and Technology
Office of Science and Technology Policy, The White House
Office of Technology Assessment, U.S. Congress
Veterans Administration
National Institute of Handicapped Research
Department of Education
Office of Civilian Health and Medical Program of the Uniformed Services

SOURCE: Office of Technology Assessment.

$200 million a year is spent on evaluation of health technologies in general. The amount spent on disability-related health technologies is probably only a minor fraction of this amount. The exact amount of this fraction is not known. However, as a point of comparison, the percentage of total Federal health care research and development

Table 7.—Non-DHHS Agencies Involved in Evaluation of Health Technology

Department of Agriculture
Department of Commerce
Department of Defense
Department of Education
National Aeronautics and Space Administration
National Academy of Sciences
National Bureau of Standards
National Science Foundation
Office of Management and Budget
Veterans Administration
White House Office of Science and Technology Policy
U.S. Congress—committees and support agencies
    Senate Finance Committee
    House Ways and Means Committee
    Senate Labor and Human Resources Committee
    House Energy and Commerce Committee
    Senate and House Veterans' Affairs Committees
    Senate Special Committee on Aging
    Housing Select Committee on Aging
    Senate and House Budget Committees
    Senate and House Appropriations Committees
    House Science and Technology Committee
    Senate Commerce, Science, and
      Transportation Committee
    Office of Technology Assessment
    Congressional Research Service (Library of Congress)
    Congressional Budget Office
    General Accounting Office

Office of Technology Assessment.

(R&D) represented by evaluation of technologies is roughly 5 percent—and that is in an area with a stronger tradition of evaluation of technologies than the disability-related area.

Three additional areas of Federal evaluation activities should be mentioned here: 1) the requirement of the Medical Devices Amendments with respect to FDA's mandate (Public Law 94-295), 2) the relatively new directives to the National Bureau of Standards (NBS) (H.R. 96-949), and 3) the consensus development conferences of NIH.

In the fall of 1977, NIH began a program of consensus development designed to improve knowledge on the safety and efficacy of medical technologies and to transmit any information gained to the practicing physician and the public. Each conference, involving scientists, practicing physicians, consumers, and others, is set up to generate conclusions and recommendations concerning specific medical technologies. The conferences are run by the various Institutes of NIH; the Office for Medical Applications of Research of NIH is the coordinating and assisting office.

Several of the topics that have been covered or are scheduled to be covered are directly relevant to the disability area—e.g., continuous ambulatory peritoneal dialysis, prevention of osteoporosis in aging, and artificial hips.

In May of 1980, the Science and Technology Committee of the U.S. House of Representatives directed NBS to "undertake a general review of its activities in the disability area, and to develop a focused plan detailing potential opportunities within NBS and for interagency cooperative, projects . . . " (23). The Bureau has, in the past, conducted evaluative projects that have had relevance to disabled people. It has developed and evaluated devices to measure slip resistance on walkways for building accessibility, conducted performance and reliability tests on hearing aids and cardiac pacemakers, developed the implant standards for acrylic bone cements and metals and, in general, has helped address technical issues related to the needs of disabled individuals. Its product performance testing and materials research experience and capabilities make it a valuable asset to the area of evaluation.

However, the degree to which NBS will be able to be involved in disability-related research and testing is yet to be determined. The major problems are time and money. NBS performs almost 40 percent of its work at the request of other Federal agencies; the work is done on a reimbursable basis when it is determined to be of mutual benefit and meets one of two conditions (23):

> The Other Agency needs measurements, standards or data for application that are so specific and programmatically focused that they would not ordinarily be carried out under the general NBS measurement mandate; or the Other Agency has a technical problem that could be most efficiently and effectively solved by using a unique Bureau expertise.

The Committee on Science and Technology encouraged NBS to continue and strengthen its activities in providing measurement technology and performance standards as they relate to devices and facilities unique to disabled and elderly people. However, in a climate where rehabilitation agencies are already operating with decreased, and perhaps further decreasing, budgets, it is difficult to see how or whether these agencies will be able to "purchase" evaluation efforts from NBS or accept the research criteria established by NBS for taking on non-NBS research projects. Perhaps, NBS will be of most appropriate use as a reference laboratory for information related to general measurements, methods, standards, and data in specialized technical and materials areas.

In 1976, Congress enacted the Medical Device Amendments to the food and drug legislation. The degree to which FDA exercises regulatory control over the development, manufacturing, and marketing process will depend on a device's potential risk and classification. Wenchel provides a good review of the three classifications and what they will entail (221):

Class I: General Controls
Use: Where controls other than standards and premarket approval are sufficient.
Scope: Applies to all devices except those specifically exempt. Prohibits adulterated or misbranded devices. Requires registration of establishment and listings of devices. Retains authority to ban certain devices. Provides for the notification of risk, repair, replacement or refund. Has requirements for good manufacturing practices including record keeping and inspections.
Examples: Dental floss, blood mixing device, tongue depressor.

Class II: Performance Standards
Use: Where general controls are insufficient but sufficient information exists or could be developed to establish a performance standard.
Scope: Includes all provisions of general controls. Requires adherence to a performance standard, when available, which may also cover construction, components, and properties.
Examples: Electrocardiograph, vascular catheter, administration kit.

Class III: Premarket Approval
Use: Where general controls or performance standards may not provide reasonable assurance of safety and effectiveness for a device that is life sustaining, life supporting, implanted, or presents a potential unreasonable risk of illness or injury or where a performance standard cannot be developed.
Scope: Requires all substantially new or different devices to obtain premarket approval.
Examples: Implantable pacemaker, infant radiant warmer.

FDA is developing for each of these categories criteria and standards that new devices will have to meet to receive approval. The importance of FDA's involvement in this area is the stimulation of evaluation activities in the areas and technologies affected. It is felt among many manufacturers that FDA's involvement will also place burdensome administrative loads on the manufacturers and will hamper innovation. According to critics, the impact on the small single- or few-product firm will be the greatest. This may be especially serious for the disability-related R&D sector, because so many of the innovators and manufacturers are in this category. In terms of industry-wide impacts, the effect of FDA's processes for premarket approval and investigational device exemptions is not known (221). Also, a factor that may possibly be more of an issue in the disability-related technology area is cost. FDA's regulations may increase the cost of technologies that go through the premarket approval process. These costs might persuade a manufacturer not to develop a technology or they may be passed on to the consumer. Disabled consumers, because of low disposable income in general, are extremely sensitive to and affected by price. However, if these increased prices help to purchase safer, more effective, and more reliable technology, then a good argument can be made in support of FDA's efforts. The debate concerning this question will continue.

The evaluation issues in the disability field mimic the problems identified for the general health care system. Adequate evaluation data are rarely available for technologies for disabled people. A study cited by NIHR found that of 300 people surveyed, over 90 percent cited a need for more buying information and advice about both special and regular goods and services that they rely on (52). Evaluation information concerning product dependability and durability, ease of use, availability of maintenance and repair services, as well as safety and efficacy information, is sorely needed by the consumer. In most cases, however, it is found lacking. Such information would prove invaluable to the users, counselors, physicians, research community, manufacturers, third-party payers, and all those who advise on the use of existing technologies or innovations.

For example, the Stanford Rehabilitation Engineering Center received a grant for a clinical evaluation project on potentially useful controls and interfaces for new aids and systems developed at the center and elsewhere (187). The project team decided to develop an evaluation model, using a retrospective study of a mobility device—wheelchairs with communication or interface components—to aid them in their future evaluation efforts. As part of this process, several evaluative criteria were selected: 1) technical performance, 2) client's life style, 3) physical environment, 4) interaction with family, friends and fellow workers, and 5) effect on client's self-image. The study team proceeded to examine the literature on the benefits identified for each of these descriptors in order to establish the data base on which to build the remainder of the study. This measurement was difficult to derive from the literature (187):

> A review of the literature indicated that clinical evaluation of rehabilitation equipment is either not being carried out, or does not appear in print. A search of the NARIC [National Rehabilitation Information Center] database resulted in just ten items. Only three were related to evaluation. The keyword "wheelchair-evaluation" is, in fact, not even in their dictionary. Other written material on wheelchair evaluation refers primarily to technical and engineering specifications. The available data on English devices is not generally applicable to the American market . . .
>
> References were found indicating the need for evaluative material. Cost and time factors, especially describing device life span and use factors, were also not available. Nor was any information found concerning the psychosocial aspects of using or assessing assistive devices.

This is one study being done on a specific area of technology application. What is surprising is the absence of information, or at least readily accessible information, regarding the major factors required for the investigators' study in an area—wheelchairs—that has received so much attention by so many organizations over the last several years.

There are a number of other specific areas/technologies that have also been identifed as being ready for evaluation (65):

- Mobility aids
  - Wheelchairs—Many models and makes are available; other than at the VA Prosthetics Center, little testing has been done in comparative evaluation or in determining prescription criteria.
  - Hand controls—Clinical studies are needed to augment VA investigations.
  - Vehicles (cars, vans, etc.)—Data are needed on the suitability of various models and makes. Clinical studies are needed to augment VA investigations of van lifts and controls.
  - Driver simulators—Studies are needed to determine their effectiveness for instructing various disability groups.
- Sensory aids
  - Sonar cane (Mowat Development, Ltd.)
  - Hearing aids having moderate bandwidth compression
  - Mowat sensor (Mowat Development, Ltd.)
  - Nottingham obstacle detector
  - ELINFA portable braille recorder
  - Kurzweil reading machine
  - Upton eyeglass aids
- Prosthetics
  - Adjustable above-knee sockets (Rancho Los Amigos)
  - Polypropylene below-knee prostheses (Moss)
  - Above-elbow osteotomy (Marquart)
- Locomotion and clinical gait
  - Gait analyser (Rancho Los Amigos)
  - Limb load monitor (Moss)
- Tissue mechanics
  - Seat cushions (many commercial models)
  - Seating systems (Rogers—Rancho Los Amigos)
  - Mattress systems (several commercial models)
  - Pressure measuring pad (Texas Institute for Rehabilitation and Research)
  - Rigid-sole rocker shoe (Carville)
  - Laser-doppler blood flow meter (University of Washington)
  - Low pressure support beds and turning beds (several commercial models)
- Activities of daily living
  - Environmental aids and controls (Prentke

Romich, VA, Fidelity)
— Page turners (several commercial models)
• Functional electrical stimulation
— Therapeutic devices and techniques (including biofeedback systems) for lower and upper extremity management and stroke
— Pain control devices
— Bladder evacuation and incontinence control systems
— Cerebellar stimulation (these devices are used extensively in some centers).

In addition to the above areas, the following area is in need of evaluation:

• Communication aids
— Non-vocal communications devices
— Writing systems for severely disabled individuals.

There are literally thousands of disability-related devices coming out of the public, private, and nonprofit sectors. Many are relatively simple and low cost items. Others are expensive, complex devices. Regardless of the technology's cost, use, or complexity, certain criteria should be applied and tested before a technology enters widespread use. The most essential are safety, effectiveness, durability, and recommended applications (65). These baseline assessments are combinations of laboratory testing and clinical evaluations. Many would argue that "life-use" testing should be an integral part of this process when a technology is past the initial research stages. Life-use testing is simply the evaluation of technology in the environment in which it will have to exist as used by a consumer. There is also an increasingly active movement toward greater "consumer" involvement in all phases of disability-related R&D, including evaluation. The major problem is that defining who the "consumer" is is not as easy as it would appear. Nonetheless, the concept is sound and has great potential.

The disabled population, Federal agencies, researchers, and corporations are acutely aware of the problems and barriers involved in these evaluation issues. An important part of both NIHR's legislative mandate and the VA's program of Rehabilitation Engineering Research and Development (RER&D) is evaluation and information dissemination. Part of the RER&D program's purpose is to work with NIHR in the areas of evaluation, information dissemination, and research coordination. VA's legislative mandate requires that its prosthetic research include testing of prosthetic, orthotic, and orthopedic appliances and sensory aids (title 38 U.S.C., sec. 4101). It also requires VA to disseminate the results and information of this program to the benefit of all disabled persons. The separation of the RER&D program from the general VA research efforts had, in part, the motive of giving focus to the rehabilitation research efforts of VA. This focus has, in turn, helped stimulate VA to devote more attention to evaluation and information dissemination activities. It should be mentioned here that NASA's technology transfer efforts have also added to the evaluation and dissemination capabilities of the rehabilitation field. Other agencies such as the Office of Special Education and Rehabilitation Services Administration (RSA) also are substantially involved with information dissemination efforts.

The major Federal effort in this area is at NIHR. The reason for this is clear. It is the lead agency in this field, by law. A sizable portion of the federally supported R&D is funneled through NIHR to the various research centers. NIHR, via these centers, is in an advantageous position to decide or direct, in conjunction with the centers, the level of resources to devote to evaluation efforts. Evaluation is, or can be, so much a part of the ongoing R&D that some form and level of evaluation effort is, or should be, always present. NIHR's 5-year plan states that the areas of clinical and laboratory evaluation of devices and systems is part of the proposed future expansion of its research support efforts (52). In essence, this is an explicit reaffirmation that formal evaluation efforts are a necessary and important aspect of research. Plans, though, are not reality. Therefore, the actual implementation of evaluation plans should be examined closely over the next few years in order to evaluate their extent, quality, and impact.

NIHR does not limit its evaluation efforts to those devices that are produced in its research centers. Innovations from federally funded organizations, private industry, and from abroad are included in its testing and evaluation efforts. The testing done in the laboratories usually focuses on characteristics such as strength, durability, reliability, technical performance, and specifications compliance. Later, in clinical testing, items such as suitability, acceptability, and durability for specific consumer applications are evaluated. NIHR has also developed an evaluation plan that it intends to apply to the testing of: 1) special classes of products and services for disabled people, and 2) general classes of products with reference to their suitability for use by disabled people. Its evaluation program will do the following (52):

- select types of products and services to be tested and compared, based on surveys of disabled consumers;
- obtain samples of products to be tested;
- carry out small-scale pilot tests for each group of products to be tested;
- determine product-use patterns;
- formulate test protocols;
- carry out full-scale physical and use tests;
- analyze test results and draw conclusions; and
- prepare and disseminate the findings.

The following three examples of NIHR and research center efforts illustrate the combination of issues and problems that are being addressed. The New York University Medical Rehabilitation Research and Training Center has ongoing projects concerned with orthotics-prosthetics, neuromuscular diseases, behavioral science, cardiopulmonary issues, and bioengineering problems. This center also is affiliated with the Spinal Cord Injury Center. The West Virginia University Vocational Rehabilitation Research and Training Center is involved in research on program evaluation, improved service models, programmatic barriers to vocational rehabilitation, affirmative action, and consumer involvement, and also maintains the Institute of Rehabilitation Issues. The University of California at San Francisco Research and Training Center in Deafness and Mental Health conducts research in areas concerning work adjustment as a function of self-image and mental health, improving clinical training for personnel working with deaf people, and evaluation of therapeutic interventions for deaf people (55).

These three centers' activities are limited, yet illustrative, examples of the diversity of research and evaluation activities that are being pursued by the Federal Government in the field of disability-related research. Other examples can be found in NIHR documents (e.g., 54).

DISCUSSION

This chapter on evaluation has been placed between those on R&D and on diffusion. That physical placement should not be taken to mean that evaluation should occur only at that point in the lifecycle of technologies. On the contrary, *evaluation is—or should be—an ongoing and integral part of the entire lifecycle.* In public policy, however, it is most visible at the late R&D stage. That is the stage where the drug and device regulation is most intense, and that is when information has to be collected for reimbursement and financing (i.e., decisions affecting use). The late R&D stage is, on the average, a good compromise point in that enough information and experience may be available for evaluation, and the technology has not yet been widely diffused; at the late R&D stage, therefore, it may be possible to affect the technology's future diffusion on the basis of evaluation.

Many of the shortcomings of evaluation in the area of technology for disabled people are similar to those in many areas of policy. Evaluation of the direct benefits, risks, and costs of technologies in general suffers from a variety of methodological, funding, and organizational problems. The weaknesses of assessment of the efficacy and safety of health-related technologies were mentioned earlier. Comparable statements could be made in the areas of, for example, education and transportation. Evaluation of cost-effectiveness and cost-benefit analyses (CEAs and CBAs) is especially fraught with methodological shortcomings. In an area where nonquantifiable measures play such an important role, extreme caution should be used in interpreting the results of these types of analysis. An approach based on using CEA to structure problems and force the explicit consideration of assumptions, however, could be very relevant to evaluation of appropriate use of technologies. This idea is covered more fully in chapter 11 in its discussion of techniques for resource allocation.

One type of evaluation that perhaps could be used effectively in the disability area is technology assessment, or comprehensive technology assessment, as it is sometimes called. It is a form of policy analysis designed to provide information on the range of effects of a technology—e.g., social, ethical, legal, political, economic, technical, and psychological effects. Technology assessment uses various methods of analysis and draws on a wide range of disciplines. Importantly, it takes into account: 1) unintended and unanticipated impacts of technological applications; 2) second and higher order impacts (i.e., indirect effects or effects caused by other effects); and 3) the full range of parties at interest and the distribution of costs, benefits, and other effects among them.

Technology assessment is little used in health care and not much more prevalent in other areas of technology. Very few assessments have been conducted in the area of technology for disabled people. Texas Tech University's study of rehabilitation technologies is the prime example (76).

The nature of policy issues in this area, however, indicates that there is great potential for using technology assessment in the disability area. *Some analytical method is needed to address, in a comprehensive manner, the intricate blend of ethical, economic, personal, sociological, technical, and legal factors involved in the application of technology for disabled people.* Work would be needed to develop appropriate methods of analysis for disability-related technologies, but such efforts might pay high dividends. Because this type of analysis looks at broad issues of the effects of technology, it could assist in developing information for allocating resources, an especially important source of problems in the disability-related area.

Not every technological application needs to be submitted to such analysis, but some warrant the effort. Systemwide telephone compatibility with hearing aids, mass transportation system accessibility, sheltered workshops, "mainstreaming" in education, and artificial organs (e.g., the artificial heart) are illustrative candidates.

There are several classes of users of evaluation information. As one moves further away from the technology-specific level of decisionmaking and closer to the broader social and political decisionmaking levels, needs for evaluation information change. For example, many levels of evaluation were and are part of the decision to provide accessible public transportation in urban areas. Political, moral, economic, and legal criteria were used to decide if, when, why, and how disabled people should have access to the public transportation system. Once these decisions were made, the process of designing, developing, and applying solutions to the policy goal was undertaken. At the policy level, the evaluation criteria were much different than the criteria at the technical solution level. At the one end, criteria such as social equity, distributive justice, ethical considerations, work force economics, political constituencies, and other decisionmaking criteria were directly or indirectly applied. At the other end, tests such as performance specification for "kneeling buses," transportation scheduling, city or State budgets, demographic considerations, cost-effectiveness calculations, number of people serviced, subway retrofitting costs, etc., became the evaluative framework in which the decisionmakers functioned.

The previous example illustrates the top-down approach to evaluation. A bottom-up example might be a communication device that is developed, tested, and found to be of use to a disabled individual. If its use increases and if wider testing proves the device to be a success, attempts are made to enlist private manufacturers or investors to put the device into full-scale distribution. At each step along the development process, the evaluation criteria change to satisfy the information needs of decisionmakers at different levels.

Safety, efficacy, convenience, usefulness, and durability issues exist at one end, and production costs, market size, patent rights, liability concerns, reimbursement, ability-to-pay criteria, and social goals operate at the other.

Some of the issues relating to evaluation are tied to the Government-private sector partnership in bringing innovations to the marketplace. Many evaluation efforts are in the exclusive domain of the private sector, yet are related to and dependent upon the performance of the various Government agencies working in the area of disability-related research. The impression OTA has gained of this process is that it is not adequately designed to support fully useful efforts at evaluation and testing. *A coherent, adequately funded, and well-focused program of evaluation is necessary at all levels of technology diffusion and adoption. Such a program does not currently exist in the disability-related technology sector.*

8.
Diffusion and Marketing of Technologies

Grace is given of God, knowledge is bought in the market.
—*Arthur Hugh Clough*

Contents

	Page
Introduction	87
Current Activities and Programs	89
Discussion	95

LIST OF FIGURES

Figure No.	Page
5. Stages in the Development and Diffusion of Medical Technologies	88
6. Organizational Chart for the Autocuer Project	91
7. The Innovation Process	97

8.
Diffusion and Marketing of Technologies

INTRODUCTION

Often, the research, development, marketing, and diffusion continuum is characterized as being loosely woven aspects of a single effort. To a degree, this is correct. However, it is also accurate to describe the diffusion and marketing aspects of technology delivery as ones requiring quite different methods, goals, and information than the research and development (R&D) efforts that have gone on before. For example, most disability-related researchers (as well as most scientists in general) have basic research orientations, training, and value systems that focus on conducting research to further the knowledge in their professional areas (147). As Dr. Goodgold of the New York University Institute for Rehabilitative Medicine explains (147):

> We're certainly concerned with utilization, but not from the point that we have a profit motive. Our profit motive is the advancement of science while agreeing that there is a need to transform research ideas in order to increase their acceptance and put them in a form which decision makers could understand and accept.

This is a point that is often overlooked in criticism of the performance of the National Institute of Handicapped Research's (NIHR's) research and training centers (RTCs) and rehabilitation engineering centers (RECs). Their mission encompasses a good deal more than product development and commercialization. In addition to having a commitment to basic and applied research, these centers are responsible for training new and existing professionals, delivering services to patients, evaluating research products developed in-house (as well as those from other RECs and RTCs), and finally, working with private firms or organizations to manufacture and market the R&D products that they have developed. Therefore, it is not entirely fair to measure their success or failure in terms of device development alone.

Even though R&D, diffusion, and marketing process can be, and is, broken up into distinct, but overlapping, approaches, there must still be a continuity to the process that allows and requires a look at the system as a whole. Any description of the entire process will be deficient in one area or another. The process is a complex one whose performance is the result of a myriad of factors, many beyond the control or predictions of the scientists, the administrators, Congress, or the market analysis. At best, a descriptive guide can be provided to cover the more generalizable features of the research, development, diffusion, and marketing process.

Many steps are involved in developing and marketing a technology. The factors affecting adoption of innovations are equally numerous and involved. An organization's potential for innovation is related to its environment—the econonomic, social, and political factors involved, the state-of-the-art of technology, and the availability of useful information (216). If barriers exist that impede the flow of information between the organization and its environment, the innovation, diffusion, and marketing process is hampered. Government (via its programs, incentives, and regulations) and the firm (using its resources, personnel, and patterns of communication and decisionmaking) are both responsible for the degree to which those barriers are overcome and innovations reach and satisfy the demands of the marketplace (216).

Combining the diffusion and marketing models used to characterize the health care system and the private sector innovation process may provide a useful guide to the vagaries of marketing of technologies for disabled people. The disability field provides an example of R&D that is stimulated by personal, economic, social, and political incentives; funded to a large degree by public and nonprofit sources; and then, usually late in the process, grafted onto the manufacturing and marketing systems of the private sector. This forced marriage is often difficult and unsatisfying to both partners, as well as to disabled people. However, when this union is successful, it is a productive, efficient relationship deserving of praise. Figure 5 depicts a typical diffusion pattern for medical technologies (165). This model may be inadequate for some disability-related technologies, but in general serves as a useful description of the process.

An ideal, or model, development and diffusion process by which technology would pass through the necessary stages to reach the consumer is as follows (164):

- discovery, through research, of new knowledge, and relation of this knowledge to the existing knowledge base;
- translation of new knowledge, through applied research, into new technology, and development of a strategy for moving the technology into the delivery system;
- evaluation of the safety and efficacy of new technology through such means as controlled clinical trials;
- development and operation of demonstration and control programs to demonstrate feasibility for widespread use;
- diffusion of the new technology, beginning with the trials and demonstrations and continuing through a process of increasing acceptance into practice;

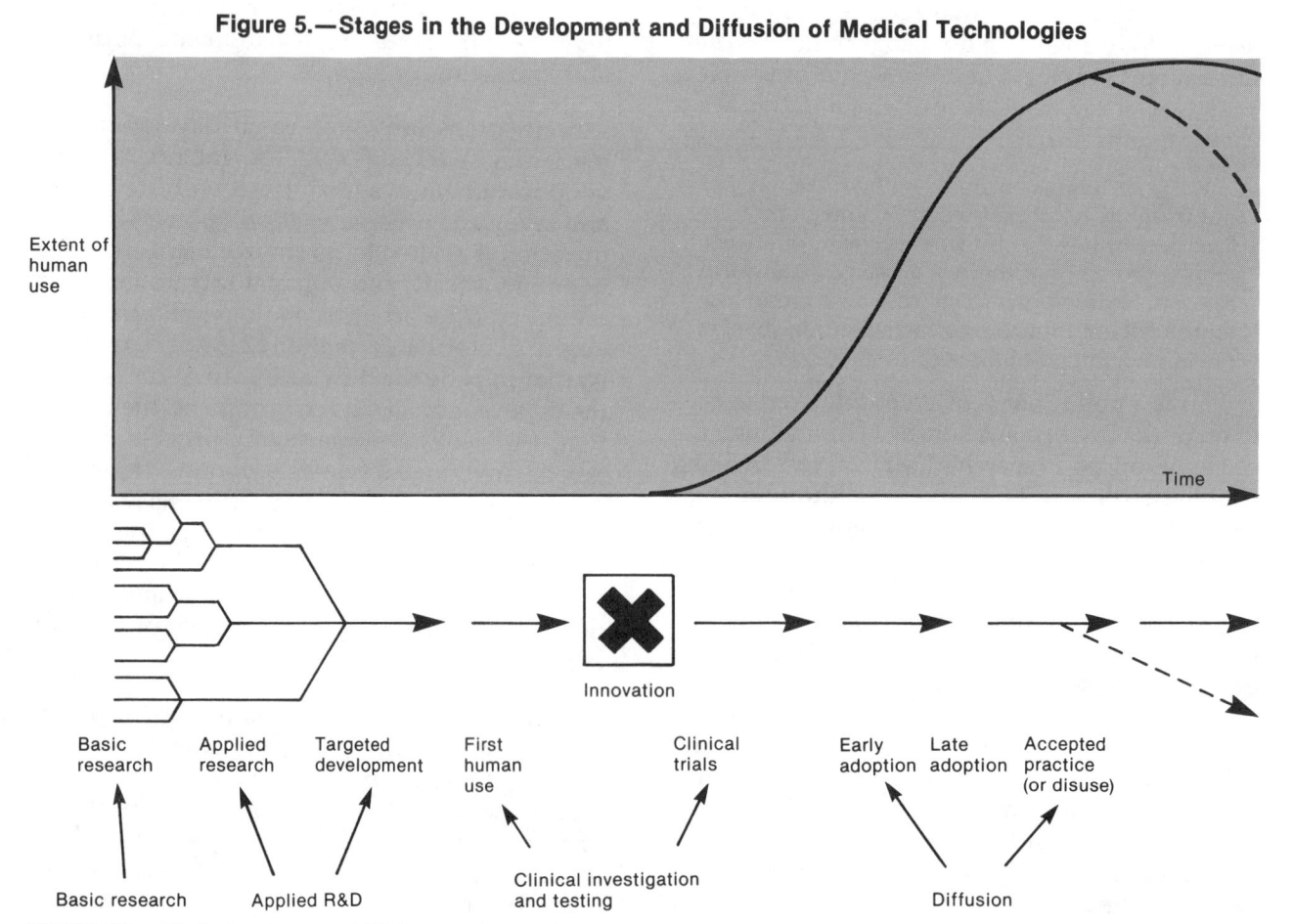

Figure 5.—Stages in the Development and Diffusion of Medical Technologies

SOURCE: Office of Technology Assessment, U.S. Congress, *Development of Medical Technology: Opportunities for Assessment* (Washington, D.C.: U.S. Government Printing Office, August 1976.

- education of the professional and user communities in use of the new technology; and
- skillful and balanced application of the new developments to the population.

Muthard cites a number of studies of utilization patterns in the rehabilitative system that were designed to determine the types of factors that have been most effective in increasing the chances of an innovation being adopted (147). Below are the factors that Havelock has suggested that account for most dissemination and utilization phenomena (105,147).

- Linkage—reciprocal relationships between resources and user systems.
- Structure—the resource system must plan its activities in a structured sequence and the user system must be organized to receive input.
- Openness—the resource system must be willing to be influenced by user needs and expose its new knowledge to inspection; the user system must actively reach out for new ideas.
- Capacity—both resource and user systems require the amount of wealth, intelligence, etc., needed to deal with a given innovation.
- Reward—both resource and user systems need kinds of positive reinforcement or benefits from the innovation to warrant the investment of time, money, and effort.
- Proximity—proximity facilitates linkage.
- Synergy—several inputs of knowledge, working together over time, through different channels and formats (purposeful redundancy) facilitate adoption.

The two lists presented above are quite different in the types of factors involved. The first set is more a description of *how* an innovation winds its way through the process, getting the appropriate and necessary "stamps of approval" along the way. It provides the framework that allows the second list of factors to operate. The second is a list of criteria that explain *why* a given innovation is used and assimilated into the system. And obviously the attributes of a technology will enhance or impede its adoption. According to Muthard, adoption will be facilitated when a technology is (147):

- inexpensive;
- time-saving;
- easy to use;
- easy to explain;
- easy to understand;
- consistent with the consumer's value system; and
- observable (its workings or effects can be demonstrated in advance to consumers).

Perhaps implicit in Muthard's list, and as mentioned in chapter 5, additional factors that could be included are perceived and actual cost effectiveness, ease of repair, and low frequency of replacement or maintenance.

CURRENT ACTIVITIES AND PROGRAMS

In the process of developing and distributing disability-related technologies, the public-private relationship is very complex and close. Each sector brings with it a full complement of beneficial and negative characteristics. These attributes assist and impede the process and require the presence of compromises and insight to make the system work. Each partner has its own set of agendas, mandates, and constituencies that it must satisfy. Often, the *organizational goals* of the various actors are not even close to being compatible, even when the basic *intentions* are similar. Federal agencies are, among other things, creations of the political process. The political process has goals and requirements that are often unique to that process. Studies, as well as common sense, tell us—not surprisingly—that private sector firms tend to innovate primarily in areas where there is a reasonably clear, short-term profit potential (216). In an area such as handicap-related innovation, where the market population is ill-defined and where, on average, the economic status of users is far below the median, the stimulus for private investment and involvement is sometimes very weak.

The imperfections in the existing market structure are numerous. Flaws in public-private sector relationship are equally abundant. NIHR, along with many others, has identified the major barriers in both the marketplace and the public-private sector relationship (52). That agency is also attempting to identify solutions to many of these problems. In the following paragraphs, the discussion will draw heavily on NIHR's summary of both the recognized imperfections and the suggested solutions to these problems. It is worth mentioning again that the Veterans Administration (VA), the Office of Special Education, and the National Aeronautics and Space Administration (NASA), among others, are also involved in efforts to address these same problems. NIHR's long-range plan is a fair representation of the general approach taking place at the Federal level.

Before turning to the negative aspects of this process and the problems that exist in the public-private relationship, it is worth noting a few of its positive aspects. The Federal Government has a number of programs in place to provide assistance to the private sector in terms of loans, technical assistance, and information transfer. The Food and Drug Administration (FDA) imposes numerous requirements on businesses of all sizes, but the smaller firms are often hit the hardest. Therefore, since 1977 it has maintained an Office of Small Manufacturers' Assistance (OSMA) to provide technical help and other nonfinancial assistance to small firms in the device and drug approval processes (221). In addition, FDA is instituting a $100 million program to assist smaller firms financially if they are involved in the rulemaking and administrative procedures at FDA (221). The Small Business Administration (SBA) is also involved in making low interest loans to small, disability-related businesses. Over the period 1973-81, SBA loaned a total of $116 million to a wide variety of firms in the United States.

The efforts of VA, NASA, and NIHR have also produced a number of "successes" in terms of taking R&D products from the Government labs to private manufacturers for mass marketing and distribution. The introduction of the commercially produced version of the Autocom, a communications device, is the result of 5 years of initial R&D at the Trace Center at the University of Wisconsin and 2 years of production engineering at Telesensory Systems, Inc. The Autocom is a example of a prototype device proving the validity of a research idea and then being "redesigned" to fit the needs of the manufacturer: 1) mass production, 2) regular production schedules, 3) high product consistency, and 4) adherence to industrial standards of quality control (189).

Rancho Los Amigos has worked with Med General in Minneapolis to transfer its research on idiopathic scoliosis to produce a device—the Scolitron—to put on the market. The University of Michigan REC has also transferred its research on transportation devices and systems to firms like Creative Controls, Inc., and the Amigo Corp. for the development and marketing of mobility technologies to aid handicapped individuals. There are many examples of where and how RTCs and RECs have been effective and successful in working with the private sector to transfer R&D prototypes and information to marketable products.*

A good example of how involved and complex this type of transfer process can be is well illustrated by figure 6, a flow chart of NASA's efforts in bringing the technology that became the *Autocuer* to the marketplace (227). This chart traces the tortuous route that a single project, involving a not unusual number of actors and organizations, took to get to the commercial stage. This schematic is a good model for this type of interagency and public-private process. Since most of the more important technologies tend to follow

---

*For an interesting account of how the Optacon technology reached the marketplace, see LaRocca and Turem's "The Application of Technological Developments to Physically Disabled People" (LaRocca & Turem, 1978). It was a 10-year project, involving DHEW, Stanford University, the Mellon Foundation, the Stanford Research Institute, and finally, the creation of Telesensory Systems, Inc., to manufacture, distribute, and service the Optacons. More than $3 million was granted to this project, which came to involve a staff of 20 to 30 people, while turning out 13 Ph. Ds. and other advanced degrees for dissertations concerning the Optacon project. A more thorough analysis of the factors associated with bringing a device to market can be found in "A Production and Marketing Strategy for Prototype Devices Developed Under the Rehabilitation Engineering Program," prepared by the Electronic Industries Foundation, March 1978, for RSA (78).

Ch. 8—Diffusion and Marketing of Technologies • 91

Figure 6.—Organizational Chart for the Autocuer Project

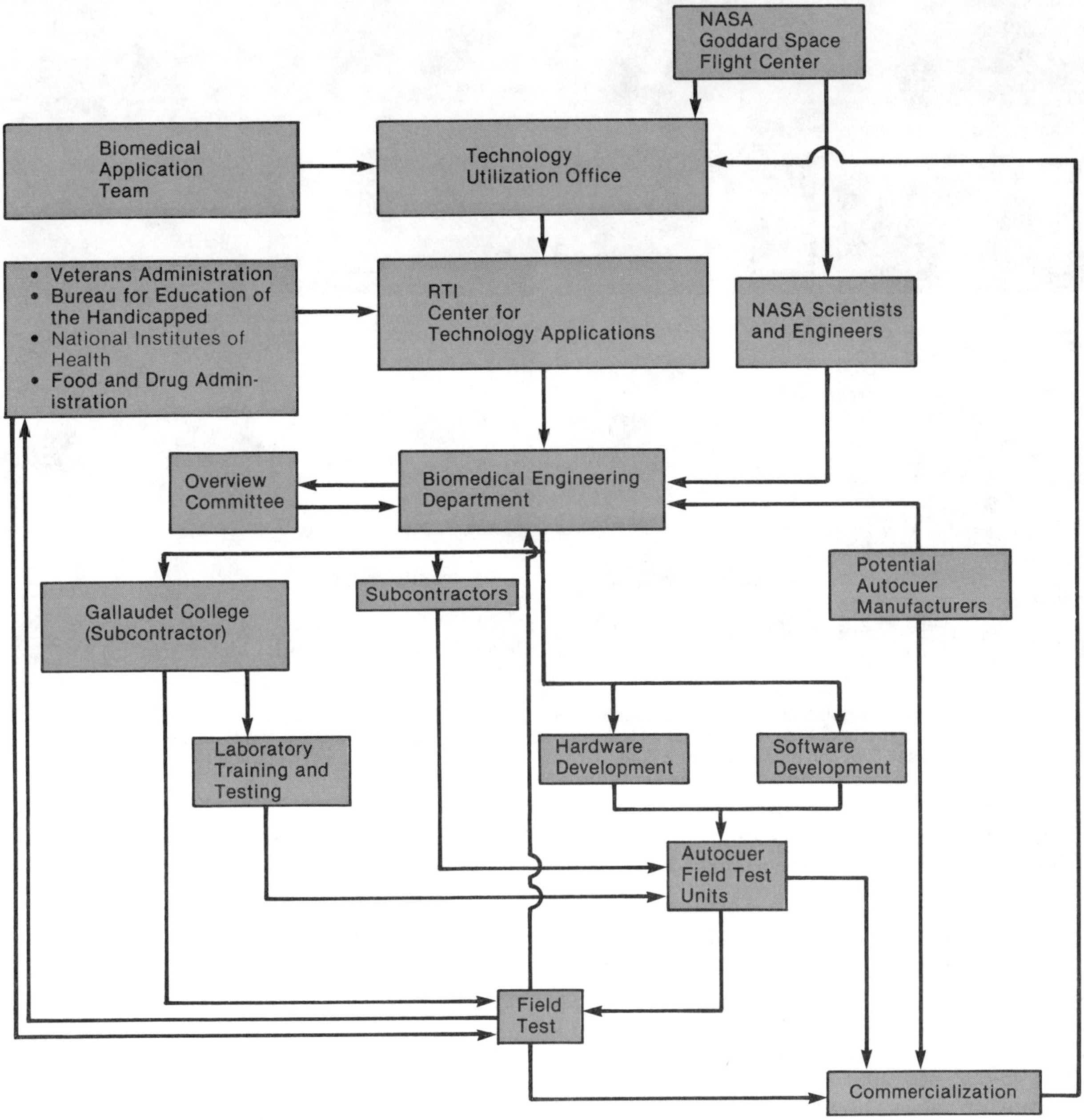

SOURCE: National Aeronautics and Space Administration.

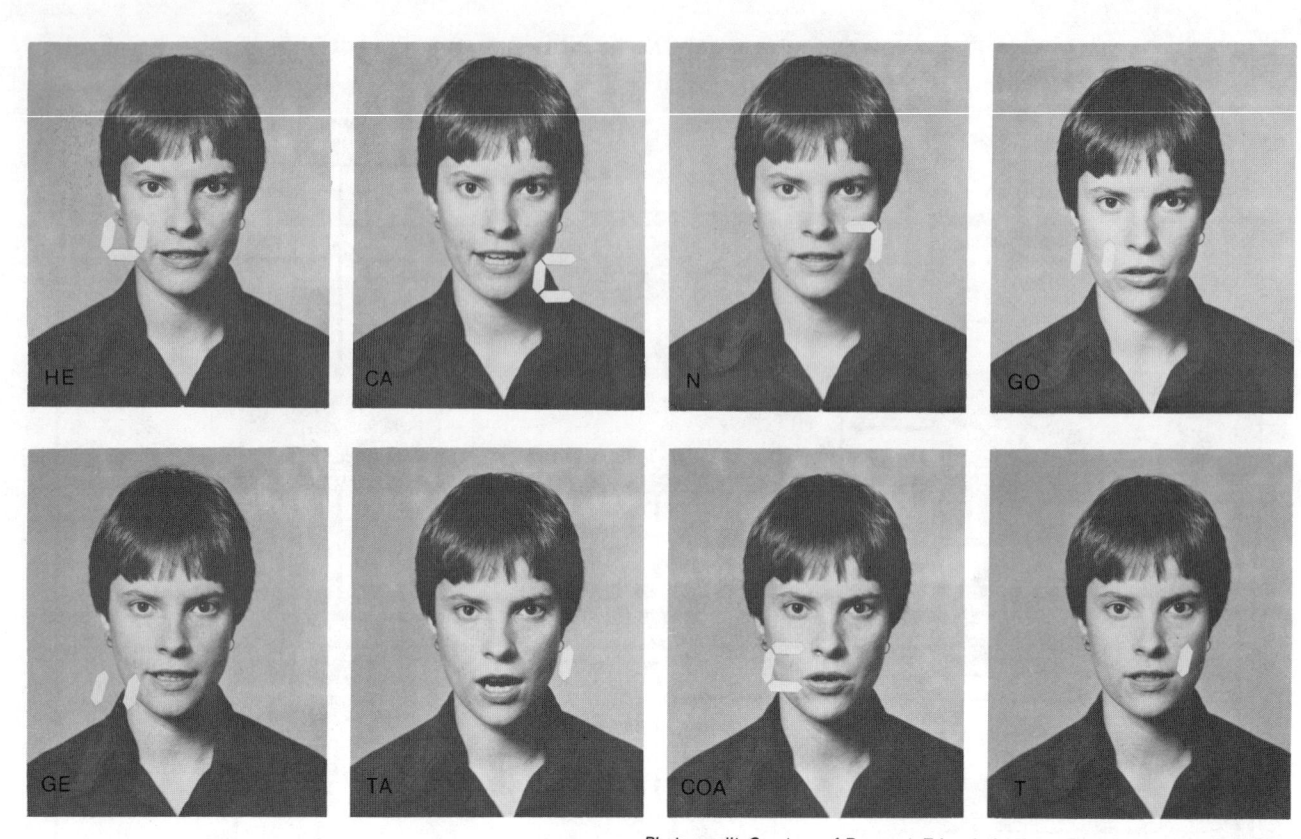

Photo credit: Courtesy of Research Triangle Institute, Research Triangle Park, N.C.

The Autocuer, a portable minicomputer, mechanically "hears" words spoken to a deaf person and projects symbols onto the lens area of a pair of eyeglasses worn by the deaf person. The symbols, shown above for the phrases "He can go" and "Get a coat," act as visual cues that lessen the ambiguity of words that look similar to a lip-reading person

this type of route, the model is an accurate general indicator of how the process works and why it can succeed or fail.

A major aspect of NIHR's mandate is to "improve the distribution of technological devices and equipment for handicapped individuals by providing financial support for the development and distribution of such devices and equipment" (Public Law 95-602, sec. 200). There are a number of significant obstacles, however, that complicate and prevent the participation of private industry in this process (170):

- lack of adequate demographic data (or market statistics) about the needs for technological aids and devices by disabled people;
- lack of commercial viability of certain ventures because of a small fragmented market and high investment costs; and
- roadblocks caused by the patent system, liability insurance requirements, and the third-party payment system.

Additional factors must be considered to the issues of reimbursement and marketing (see the following chapter). The Government may provide a fairly large guaranteed market for numerous medical and rehabilitative technologies. VA and the vocational rehabilitation systems alone provide a ready market for medical and rehabilitative devices. The Government, as purchaser and as arbiter of performance and design standards, can to a large extent determine what technologies will qualify to enter the marketplace. There is some concern that FDA, the Rehabilitation Services Administration (RSA), and VA accept specification and standards of existing technologies on the market as the criteria for evaluation and (in the case of VA and of vocational rehabilitation systems)

Ch. 8—Diffusion and Marketing of Technologies • 93

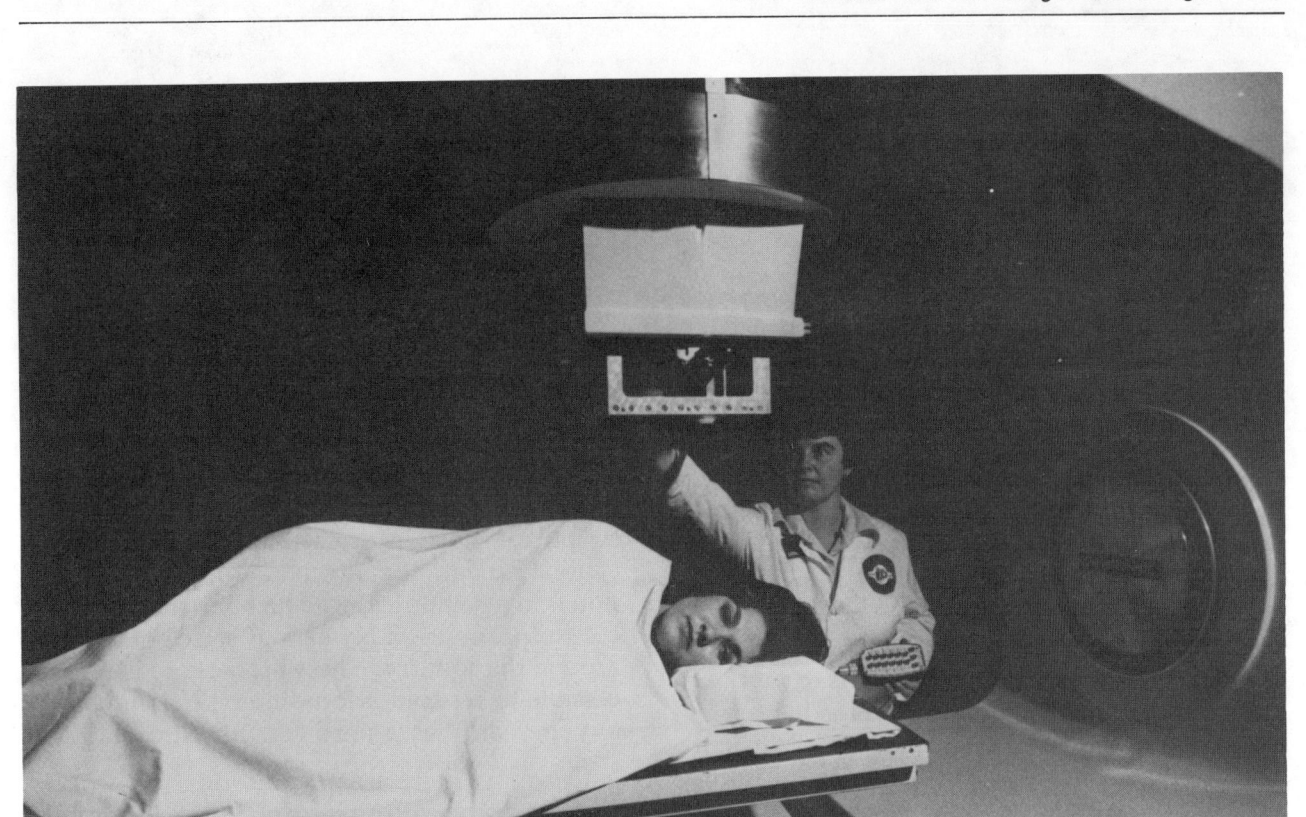

Photo credit: Courtesy of the National Institutes of Health

An arthritis patient is being set up to receive radiation treatment from a high-energy X-ray machine. Total lymphoid irradiation is currently being tested for its effect on reducing disability of people with severe rheumatoid arthritis

purchase of new rehabilitative devices (141). This situation makes it even more difficult for emerging technologies that are different in design or performance levels to enter the general marketplace, especially the large VA market. If a device can enter into the "medically necessary" category in the Medicaid reimbursement process or be included as a necessary rehabilitative device in the VA or vocational rehabilitation systems, a significant obstacle is overcome for the manufacturer. Reimbursement is then guaranteed for their product. If a technology is not found to be "therapeutic," "medically necessary," or does not meet the standards established by FDA, RSA, or VA, then the production and marketing outlook is much less optimistic given the relatively poor financial status, low employment levels, and ill-defined target populations that characterize disabled people as a market.

There are relatively few commercial products available to disabled people despite the millions of public dollars dispersed yearly for handicap-related R&D. A major problem is that *the Federal Government does not have consistent, formal mechanisms in place to link research investment to the production and distribution needs of the marketplace.* The exception is a formal mechanism for accomplishing this task within NASA that works quite well when applied correctly. One critical aspect of the NASA system is that it sometimes uses a "co-contracting" process with both researchers and potential marketers involved. NIHR and VA are trying to move in this direction, to the extent possible, by redirecting the development process to accommodate and include marketplace considerations. NIHR is examining a number of initiatives to promote and facilitate private sector involvement (170):

- demographic and market research,
- low-cost loans or grants,
- tax incentives,
- studying the experience of European systems, and
- contracting arrangements.

NIHR is also investigating ways to overcome the disincentives that have discouraged private sector involvement, such as patent policy, product liability issues, and the third-party payment system. Patent policy, for example, is seen as a disincentive for many firms who are in, or who might enter, the production of disability-related technologies. The patent process is expensive and lengthy. Numerous challenges of patent rights in court have resulted in a situation of uncertainty regarding the amount of protection of a design afforded by a patent. There is also uncertainty regarding the granting of patent rights to products or techniques developed in whole or in part by Federal funds. These considerations are heightened by the fact that a great many firms in this area are small and cannot easily afford the costs involved in a lengthy patent process. Additionally, in a rapidly evolving field of technology such as this, patents may be out-of-date rapidly, thus lessening the incentives to go through the process of securing them. Nevertheless, a streamlined and less costly patent process, combined with a more consistent and explicit Federal policy toward the assigning of rights to products developed with Federal funding, could make some firms less reluctant to enter the market with new products.

It remains to be seen whether this Federal attention will be translated into federally supported action. One final problem that NIHR has already begun to address is information collection and dissemination. This is not to say that there is, at present, an absence of disability-related information collection and dissemination in this country. On the contrary, there are numerous public and private reference centers, information dissemination networks, nonprofit organizations, bibliographic services, etc., that can provide a wealth of information on a wide variety of topics. Nevertheless, finding product information that is up-to-date, complete, and accurate remains a substantial problem.

The most recent addition to the information collection and dissemination system is the computer network ABLEDATA. This is an NIHR-funded, product information system operated as a service of the National Rehabilitation Information Center based at Catholic University in Washington, D.C. Most product information is available only through manufacturers' catalogs or from distributors. Normally, these data consist of technical specifications, selection choices, etc. The ABLEDATA system collects manufacturers' data and adds updated information regarding local availability of products, names of manufacturers, where the distributors are located, product descriptions, cost information, and any relevant evaluation data that are available. This information is in a computerized data bank that is accessible to information brokers at selected locations around the country. These brokers are in turn accessible to rehabilitation centers, individuals, or anyone who has a need for that information.

Currently there are nine information brokers. In their searches (for information for clients or users), these brokers access the on-line data base as well as conduct manual searches through documents containing information not yet entered into the computer data bank. As of November 1981, information on 3,200 items was entered into the system, and another 2,000 entries were expected shortly. The amount of information that can be entered is constrained by the limited staff time available to obtain the information and process it. There are 15 centers, including private rehabilitation centers and NIHR-funded RECs, that assist the ABLEDATA staff in obtaining manufacturers' literature. For example, the University of Virginia is responsible for contributing wheelchair data to the information bank. The University of Michigan submits information regarding personal transportation technology. The Smith-Kettlewell Institute contributes data regarding technologies for deaf-blind individuals. And, New York University covers environmental technologies for personal use.

The information contributed by RECs will include relevant R&D and evaluation/performance information they have developed in their program areas. Surveys of manufacturers, consumers, and other relevant persons, will be conducted to supplement these efforts, as well as to keep the product listings and information current. For each product, there will be a section for general comments regarding the technology's use. These comments may include information provided by the manufacturer but not printed in the product's literature, suggestions by consumers and professionals regarding modifications that can be made to the product, and tips regarding the product's safe use.

The concept and approach of ABLEDATA are excellent. However, primarily due to low levels of funding for start-up and for continuing operations, effective implementation of this program is likely to be quite difficult. The number of entries is extremely limited, and the comment and evaluation fields (areas of the forms used) for each product are currently incomplete. Furthermore, there is no procedure in place to systematically update the information. As with the original product entries, the reason for these limitations appears to be a lack of funding for additional staff time. They are not due to a lack of need or to the existence of severely limiting technical problems.

Summarizing NIHR's priority research and demonstration activities in the marketing and diffusion area also serves the purpose of summarizing the major issues that confront the disability-related development and marketing system in general. The research goals and projects identified below represent the distillation of concerns collected from relevant participants in the field (170):

- Conduct a comprehensive demographic survey of the Nation's disabled population to determine the number and the character of subgroups according to precisely defined impairment and/or functional needs.
- Conduct a comprehensive study of incentives to promote business investment in ventures that potentially have high social benefit but which at present are not profitable. Incentives to be studied include: 1) low-cost loans or grants, 2) tax abatement, and 3) contracting arrangements related to Government purchases.
- Conduct a study of disincentives to business investment including: 1) patent policy, 2) product liability, and 3) third-party payers.
- Establish a testing and evaluation program (minimum of two centers per year) to assess suitability of products for use by disabled persons. This program is to include input from disabled consumers.
- Develop and establish minimum performance specifications for products. This will offer producers criteria for manufacturing, and furnish a framework for testing and evaluation.

DISCUSSION

One of the key driving forces usually behind the innovation process are consumer demands and needs *as perceived by the Government or private sector*. Note that it is not as common for needs *as perceived by the user* to be a key driving force. To a major degree, new scientific or technological advances and opportunities have also stimulated important innovations (216).

The obstacles to getting new products onto the marketplace are many. Booz, Allen & Hamilton, Inc., found that of every 58 new product ideas, 12 pass the initial screening test, seven remain after a thorough evaluation of their profit potential, three survive the production stage, two survive the test marketing phase, and only one becomes commercially successful (15). Coupling these statistics with the knowledge that 8 of every 10 new small (general) businesses fail within their first 5 years makes it apparent that new business and products (of any type) have very significant survival problems. These statistics are especially relevant to the handicap and disability-related area, since many of the firms that produce technologies in this area are relatively new and very small, with a fragile capital base and narrow market structure. Businesses and products existing primarily for disabled persons may encounter additional difficulties due to the sometimes limited and almost always ill-defined market segments that characterize this area. These factors also present further complications when a business tries to raise venture capital to support an uncertain or risky business proposition. The market demands and needs may be present, but so are a host of other considerations that make the production, diffusion, and marketing of innovations quite difficult. Below is a set of actual or perceived reasons why manufacturers avoid producing disability-related devices (123):

- the cost of design for production may not be recoverable;
- the cost of special modifications that may be necessary in individual situations;
- the cost of training that may be involved in the use of the technology;
- the costs associated with assuring that the technology meets functional, technical, reliability, and safety requirements;
- liability and legal concerns (lawsuits due to malfunctioning devices);
- the cost of developing maintenance systems for technologies whose market potential is difficult to identify and quantify; and
- fear that informed consumer demand, for better or new products or services, does not exist.

A dilemma that also adds to the uncertainty of being a manufacturer in this area is the occurrence of special problems *within* existing problem areas for business. Different populations (e.g., children, elderly people, active young adults) may have the same underlying condition or disability, and yet will not share the same lifestyles, educational needs, employment aspirations, and so on. Thus, a technology to assist, for example, a deaf young adult may have quite different demands placed on it than one to assist a deaf or hearing-impaired senior citizen. The specific requirements for an assistive device will often be quite different. Are the "numbers" of deaf people relevant to the manufacturer if that firm does not know the subsets of the market, their various disability levels, and their lifestyle requirements?

Figure 7 provides more graphic illustration of the dynamics and requirements involved in private sector efforts to bring research ideas, information, and products to the consumer (147). Diffusion of information is a critical aspect of any such process. Information transfer needs are found along the continuum of R&D, diffusion, and marketing. Outlets for information include scientific journals, meetings, radio, periodicals, computer networks and data bases, reports, advertisements, catalogs, television, and books. Despite the extensive array of possible information sources, considerable attention has been focused on the many weaknesses of the information transfer system.

The complexity of the general research, diffusion, and marketing process is increased by the special requirements of the area of technology for disabled or handicapped people. If one examines just the engineering obstacles of adapting technologies to the human system, the barriers to diffusion *seem* monumental. The testimony of James Reswick illustrates the frustration involved in this process (123):

It is virtually impossible for any one person clearly to state specifications of a device to meet a patient's need in engineering terms. An initial attempt can be made by an effective team which includes medical, engineering and the associated health professionals and technical persons associated with clinical operation and testing. Such a medical engineering team can set down initial performance goals and proceed from these goals to define research and development tasks. Still, the inescapable fact remains that *it is not until the device is first tried in the clinic on a patient that many aspects of the problems not recognized in the beginnning become clear, after which it may be possible to define the specifications in engineering terms.*

Inevitably, the first prototype must be redesigned and redeveloped, and it is seldom that only one cycle of this process is required. Rather, the process becomes a continuous one, with new and improved models being worked on and evaluated. It often is difficult for a developer to accept that his designs must be frozen for production at a time when he still is working on various improved versions. But at some point, a manufacturer or other agency must reach a decision that a product or a device has attained a level of development sufficient to warrant production and distribution for profit. It is absolutely vital that this occur if the firm or agency is to be able to encourage a continuing R&D effort in the first place.

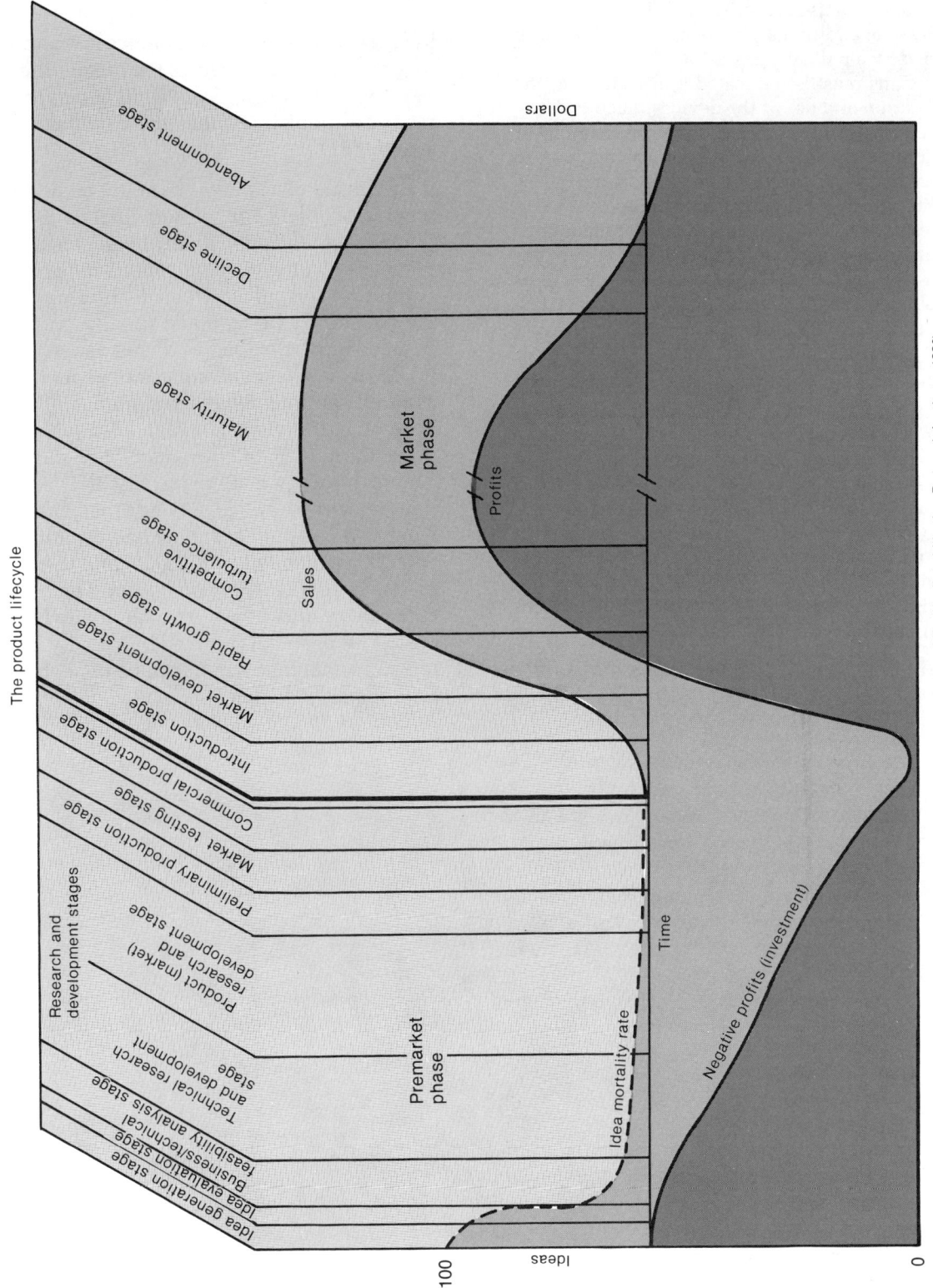

Ch. 8—Diffusion and Marketing of Technologies • 97

Figure 7.—The Innovation Process

The product lifecycle

SOURCE: J. E. Muthard, "Putting Rehabilitation Knowledge to Use" (Gainesville, Fla.: University of Florida Rehabilitation Research Institute, 1980).

Presuming that the manufacturer is successful in producing a useful biomedical product, he then faces some additional problems not usually prescribed by a patient's physician. This means that physicians must be educated and trained in the application and use of the devices. Such training and education are costly and the physician must be completely sure of the performance of the device before he can fulfill the ultimate of responsibility which the doctor-patient relationship requires of him. Thus the device development must occur in the context of a respected teaching-clinical facility if reported clinical experience is to be considered reliable by the prospective prescribing medical community.

A second problem facing the manufacturer is the fact that no electromechanical device ever improves with use and age. These devices inevitably require maintenance and repair, and the manufacturer must assume responsibility for this service. The establishment and maintenance of such a service in a limited market may well be too costly to justify. Therefore, many small firms with limited marketing, distribution, and service capability refrain from producing medical engineering devices even though many have the technical capability and interest.

Additional steps in this process are the premarket approval evaluations required by FDA for medical devices. The cost of just the process is considerable. Reswick estimates that the investment required to move a device beyond the prototype stage is as much as four times the original development costs (123). NIHR places this investment at about five times the original cost of research (51).

The issue of rapidly changing technology is a serious problem for manufacturers in this field. Sometimes, though, it can be a benefit as well; especially in those areas served by or related to computer and microcircuit technology. Devices are constantly being made smaller, more sophisticated, more flexible, and cheaper. At the Tufts RTC, researchers and subcontractors have made available an Interactive Communicator for use by nonvocal individuals (147). They never build more than 10 to 20 devices of the same design. The technology changes so fast that each year a new feature is added. As another example, the Kurzweil Reading Machine had an initial cost of $50,000, which fell to $25,000; and there are now plans to reduce the price much further as new technology and "mass" production help lower its cost. The problems created by rapidly expanding technological innovation can be offset by the benefits it helps deliver.

9. Delivery, Use, and Financing of Technologies

The first of earthly blessings, independence.
—*Edward Gibbon*

Contents

	Page
Introduction	101
Current Activities and Programs	102
Public Programs	102
Income Maintenance	102
Health and Medical Care	108
Social Services	112
Education Services	114
Vocational Rehabilitation and Independent Living	117
Nonpublic Programs	119
Discussion of General Issues	120
Coordination and Consistency of Services and Funding	120
Gaps in Enrollment	122
Maintaining Medical/Rehabilitative Device Technologies	122
Consumer Involvement in Service Delivery	123
Shortage of Rehabilitation Providers	123

TABLES

8. Federal Expenditures for Disabled People Under Selected Programs ... 103

9. Delivery, Use, and Financing of Technologies

INTRODUCTION

The desired result of research, development, evaluation, and diffusion of technologies is the *use* of these technologies by disabled individuals. In order to develop a framework for examining the fit between the individual disabled person's needs, desires, and capabilities and specific technologies, it is necessary to assess the current system of use of technologies. This system includes selecting technologies, providing technologies, and paying for them. Assessment of this system also relates directly to issues of resource allocation.

The use of technologies by disabled people appears to depend primarily, but certainly not entirely, on the public and nonpublic programs and services for which the individual users are eligible. Through their affiliation with these programs and services, users either receive technologies directly, have them financed, or learn about them. "Public programs" are those provided by the governmental sector, whether at the Federal, State, or local level. "Nonpublic programs" are those provided by all other sectors of society. The nonpublic (or "private") sector may be further divided into the "for-profit" sector (which would include manufacturers and commercial insurance companies) and the "not-for-profit" sector (which would include foundations, voluntary health agencies, universities, and professional associations).

One reason the use of technologies is dependent on eligibility for programs is that many disabled persons are poor. Three-fifths of disabled adults of working age earn incomes at or near the poverty level (17). In 1977, the median family income (including public assistance) for severely disabled individuals was slightly over half that of the nondisabled (70). These figures must be kept in perspective, however, because they may be excluding the many disabled people who have higher incomes and are thus not in programs from which much of the data is drawn.

Furthermore, of 15 million disabled Americans between ages 16 and 64, more than 7.7 million are either out of the labor force by choice or unemployed (17).

A second reason the use of technologies is dependent on eligibility for programs is that information on available technologies reaches potential users primarily through the variety of programs that exist. One type of program provides the technologies directly, with the professionals on staff either disseminating information on possible choices or prescribing professionally selected technologies, training the client in their uses, and monitoring their effectiveness. Another type of program serves as an information source for eligible clients.

This chapter describes the significant public and nonpublic programs that affect the use of technologies by disabled people. Programs legislated and funded by the Federal Government are emphasized. Because this chapter covers a range of programs, issues pertaining to particular programs are discussed following the relevant program description. Issues pertaining to the service delivery system as a whole are then discussed separately.

CURRENT ACTIVITIES AND PROGRAMS

Public Programs

There are many public programs that serve disabled individuals at the Federal, State, and local levels. These programs vary in their purpose, origin, definitions of disability, and criteria for eligibility. Some serve specific disability groups, others serve all disabled people who meet non-diagnosis-specific eligibility criteria, while others serve disabled persons through funds earmarked from broader programs. Programs also differ in their methods of providing services (which include alternatives such as funding only, funding plus referral to services, or direct service provision), in their financing, and in their administration.

In 1975, the Office of Handicapped Individuals of the Department of Health, Education, and Welfare (DHEW) surveyed all Federal programs that serve disabled people, and it found 75 programs that focused on serving disabled people, 6 programs that were not exclusively for disabled people but emphasized serving them, and 45 programs that mandated serving disabled persons but on the same basis as able-bodied people (83). A more recent survey (1981) found 83 programs targeted to disabled persons and 50 that include these individuals as beneficiaries (122). Thus, in recent years, the number and diversity of Federal programs serving disabled people has remained fairly constant. These programs are administered by 22 Federal agencies and are concerned with nearly every aspect of a disabled individual's life. It should be noted that authority for more than one program may stem from a piece of legislation.

Although there are over 100 different Federal programs serving disabled people, the majority of public services are in the form of: 1) income maintenance, 2) health and medical care, 3) social services, 4) educational services, and 5) vocational rehabilitation and independent living. Other services, not discussed in depth in this report, include special housing programs and transportation systems. Clearly, the greatest expenditures for disabled people have been and continue to be made for income maintenance and related transfer payments and health and medical care (8,83,122,130, 208). For most programs, the majority of dollars come from the Federal Government; Federal funds are often supplemented by mandatory or optional State or local matching funds. The Urban Institute estimated that in 1973, $15.3 billion in public funds was spent on income maintenance and related transfer payments, $7.9 billion was spent on health and medical payments, and $1.1 billion was spent on other direct service payments (including education and social services) (208). In 1977, these figures increased to $29.8 billion for income maintenance and transfer payments, $7.7 billion for health and medical payments,* and $2.4 billion for direct services (8). Thus, similar proportions of total funds were spent in each area. In the case of funds spent on children only, the greatest amount is spent on special education, followed by lesser amounts for transfer payments and medical care (118). A summary of Federal expenditures for disabled people under the programs discussed in this chapter is presented in table 8.

Income Maintenance

The major income maintenance programs for persons with disabilities are the Social Security Disability Insurance (SSDI) program, the Supplemental Security Income (SSI) program, Veterans Administration (VA) compensation for service-connected disabilities, and VA pensions for nonservice connected disabilities.** In fiscal year 1980, Federal expenditures for disabled recipients were $15.0 billion under SSDI and $3.9 billion under SSI.*** There were 4.8 million SSDI and 2.3 million SSI beneficiaries (130). For the VA programs, $6.1 billion was spent for 2.3 million vet-

---

*Different authors categorize expenditures in different ways, depending on their assumptions and definitions. Thus, it is difficult to compare figures from source to source, although they may be useful in examining the magnitude or direction of the spending. In this case, it is unlikely that medical payments due to disabling conditions decreased from 1973 to 1977, but rather, it is certain that some programs included in the 1973 figure were not in the 1977 figure. It should also be noted that the latest year for which figures are available varies from program to program.

**State-run worker's compensation programs are an additional source of aid to handicapped people. Since these programs are outside of the Federal Government, they will not be discussed in depth. They operate in all States to provide benefits for work-related impairments or death in the form of cash assistance and/or medical care (130). In 1977, $5.1 billion was spent for income maintenance payments and $2.5 billion was spent for medical care (8).

***These figures exclude administrative expenses.

Table 8.—Federal Expenditures for Disabled People Under Selected Programs[a]

Program	Amount of expenditures[b] (000s)	Number of beneficiaries[b] (000s)
Income maintenance		
SSDI	$15,000,000 (FY 80)	4,800
SSI	$3,900,000 (FY 80)	2,300
Veterans Administration		
Compensation	$6,100,000 (FY 80)	2,300
Pensions	$800,000 (FY 80)	900
Health and medical care		
Medicare		
Related to disabling conditions	$1,400,000 (1977)	3,300 (FY 80)
Total benefits for disabled people	$4,000,000 (FY 80)	
Medicaid		
Related to disabling conditions	$2,800,000 (1977)	3,300 (FY 80)
Total benefits for disabled people	$3,500,000 (FY 80)	
Veterans Administration		
Related to disabling conditions	$816,000 (1977)	600 to 1,300 (FY 80)
Total benefits for disabled people	$3,000,000 to $5,600,000 (FY 80)	
Other programs		
Developmental Disabilities	$62,400 (FY 80)	3,600[c]
Title XX	$841,000 (1977)[d]	Not available
Education for all Handicapped Children	$951,000 (FY 79)	3,900
Vocational Education	$55,000 (FY 79)	2,100
Title I, Elementary and Secondary Education Act	$143,000 (FY 80)[e]	222
Handicapped Children's Early Education Act	$20,000 (FY 80)[e]	Not available
Vocational Rehabilitation	$1,400,000 (FY 80)	1,100

NOTE: Numbers from refs. 8, 58, 122, 128, 129, 132, 215.

[a] These programs include those discussed in ch. 9. Other programs for disabled people, such as those under the Department of Labor, Department of Transportation, and Small Business Administration, for example, are not included. Generally, expenditures under omitted programs are significantly lower than those presented.
[b] Many of the dollar and beneficiary figures are estimates rather than actual counts. They are also from different years and sources and should be used to compare magnitudes rather than added to obtain total counts. Unless otherwise noted, the year of the beneficiary count is the same as the year for the money spent.
[c] This figure represents the DD population, not the number of beneficiaries. Some disabled people who do not meet the criteria to be classified as developmentally disabled receive services from DD agencies, (184).
[d] This figure includes State funds.
[e] These figures represent appropriations rather than expenditures.

SOURCE: Office of Technology Assessment.

erans under the compensation for service-connected disabilities program (122,215), and $0.8 million was spent for 0.9 million beneficiaries under the pensions for nonservice-connected disabilities program (130). As will be noted below, these programs are important for recipients not only for the income they provide but also for supplemental benefits and referrals to other services. Both physical and service technologies are provided under the supplemental benefits. The income itself allows the recipients to purchase technologies not covered by the supplemental benefits.

SSDI is a Federal social insurance program for workers who have contributed to the social security retirement program and become disabled before retirement age. In order to become eligible for benefits, a worker must have 20 quarters of coverage in the 40 quarters prior to the onset of disability and must meet the statutory test of disability or blindness. Under the statutory test for disability, the individual must be unable to engage in *any* substantial gainful activity (SGA) due to a *medically determinable* physical or mental impairment expected to last at least 12 months or result in death (58). If a blind individual meets the statutory test for blindness, he or she may be declared eligible for benefits if unable to engage in SGA comparable to *previous* gainful activity in which engaged (213). Once application is made, there is a 5-month waiting period for receipt of benefits. Disabled spouses and dependent children may receive benefits upon the retirement, disability or death of the primary beneficiary.

Individual SSDI beneficiaries receive cash payments with no restrictions on their use. These payments are distributed by the Federal Government (although eligibility determinations are made by State vocational rehabilitation agencies) from the Disability Insurance Trust Fund, which is financed by a payroll tax. In addition to cash payments, beneficiaries receive two other benefits—health insurance coverage under title XVIII of the Social Security Act (Medicare) and referral to, and thus use of, vocational rehabilitation services. Medicare coverage begins after 24 months of SSDI payments; funds are transferred from the Disability Insurance Trust Fund to State vocational rehabilitation agencies. Federal dollars cover 100 percent of the cost of vocational rehabilitation services for eligible SSDI recipients. In fiscal year 1979, $102 million was expended (138).

The SSI program is a Federal cash assistance program whose purpose is to guarantee needy aged, blind, and disabled individuals a minimum income. Although the statutory definition of disability is the same as that under the SSDI program, SSI exhibits an important difference from SSDI, because eligibility for SSI is based on the individual's current status without regard to previous work or contributions to a trust fund (83). In order to qualify for benefits, an applicant must first fulfill the definition of disability, then pass an income needs test (which, in reality, is included in the determination of disability), and must not have personal resources which exceed statutory limits. Certain children under 18 are eligible for benefits, but there is no provision relating to the eligibility of widows or widowers.

The SSI program originated from several State programs for disabled, aged, and blind persons. In 1972, the Federal program was enacted; it is administered by the Social Security Administration and funded out of general revenues. States may supplement the Federal program by adding to the Federal cash benefits or by broadening eligibility limits. This supplemental program may be administered federally at each State's request, in which case the administrative costs are borne by the Federal Government. If States select this option (27 have), they must agree to provide supplements for all SSI recipients of the same class (127).

Like SSDI beneficiaries, SSI beneficiaries receive unrestricted cash payments. They also receive numerous welfare-related services, including health insurance coverage under title XIX of the Social Security Act (Medicaid), social services under title XX of the act, and food stamps. Certain beneficiaries may receive vocational rehabilitation services. Finally, beneficiaries who require care in personal care homes or domiciliary care facilities may have their Federal SSI or State supplemental payments made directly to their institutions (66).*

Clearly, the method of determining eligibility for the SSDI and SSI programs greatly affects the number and severity of beneficiaries and disabilities and thus, use of technologies. As noted earlier, the statutory definition of disability is the same for both programs, although the basis for each program is different (one is an insurance program and one is a welfare program). By law, the definition is meant to be a strict one so that only the most severely disabled individuals can meet it (213). It is the regulations rather than the statute, however, which specify how the definition is to be applied in individual cases. The State vocational rehabilitation agencies make the initial determination of disability based on medical considerations alone or on medical and vocational factors.

First, the agency makes a determination of whether or not an individual is engaging in SGA. Earnings below $190 per month are considered not to be SGA, while earnings above $300 per month automatically cause a finding of no disability.

---

*These institutions provide a lower level of skilled care than intermedicate care facilities and as such are not covered under Medicare or Medicaid. Generally, room and board as well as some supervision in activities of daily living are provided.

Earnings beween the two amounts must be evaluated further. If the individual is not engaging in SGA, a determination of whether or not the individual has a severe impairment—one which limits his or her physical or mental capacity to perform basic work-related functions—must be made. Past relevant work is not considered at this step. If a severe impairment is found, it is checked for inclusion on the Social Security medical listings for comparability and duration. At this stage, as long as the impairment is included in the listings or determined to have a medical equivalent in the listings, a finding of disability is made. In cases where the SGA and medical tests do not point to a clear finding of "disability" or "no disability," vocational factors, such as ability to do past work or adjust to different work, are considered.

According to the Subcommittee on Social Security of the U.S. House of Representatives, there is good reason to believe that the process of disability determination is not uniform across the country. Furthermore, there is disparity between two levels of eligibility determination—the initial application at the State agency level and the appeal (permitted if a denial is made at the initial application) at the administrative law judge level. State agencies are denying benefits to 67.4 percent of initial applicants, yet administrative law judges are reversing these decisions at a 60-percent rate. The subcommittee also noted that Federal supervision and knowledge of the program have been weakened by a number of executive branch reorganizations since 1975 (212). A recent General Accounting Office (GAO) study (95) found a problem with removing individuals who are no longer disabled from the SSDI rolls. GAO estimated that as many as 584,000 beneficiaries who do not currently meet the eligibility criteria may be receiving benefits.

At the heart of the definition of disability under SSDI and SSI is the determination of an individual's ability to engage in SGA. Under SSDI, although there is no "means test" to determine eligibility, benefits are terminated if a recipient earns more than $300 of counted income per month. Under SSI, since the program is designed to guarantee a minimum income, there is a reduction in benefits for dollars earned. It has been noted that SGA is less than the poverty level and thus provides a significant disincentive for beneficiaries to work (17,83). Furthermore, *the potential loss of supplemental benefits when SGA is declared, particularly the health insurance benefits under Medicare or Medicaid, provides an additional disincentive to work* (17).

Elimination of disincentives to leave the disability rolls and return to work has been widely discussed in the literature (12,17,68,83,104,130,138, 146,156,213). One suggestion has been to raise the level of SGA (which has been done periodically since the SSDI program was enacted). In theory, a higher SGA level would mean that once a beneficiary was terminated from the SSDI or SSI roll, because of performance of SGA, his or her earnings would automatically allow financial self-sufficiency. Yet a special study by DHEW of the increases in the SGA level in 1966, 1968, and 1974 found that these increases were not accompanied by increases in beneficiary earnings (213). One apparent reason for this finding is that most disabled beneficiaries' earnings are substantially below the SGA level, and raising that level does not increase those earnings. Another suggestion has been to increase the wage-to-benefit ratio. This ratio can be increased by lowering benefits or by improving wages by liberalizing the provisions of the trial work period (to be discussed below), by improving the performance of rehabilitation counselors, and by making the labor market more receptive to the rehabilitated disabled population (104). Improving wages appears to be the preferable method—first, it is more equitable, and second, high benefit levels are not always the result of SSI or SSDI benefits. A study of SSDI beneficiaries showed that in 1971, 44 percent of those receiving SSDI benefits for 1 year or longer also received cash benefits from at least one other source. Furthermore, the average total benefits paid to those receiving multiple benefits were double the amount paid to those receiving only SSDI (146).

The Social Security Disability Amendments of 1980 (Public Law 96-265) attempted to strengthen work incentives in several ways (68,130). Many of the law's provisions affect both SSDI and SSI, although some apply only to one program. One provision is that extraordinary work expenses due to disability—such as those for attendant care services, medical devices, equipment prostheses, and similar items and services—will be excluded from the calculations of whether the individual is engaging in SGA. A second provision is that a person's status as a disabled individual will be extended for 15 months after he or she has successfully completed a 9-month trial work period. Although the individual cannot receive cash benefits for more than 3 months of the extended benefit period, active benefit status can be reinstated if the work activity fails or the SGA level of earnings is not maintained. Prior to Public Law 96-265, there was a trial work period of 9 months after which the beneficiary's case was closed; new application and waiting periods were subsequently applicable.

A third important set of provisions in Public Law 96-265 relates to health insurance benefits. Indeed, potential loss of these benefits has been noted as one of the strongest disincentives to return to work. Their value alone is often more than the disabled recipient is able to purchase through his or her earnings, since the average cost of medical care is three times more for disabled persons than for able-bodied persons (17). Public Law 96-265 extends Medicare coverage for SSDI beneficiaries for 24 months *beyond* the automatic reentitlement period as long as there has been no medical recovery from disability. Furthermore, it eliminates the 24-month waiting period for Medicare for persons previously receiving SSDI who become eligible a second time. For SSI recipients, a 3-year demonstration program was authorized. Under this program, people who have completed the trial work period and continue to earn SGA receive a special benefit status that entitles them to retain Medicaid and social services benefits and in some cases, special cash payments. On a case-by-case basis, the Secretary of the Department of Health and Human Services (DHHS) is authorized to determine that former SSI recipients require Medicaid and/or social services to maintain employment or to provide for themselves a reasonable equivalent of SSI benefits. It is too early to assess the effects of these amendments on abolishing disincentives to work. A full report by the Secretary of DHHS to Congress on the effects of these amendments and on the programs in general is due by January 1, 1985.

As mentioned above, certain SSDI beneficiaries may receive vocational rehabilitation services under the Beneficiary Rehabilitation Program (BRP), and certain SSI beneficiaries receive such services under the SSI-Vocational Rehabilitation (SSI-VR) program. Under both programs, the services are provided by State vocational rehabilitation agencies and funded totally by the Federal Government (as opposed to the general Vocational Rehabilitation program under which States must contribute 20 percent). The primary purpose of funding the two programs is to save trust fund and general revenue dollars as a result of rehabilitating individuals into productive activity. Thus, the following criteria were developed for selecting beneficiaries to receive services (213): 1) the disabling physical or mental impairment is not expected to progress so rapidly as to outrun the effect of the vocational rehabilitation services or preclude restoration of the individual to activity; 2) without the services, the disability is such that the individual is expected to continue needing SSI or SSDI payments; 3) a reasonable expectation exists that provision of the services will restore the person to gainful activity; and 4) the predicted period of work is long enough that the benefits saved and future contributions to the trust fund are greater than the cost of the services provided. These criteria imply that only the least severely disabled beneficiaries in the SSDI or SSI program, who by definition must be severely disabled, are eligible for the BRP or SSI-VR programs. Indeed, in fiscal year 1979, there were only 94,936 beneficiaries in the BRP (138) out of a total 4.77 million beneficiaries on SSDI (69).

At issue currently is whether the Federal Government should continue to support vocational rehabilitation services as part of the income maintenance programs (96,129). One question is whether the programs are cost effective—i.e., whether the costs of services provided are less than the savings of cash benefits plus the contributions to the trust fund. A study of savings to the trust fund using vocational rehabilitation case data and SSDI benefit histories found the savings to be between $1.39 and $2.72 per $1.00 of cost for SSDI beneficiaries who completed their vocational rehabilitation service period in fiscal year 1975 (138). The same study found that the cost of vocational rehabilitation services would be fully repaid in 10 years. However, it also found that the loss of savings due to individuals returning to the SSDI rolls is substantially greater than the increased payroll tax revenue received during post-vocational rehabilitation employment. In contrast to the generally positive findings of the study of the BRP, a GAO study of the SSI-VR Program (96) found that the Federal funds spent greatly exceeded reductions in SSI payments. Furthermore, in 55 percent of cases studied, there were no reductions in SSI payments that could be attributed to a beneficiary's increased earnings. Similarly, a study of disability benefits and rehabilitation services found that persons who receive SSI benefits, SSDI benefits, or both, are rehabilitated (gainfully employed and removed from the benefit rolls) less frequently than nonbeneficiaries receiving the same vocational rehabilitation services, including other severely disabled vocational rehabiliation clients (12). The authors of that study note, however, that many SSI or SSDI beneficiaries who complete the vocational rehabilitation program remain on the benefit rolls, because the severity of their disability may prevent employment in the competitive market or because the disability benefits reduce their incentives to work.

A second question is whether the current recipients of vocational rehabilitation services under either the BRP or SSI-VR programs would be able to receive such services under the general vocational rehabilitation program. The general vocational rehabilitation program is now mandated to focus on severely disabled persons, which would include SSDI and SSI recipients. In addition, criteria for selection under the general vocational rehabilitation program are not as stringent, since it includes independent living as a goal (and not only gainful employment). However, the rehabilitation costs for income maintenance beneficiaries are roughly twice that for nonbeneficiaries. Thus, if scarce funds are not earmarked for those currently in the BRP and SSI-VR programs, there is less chance for those individuals to be selected for services (129).

The income maintenance programs for *disabled veterans* are completely separate from the civilian programs and have completely different bases for determining recipients' eligibility than the SSDI or SSI programs have. Both the compensation for service-connected disabilities and pensions for nonservice-connected disabilities programs are administered by the VA and funded out of general revenues. There are no State or local supplements for either program. Similarly, there is no participation by State or local agencies in determination of eligibility.

Compensation for service-connected disabilities is a program whose purpose is to provide economic relief to veterans whose earning capacity is impaired due to their military service. The amount of compensation depends on the degree of disability which the impairment causes in earning capacity in a civilian occupation. Additional compensation is provided for dependents. To become eligible, a veteran first must have contracted a disease, suffered a nonmisconduct injury, or aggravated an existing disease or injury in the line of duty during active war or peacetime service. Proof of disability is based on the service medical records. Service connection may be granted by presumption if a veteran develops one of the specified chronic diseases within 1 year of discharge from service, tuberculosis or Hansen's disease with 3 years, or multiple sclerosis within 7 years. Once service connection has been established, the percentage of disability is assigned by VA from an established "Schedule for Rating Disabilities." Percentaged range from 10 to 100 (215). Thus, the establishment of eligibility is based entirely on medical criteria (in addition to proof of service). No vocational factors are considered in individual cases. (Vocational factors were considered only when the "Schedule for Rating Disabilities" was developed.) Furthermore, the individual veteran does not have to show a lack of ability to earn an income or an inability to support himself or herself with unearned income.

Pensions for nonservice-connected disabilities is a program to provide an income to totally and permanently disabled veterans and their dependents whose income is below an established standard. To become eligible, veterans must have served at least 90 days including 1 day of wartime service, must meet a medical determination of disability, and must have personal resources and income below a legislated amount. At age 65, veterans are deemed to be disabled regardless of their physical condition. Disabled survivors of veterans may also receive benefits if the income test is met (127). As noted earlier, this income-tested program is smaller than the nonincome-tested one. Eligible veterans receive cash payments (the amount is determined by statute), medical and social services under the VA system, and housing and education benefits.

Erlanger, et al. (82) note that while distinction between service- and nonservice-connected disabilities has always been made in discussions on veterans' benefits, the legitimacy of veteran pressure for benefits has never been seriously questioned. An examination of the hearings on the Veterans' Disability Compensation and Survivors' Benefits Amendments of 1980 supports this comment (215). The veterans' disability programs have always been separate from the civilian programs and have had better benefits and less strict eligibility requirements. The major issue of concern to policymakers has been the cost of the policy of providing all eligible disabled veterans with all necessary services (82).

Health and Medical Care

The major publicly financed health and medical care programs serving disabled individuals are programs that serve able-bodied individuals as well. They include Medicare, Medicaid, and VA medical services. Expenditures attributed to disabling conditions are significant. Berkowitz estimated that in 1977, $1.4 billion was spent under Medicare and $2.8 billion was spent under Medicaid (8). Another $816 million was spent by VA. These figures do not represent total medical care benefits to disabled people funded under the three programs; rather, they represent only those medical care expenditures incurred by disabled persons directly related to their underlying impairments (8). Total health and medical care expenditures (not due only to disabling conditions) for disabled people under these programs are even higher. In fiscal year 1980, the Federal Government spent $4.0 billion under Medicare for 3.3 million disabled beneficiaries, $3.5 billion under Medicaid for 3.3 million disabled beneficiaries,*

---
*State supplements to the Medicaid program are not included in these figures.

and $3.0 billion to $5.6 billion for 0.6 million to 1.3 million disabled beneficiaries under the VA medical system (129). As will be discussed further, the use of technologies by disabled people is significantly affected by the amount of funds provided by these programs, either to individuals or providers, by the methods used to authorize payments, and by the organization of provision of services.

The Medicare program authorizes health insurance benefits to cover the cost of hospitalization and medical care for eligible elderly and disabled persons, including services by physicians, some allied health professionals, outpatient clinics, rehabilitation facilities, skilled nursing facilities, home health agency services, and some medically necessary drugs and devices (58,208). As noted in the previous section, individuals who are eligible for SSDI benefits for 24 months can receive Medicare benefits. Other eligible disabled persons include those severely disabled during childhood who are the dependents of deceased, retired, or disabled social security beneficiaries, disabled widows or widowers over age 50 whose deceased spouses were fully insured, and individuals with end-stage renal disease. Unlike the determination of eligibility process under SSDI or SSI during which medical factors, vocational factors and earnings were examined, eligibility for Medicare is strictly categorical with the categories mandated by statute. The determination *process* under this program is not as important for the use of technologies as it is under SSDI or SSI, although categorical eligibility clearly depends on the earlier determination process.

Under part A of the Medicare program (the hospital insurance program), participating hospitals, skilled nursing facilities, and home health agencies (institutional providers) are reimbursed for the reasonable cost of providing medically necessary inpatient and home care visits. The providers receive the reimbursement directly. Part A is financed by a payroll tax. Under part B (the Supplementary Medical Insurance program), reimbursement equals 80 percent of the reasonable charge for covered services, including physicians' services, outpatient physical therapy and speech pathology services, and other medically necessary services, including some drugs and devices. The payments are financed by participants' premiums and by general Federal revenues. They are paid either to the providers directly or to those who receive the services (58).

The Medicaid program authorizes Federal payments to States to cover the costs of medical care and related services for eligible recipients. The program is administered by the State and financed jointly by Federal and State contributions; the Federal portion varies according to a formula that considers State wealth and according to participation in optional parts of the program. Most persons receiving SSI are eligible for Medicaid assistance (categorically needy). States *may* elect to use more restrictive criteria for Medicaid eligibility than SSI. However, States may elect to cover other individuals whose incomes are higher than the SSI maximum but who can not afford medical care (medically needy); Federal contributions are received for these beneficiaries. Participating States are mandated to provide certain services, including hospital and physician services, but they are permitted to provide optional services. The provision of prosthetic devices and rehabilitation services are considered optional services. The Medicaid program has emerged as a primary source of funding for services to disabled people. This is both because the incidence of disability is higher among low-income groups and because amendments to the act added specialized benefits for institutionalized mentally ill and mentally retarded persons (58). The primary example of such specialized benefits is the Intermediate Care Facilities for the Mentally Retarded (ICF/MR) program. The ICF/MR program was added to Medicaid in 1971 as an optional service; it will be discussed further below.

There are several important policy issues that affect eligible, disabled Medicare and Medicaid recipients. First, what technologies are covered and how are those decisions made? Under the present coverage mechanism, funds are passed from the Federal Government to contractors (called fiscal intermediaries for Medicare, part A, and carriers for Medicare, part B) who reimburse the providers.* It is the contractors who are initially responsible for identifying coverage issues (166). When the contractors feel unable to judge whether or not to cover a particular service, the case is referred to 1 of 10 regional offices in the case of Medicare. If the regional office is unable to settle the issue, the case is submitted to the central office for a decision. Yet, decisions are often made on a case-by-case basis and thus may vary from region to region (or State to State).

Coverage for certain technologies (including procedures, services, and devices) is mandated by statute or regulation. For example, necessary curative physician services in or out of the hospital are covered nationwide. However, many individual technologies are not specifically covered in a list or set of lists.** Their coverage depends on determination by the contractor that their use falls within a category of covered technologies. For example, prosthetic devices (a category of technologies) may be covered under part B of Medicare if they replace all or part of an internal body organ or replace the functioning of a permanently inoperative or malfunctioning organ (108). Communication aids, which are considered by numerous health professionals to be prosthetic devices, are not specifically covered under part B (47,108). At present, no agencies or programs are specifically mandated to fund the purchase of communication aids (108), although they may be covered under some programs once precedent-setting cases have been experienced. (See separately issued OTA Background Paper on "Assistive Communication Aids" for additional discussion on this topic.)

According to an earlier report by OTA (166), coverage decisions on a particular technology appear to be based on the technology's stage of development and its general acceptance. A technology that is perceived to have moved beyond experimental status to clinical application and to be accepted by the local medical community is considered "reasonable and necessary" and thus is

---

*The contractors may also reimburse individuals whether or not they have already paid the providers under the part B program. However, decisions on what is covered and what types of professions or institutions are recognized as providers are not affected by and do not affect whether or not the public funds are paid directly to the provider or to the individual.

**Congress and the agencies often avoid such lists in drafting laws and regulations, because it is very difficult to be comprehensive. Usually some examples are included followed by phrases such as "other necessary services" or "other health impaired persons requiring special education and related services."

covered if it is not specifically excluded from coverage. The standards for the criteria used—stage of development and general acceptance—depend on judgments made on the technology's medical safety and efficacy. These judgments are made by the contractors' or regional offices' medical advisors; they may be based on personal knowledge, on recent literature, or on advice by advocates of the technology (166). *They are rarely made on the basis of a consistent national policy, and they vary widely from contractor to contractor* (22,166).

Technologies that are covered must then be deemed "medically necessary" by the medical community for individual users. Lack of proof of medical necessity is often a reason for denial of funding even if the services are necessary for the comfort or convenience of the patient. Even if necessity is established, contractors do not always agree with clients and their providers over whether the need is medical in nature. Consultants employed to assist the contractors in their decisions rarely have experience with rehabilitation and do not fully understand its function. As a result, funding is often denied rather than justified. This is a particularly important problem for those disabled people whose needs for services and devices are not in response to curing a medical problem (even if it is a disease that has caused their impairment). Preventive services generally are also not covered. For example, a new electronic personal response system for disabled and elderly people that has been shown to be effective, called Lifeline (196), is not covered by Medicare or Medicaid because it is considered to be preventive but not "medically necessary."

A second issue affecting Medicare and Medicaid recipients is what types of professions and institutions are recognized as providers, because only those who are recognized as providers by law or regulation may prescribe the medically necessary services. While it may be clear to those outside the medical community that some technologies are medically necessary (and thus reimbursed), the recognized providers may not be the best suited to match a particular technology with an individual. The use of durable medical equipment (DME) may illustrate this point. DME, covered under part B of Medicare, refers to equipment that: 1) can withstand repeated use, 2) serves primarily a medical purpose, 3) is not generally useful in the absence of an illness or an injury, and 4) is appropriate for use in the home (116,170). In 1977, an estimated $73 million to $130 million was spent on DME (115). Examples of DME include hospital beds and accessories, wheelchairs and accessories, and canes and crutches. For DME to be paid for, it must be prescribed by a physician. The prescription must include a diagnosis and prognosis of the patient's condition, the reason for prescribing the equipment, and the estimated duration of medical necessity (116). However, the actual matching of DME to the patient's needs is often done by providers such as social service workers, visiting nurses, orthotics specialists, and others who transmit the pertinent information to the prescribing physician. The carriers often check claims with these additional providers, and due to the number of individuals who must be contacted, the claims are up to five times more costly to process (169). There are, however, those who believe that the physician prescription is an important element in getting an appropriate fit between the technology and user and in obtaining funding (41). Although there are numerous other reasons for denial of funding, prescriptions that are not detailed are often initially denied or referred for followup. Carefully detailed physician prescriptions may, and have, assured funding (41).

Another problem pertaining to the issue of which providers are recognized for funding is that, although a class of institutions may be specifically recognized, the determination of whether an individual institution qualifies as a provider is not always clear cut. Thus, for example, intermediate-care facilities for the mentally retarded (ICF/MRs) were mandated as providers under the Medicaid program in 1971. While the law contained a definition of ICF/MRs, the definition was modeled on large publicly operated institutions for the mentally retarded. Initially, it did not specify criteria for including small publicly and privately funded community residences. Regulations promulgating the ICF/MR program in 1974 stipulated that facilities of 15 or fewer residents could qualify, but very little guidance was provided to States in certifying small community residences.

The updated regulations in 1977 were not much more specific (2).

A third issue affecting Medicare and Medicaid recipients is the amount reimbursed for the cost of covered, medically necessary technologies. The fact that a technology is covered does not ensure that it will be fully reimbursed. The amount authorized for Medicare or Medicaid reimbursement may be such that indigent clients needing expensive equipment (and, by definition, Medicaid recipients are indigent) may effectively be denied access to it (116). A study of DME claims flow and subsequent payment found that there was payment of only 52.3 percent of all submitted charges (116). The reasons for this figure included: a claims denial rate of 13.4 percent, requirements for deductibles and coinsurance, and reductions of the actual charges to allowed charges. The allowed charge is a result of a comparison among the actual charge, the customary charge of the individual supplier, the prevailing charge in the area, and the lowest charge level in the area for certain specified items (116). The Omnibus Budget Reconciliation Act of 1981 removed the Medicare reasonable charge limitations on Medicaid reimbursement. It is too early to assess the effect of this charge on indigent disabled people receiving technologies.

A recent GAO report on DME reimbursement found that standard DME items often cannot be bought at the amounts allowed and recommended that the lowest charge level screen be discontinued. That report also found inconsistencies in the reimbursement and coverage screens used in different regions of the country. The agency's recommendation was to make DME reimbursement policy more consistent (94).

A final important issue is that the Medicare and Medicaid programs have great influence on the type and location of services provided to disabled beneficiaries. Historically, reimbursement policies have promoted care in institutions both for disabled and elderly persons when coverage of home care and/or attendant services would have permitted some of those institutionalized to remain at home (2,14,66). While the current public policy rhetoric has shifted to a focus on community-based home health care, the policy reality is that the incentives for institutionalization remain stronger than the rhetoric. One reason for this is that Medicare and Medicaid remain physician-driven medical programs to support curative care which were not designed to support the social (nonmedical) needs of beneficiaries (14). Most disabled individuals do not have a disease of which they may be cured. Another reason is that Medicaid eligibility may be easier to obtain when applicants are in institutions. In 16 States, disabled and elderly persons living in the community may not receive Medicaid unless their income is so low that they receive public cash assistance. These same persons *can* receive Medicaid with somewhat higher incomes if they are in nursing homes (66). An example may illustrate the incentives for institutionalization. While home health services are covered under Medicare, they may be provided only after an *acute* illness and to those who need *skilled* nursing care on an intermittent basis. This limited benefit is a very small part of the total Medicare program; in fiscal year 1979, only 2.1 percent of the Federal Medicare budget was expended on home health care (14). The home health aides who provide the service are not generally permitted to do housekeeping or general chores. Homemaker services, including chores, may be covered under Medicaid, although only 15 States have elected to do so (66).

VA provides comprehensive medical and rehabilitative services to all veterans with service-connected disabilities and to all veterans with non-service-connected disabilities who are unable to obtain or pay for needed medical services (208). Funding is 100 percent Federal. Unlike the Medicare and Medicaid programs, VA medical programs provide services directly in a variety of VA-run settings—including hospitals, nursing homes, domiciliary care homes, special rehabilitation centers for blind persons, and rehabilitative engineering and development centers. Priority for any services is given to veterans with service-connected disabilities. Veterans with nonservice-connected disabilities must prepare a statement declaring that they cannot pay for necessary medical expenses. This statement is used to establish an income limit for hospitalization, outpatient care, and nursing home care. Currently, approximately 80 percent of VA patients are veterans without a service-connected disability (127).

Benefits provided include prehospitalization care, hospitalization, posthospitalization care, prosthetic devices, nursing home care, medical devices, transportation services, domiciliary care, outpatient medical services, and prescribed drugs. Unlike coverage decisions under Medicare and Medicaid, all technologies suited to a veteran's circumstances and needs are made available (123). Of course, determinations about circumstances and needs still need to be made. VA policy is to provide blind veterans with all necessary services and devices to *overcome* their handicap and to provide other disabled veterans with technologies deemed *medically necessary*. As with disability compensation and pensions, the major issue of concern to the users and policymakers is the cost of the policy of covering all available technologies. It should be noted, however, that there are funding restrictions for some services for veterans without service-connected disabilities. For example, a foster home program found to be effective is only available to those veterans who can afford to pay its cost with personal resources (149).

Social Services

Social services programs serve disabled individuals by the direct provision of services, funding of services, or both, at the Federal, State, and local levels. The two programs with the highest level of funding are the Basic Social Services program authorized under title XX of the Social Security Act and the Developmental Disabilities program authorized under the Developmental Disabilities Assistance and Bill of Rights Act, as amended. Since the title XX and other social services programs serve the able-bodied as well as disabled individuals, it is difficult to estimate the expenditures for disabled people under these programs. Berkowitz provides a very rough estimate of $841 million in 1977 (8). Total program expenditures were over $2 billion.* In fiscal year 1980, $62.4 million was expended under the Developmental Disabilities program (122). There were approximately 3.6 million beneficiaries (184).** Clearly, the amount spent on these services is far less than that spent on income maintenance or health care services.

Social services comprise a wide variety of activities, including counseling, guiding, and informing individuals to enable them to use other public and private programs; referring individuals to other community resources; and providing identifiable services to individuals such as day care, personal attendant care, legal aid, and meals, which give them the opportunity to make use of other programs (208). The funds for social services programs may be used to pay for the programs' administrative costs, the providers' salaries, and actual physical objects needed by the programs' clients such as speech prostheses. The receipt of social services has been traditionally linked to eligibility for public income maintenance programs as well as some other measures of financial need. Individuals and families not receiving income from such programs may also receive services, although fees are usually charged if they have the ability to pay.

The title XX program authorizes Federal assistance to help States provide social services to public assistance recipients, including those who receive SSI. The Federal Government provides 75 percent of the funding (90 percent for family services and 100 percent for a portion of child day services) up to an appropriated ceiling. The funds are apportioned among the States on the basis of population. Within Federal guidelines, the States may establish eligibility criteria. Thus, while SSI and Medicaid recipients must be covered, other needy disabled people may be eligible. The States have broad discretion to define the services provided under this program as long as they meet one of five statutory goals: 1) achieving or maintaining economic self-support to prevent or eliminate dependency, 2) achieving self-sufficiency, 3) preventing or remedying neglect or abuse of children and adults unable to protect their own interests, 4) preventing or reducing inappropriate institutionalization, and 5) securing referral for or providing institutional care when other forms of care are not appropriate. Certain activities are specifically prohibited. These include major construction or renovation as well as medical or remedial services that can be funded under Medicare or Medicaid (unless such services

---

*This figure was estimated using the fiscal year 1980 appropriation of $2.7 billion (58).
**This figure represents the estimated population of developmentally disabled persons.

are an integral and subordinate part of a broader service not supported by the medical programs) (58).

Although the breadth of the range of services that may be funded under title XX may mean that some clients receive a comprehensive program, it also means that providers and clients often need to learn the intricacies of the regulations in order to assure that necessary services are funded. This process is usually quite time-consuming. Another result of the wide range of possible services is that clients with similar situations in different States will receive different care. Finally, the range of services has resulted in title XX being used to fill gaps in funding services not completely paid for under other programs. Examples include radio reading services for blind people and otherwise print-impaired people (134), intermediate care facilities for mentally retarded individuals (2,14,39) and foster home care (66). This use of title XX funds exemplifies a significant problem in the total "system" of delivery and use of technologies for disabled people—a lack of coordination in funding and delivery of services.* Furthermore, reliance on title XX funds to fill gaps in funding can be problematic, because unlike Medicare or Medicaid, title XX has a closed-end budget (14).

The Developmental Disabilities program authorizes Federal formula grants to States to support planning for services to persons with developmental disabilities. States also receive grants for the establishment of a system to protect the rights of developmentally disabled people. In addition, university-affiliated facilities for developmentally disabled persons receive grants to support their operation and administration. Special project grants to State and local public agencies and nonprofit organizations may also be awarded.

The current Developmental Disabilities program evolved from the Mental Retardation Facilities Construction Act of 1963. That act initially provided funds for construction of community-based mental retardation facilities and later supported the provision of comprehensive services (58). States are required by statute to select one priority service area out of the following: case management services, child development services, alternative living arrangement services, and non-vocational social-developmental services. Under certain circumstances, a second priority area may be chosen. Services that may be provided are similar to those authorized under the title XX program. Service activities, as defined by law, include delivery of services, model service programs, activities to increase the capability of agencies and institutions to deliver services, coordinating with other services, outreach, and training of providers (58).

Eligibility for services depends on meeting the definition of developmental disability. Until 1978, a developmentally disabled person was one with a substantial disability attributable to mental retardation, cerebral palsy, epilepsy or other neurological conditions closely related to mental retardation that originated before the individual reached age 18 and was expected to continue indefinitely. In 1978, however, the definition of developmental disability was changed to shift the emphasis from etiological categories to functional impairments. The new definition includes disabilities attributable to mental or physical impairments that are manifested before the person reaches age 22 and result in substantial functional limitations in three or more of the following categories: self-care, receptive and expressive language, learning, mobility, self-direction, capacity for independent living, and economic sufficiency (58).

The change in definition of developmental disability was enacted by Congress after intensive lobbying by advocates of disabled citizens. While it is too early to definitively determine the effects of the change, there have been several significant occurrences (224,225). First, the *original* targeted population has been approximately halved, primarily due to the fact that mildly mentally retarded people are no longer being considered developmentally disabled. Second, the *potentially* eligible population has been broadened considerably due to the inclusion of physical disabilities and mental illness under the new definition. As a result, one State (so far) has withdrawn from the program. Another has specifically excluded chronic mental illness from the definition of developmental disability in the State

---
*This problem will be discussed in depth later in this chapter.

statutes (2). Third, coverage of some of the services jointly funded under the Developmental Disability and Medicaid programs may have to be abolished due to the broadening of the definition. An example is the funding for the intermediate care facilities for mentally retarded people (who are developmentally disabled). The ICF/MR program was never intended to cover mentally ill or learning disabled persons. Thus, not only are funds insufficient, but the standards are not applicable to the new groups (2).

Education Services*

The two largest programs that provide education services for disabled individuals are authorized under the Education for All Handicapped Children Act (Public Law 94-142) and the Vocational Education Act. In fiscal year 1979, the Federal Government spent $951 million under the Education for All Handicapped Children Act's authority for approximately 3.9 million disabled children. States and local school districts added approximately $5 billion to that amount (128). Under the Vocational Education Act, the Federal Government spent at least $55 million in fiscal year 1979 for approximately 2.1 million special education students (132).** State and local governments provide substantial supplements; in fiscal year 1979, they provided 91.5 percent of the total funds spent for vocational education programs (132).

Three additional programs, which will not be discussed in depth, are significant education services programs.*** Part B of title I of the Elementary and Secondary Education Act (Public Law 89-313) authorizes grants to State agencies operating or supporting schools for disabled children.

---

*Education services refer to those education services, such as elementary and secondary education as well as vocational training, provided and funded outside of the Federal-State Vocational Rehabilitation program.

**This figure is for fiscal year 1978; it is an estimated figure. Special education students include disadvantaged and handicapped pupils.

***While there are many programs that provide education services for handicapped people, the Education for All Handicapped Children and Vocational Education Acts are those that serve the most disabled individuals. Thus, they were selected for highlighting in this report. Furthermore, problems and opportunities relating to those two programs are characteristic of problems and opportunities found in other smaller programs.

Federal appropriations for fiscal year 1980 were $143 million (58). These funds supported over 222,000 children (122). The Handicapped Children's Early Education Act authorizes grants for demonstration programs for preschool disabled children and their parents. This program received $20 million in fiscal year 1980 appropriations (122). It has been in existence since 1968. Finally, the Comprehensive Employment and Training Act of 1973 authorizes a number of programs to assist unemployed persons, including disabled persons, to develop job skills and work potential. While there are no programs specifically for disabled people, they were specifically recognized in the 1978 amendments to the act as a targeted population (58). During the Reagan administration, it is the training portion of the program that will be emphasized; appropriations for the employment programs have been substantially cut.

Basic education services for disabled persons, usually in the form of special education, were considered the primary responsibility of State and local education agencies until 1966. Congressional hearings that year revealed that only one-third of the country's disabled children were receiving appropriate educational services. Thus, a new title was added to the Elementary and Secondary Education Act (the Federal program of grants to States to support elementary and secondary education for all children) which authorized grants to States specifically to assist in the education of disabled children. In 1975, the Education for All Handicapped Children Act, as amended, expanded the original program to a major multibillion dollar commitment of the Federal Government to assuring all disabled children free appropriate public education in the *least restrictive environment*. Since enactment of the act, disabled children are to receive special education as well as any related services necessary to benefit from the education. An individualized educational program (IEP) is mandated for each disabled child (58). It is these provisions of the act that have significant effect on the use of technologies by disabled children.

The least restrictive environment (LRE) requirement is central to the act's mandate of a free appropriate education. The concept itself is simple—disabled children must be educated to the maximum extent appropriate with nondisabled children. It is the word "appropriate," however, which makes LRE a complex issue (49). Appropriateness is the factor that determines whether a child will be educated in the regular classroom or in another setting such as a special classroom, a special (separate) school, at home, or in the hospital or institution. The interpretation of appropriateness naturally varies from child to child, from school district to school district, and from State to State. In the 1977-78 school year, 93.9 percent of school-aged disabled children were educated in schools serving nondisabled children. Of those children, over two-thirds received educational services in classrooms along with nondisabled children. The proportion of children placed in regular schools and the proportion of those children placed in regular classrooms increased slightly over the previous year (49).*

To keep these children in their current placements or to move them closer to a regular classroom, available technologies in the form of aids and services must be provided. Under Public Law 94-142, these aids and services are entitled "related services." Determining what may be included as "related services" and who is responsible financially have been very difficult issues and certainly a source of confusion and long debate for policymakers, providers, and consumers. One reason for this difficulty is that the law and subsequent regulations suggest some examples of related services, but the list is intentionally not exhaustive (222). The examples themselves are not well defined; they include transportation, developmental and corrective services, speech pathology and audiology services, psychological services, physical and occupational therapy, medical services for diagnostic or evaluation purposes, school health services, social work, and parent counseling and training (194). Decisions on what may be included under each example category still need to be made by local and State agencies and, ultimately, the courts. For example, a case on whether catheterization (a medical service) must be provided is still being fought in the courts; the current status is that States do not have to provide that service (222). A second reason that "related services" has been a difficult issue is that education agencies now have the responsibility for providing services that have historically been the domain of the medical community (194). Under Public Law 94-142, a child needing physical therapy would have that need determined by a team of educators instead of the traditional physician. In many States, a physician would still need to prescribe the physical therapy services** (without having first determined the need) and then have that prescription's outcome subject to an educational fair hearing process.

The mandate that each child must receive an IEP clearly affects the delivery and use of technology, since it is the IEP that details the current capabilities of the child, the annual and short-term instructional goals, the particular services to be provided, and the extent to which the child is to participate in the regular classroom program. Related services are prescribed in about 13 percent of the IEPs (49). One issue relating to the IEP that is often discussed is the cost of its development. Those who believe it is too costly due to the number of hours and personnel needed*** argue that the requirement should be deleted unless Federal funds are allocated specifically for that purpose. Others argue that its cost is only too high if the IEP system is placed on top of the placement and classification systems already in place and that, ultimately, less professional time might be needed than under the former placement systems (128). Another issue relating to the IEP concerns the methods by which it is developed (49,171). On one hand, the IEP process requires a move towards educational programing and use of related services based on a functional assessment of an individual child's abilities and disabilities and away from special education classes for categories of disabled children (such as "mentally retarded" or "deaf"). On the other hand,

---

*The increase does not necessarily represent a change in policies or implementation relating to the least restrictive environment requirement, but rather may represent an increase in the number of mildly handicapped children served.

**In these States, the Medical Practices Act does not allow physical therapists to provide services without a medical prescription (194).

***A national survey of IEPs found that there was an average of 4 participants in the development of IEPs, with the greatest number reported as 15. These participants included representatives of the school district (usually principals), special education teachers, regular classroom teachers, physical and/or occupational therapists, speech therapists, school psychologists, social workers, school counselors, parents, handicapped students themselves, and others (49).

however, the IEP process in its focus on the individual child tends to devote too little time to an assessment of the child's environment as a continuing source of the handicap.

While studies of the implementation of Public Law 94-142 indicate that more disabled children are receiving a free appropriate education than ever before (49), there is evidence suggesting that the congressional intent remains unfulfilled. It does not appear that all disabled children are being served. Seven percent of school enrollees are disabled, yet 12 percent of the total school-aged population is disabled (17). (Keep in mind, however, the frequently inadequate state of data in the disability area.) Many of these disabled children who are enrolled in school remain unnecessarily segregated in special classes or whole schools (77). There appears to be a substantial yet undetermined number of children who need but who do not have access to special education (93). In addition, disabled children are often denied essential related services; in some school districts, related services provided have been based on what was available instead of what was needed (49,77). A number of disabled children are waiting for an IEP (77). Others are reportedly suspended for periods of up to 2 years (77). There continue to be shortages of adequately prepared special education teachers and support personnel (49,128). Finally, while the law guarantees rights to disabled children and their families, the funds for its enforcement have been called inadequate (16,121). (See separately issued Background Paper for a case study on "The Educational Context and the Least Restrictive Environment" for a more complete discussion of Public Law 94-142.)

The Vocational Education Act, as amended, authorizes a program of grants to States to support vocational education. While the Federal Government has supported State vocational education programs since 1917, it was not until 1963 that the funding structure and legislative language recognized the needs of special groups, including disabled people, and not until 1968 that disabled people were specifically targeted as beneficiaries. In 1963, the focus of Federal funding shifted from support of occupation-specific training programs to support of general planning for and operation of a wide range of secondary and postsecondary vocational education programs and auxiliary services (48). This shift allowed States to develop programs that included disabled and disadvantaged students who had been excluded by virtue of the types of occupation-specific programs previously provided. Since 1968, 10 percent of each State's basic grant funds must be targeted to disabled students. In addition, Federal funds ($20 million in fiscal year 1981) are appropriated for special programs for disadvantaged students (132).

Although specific devices are not provided with vocational education funds, vocational education programs are important for the use of technologies by disabled students, because effective use of technologies in the employment setting is one objective of the education services received. In addition, vocational education programs often serve as a source of information on what technologies are available to assist disabled individuals in employment. Evaluation of the effects of vocational education programs on their students is quite difficult, because many factors other than the program curriculum affect the economic and noneconomic experiences of the students once they leave the programs (48). One report on the state of the art of vocational education of disabled students (112) identified six areas needing improvement: 1) interagency cooperation, 2) personnel preparation, 3) amount of funding, 4) availability of a choice of service delivery and program options for disabled students (i.e., regular vocational education programs, adapted programs with special support services and materials, special education programs, or individualized vocational training in a variety of settings), 5) program evaluation, and 6) delivery of services to Native Americans and other minority disabled youth. Another report found that it is necessary to look at programs not necessarily designated as vocational education programs since most special education courses for postelementary students have vocational content (159).

From a national perspective, there are several issues of concern regarding the Vocational Education Act and disabled people. Bowe has stated that vocational education is the most blatantly discriminatory aspect of public education, since only 1.7 percent of those receiving vocational education services are disabled while 10 to 12 percent of the population eligible by age are disabled (17). He reported that this discrimination has been due to a lack of appropriations for monitoring and enforcing the full access requirements of the law. Additional factors have been suggested as contributing to the low percentage of disabled enrollees, including severe shortages of personnel training in both special education and vocational education, limited types of vocational education programs and service delivery options, and a limited funding base (112). Another issue of concern is that the procedures mandated for the States to distribute Federal dollars to local education agencies and other eligible recipients are extremely confusing and, in part, contradictory (48,132). One set of criteria is used for determining the priority of applicants and another set, similar but not the same, is used for distributing the funds. This situation exists because the Education Amendments of 1976, which amended the Vocational Education Act, combined a Senate bill with a House bill without reconciling them. A third issue is whether the Federal Government should continue its involvement in vocational education. Arguments against continued involvement include noting that more services are being provided with a smaller percentage of Federal funds each year. Arguments for continued involvement include noting that only the Federal program have required planning for targeted populations and that relatively small amounts of Federal funds have been effective in advancing Federal goals and affecting and/or redirecting State efforts.

Vocational Rehabilitation and Independent Living

The stated goals of the vocational rehabilitation system are: 1) to assist vocationally disabled individuals to enter or return to gainful employment and 2) to assist those individuals whose disabilities are so severe that they do not have the potential for employment, but who may benefit from services, to live and function independently. The Rehabilitation Act of 1973, as amended, authorizes a variety of service, demonstration, research, and training programs to accomplish these goals.

The largest program provides Federal grants to designated State rehabilitation agencies to provide basic rehabilitation services to disabled persons. The Federal Government provides 80 percent of the funding for the Federal-State program (208). In fiscal year 1980, $1.4 billion Federal dollars were spent for 1.1 million beneficiaries (130). Eligibility for vocational rehabilitation services is usually determined by a rehabilitation counselor, in consultation with the client, based on meeting three criteria: the presence of a physical or mental disability, the presence of a substantial handicap to employment, and a reasonable expectation that the vocational rehabilitation services will allow the individual to become gainfully employed. For each client accepted, an individual written rehabilitation plan must be developed. This plan defines the individual's long-range employment goal and lists the specific intermediate services to be provided to achieve the goal.

In addition to counseling and guidance, the vocational rehabilitation client may receive physical and mental restoration services; prevocational evaluation and training; vocational and other training services, including personal and vocational adjustment services, books, tools, and other training materials; maintenance allowances during the rehabilitation process; transportation; services to the client's family if they are necessary to the adjustment of the client; interpreter services for deaf persons; reader, orientation, and mobility services for blind clients; telecommunication, sensory, and other technological aids and devices; work adjustment and placement counseling; placement services; occupational licenses, tools, equipment, initial stocks, and supplies; and any other goods and services which may reasonably be expected to assist in the employment of a disabled individual (58). In essence, then, any technology that can be proven to be of value in preparing an individual for employment or in maintaining that employment *may* be provided under this program. The goods and services are provided by the State rehabilitation agencies themselves, by other public service agencies, and by private agencies who serve the general public. They are paid for out of the Federal-State vocational rehabilitation funds unless the individuals are eligible for support under some other program (208). An example of another program is the Beneficiary Rehabilitation Program funded under the SSDI program.

The key issue in the vocational rehabilitation program is eligibility, since the range of technologies available to and funded for eligible disabled individuals is clearly extensive and varied. By mandate, vocational rehabilitation agencies now must focus attention on severely disabled people. Yet a possible conflict with this requirement is the eligibility criterion that requires evidence of a reasonable expectation that rehabilitation service will result in gainful employment. In 1975, the Urban Institute (208) found that only 41 percent of all vocational rehabilitation recipients could be considered severely disabled. The same study noted that critics of the system suggest that rehabilitation counselors select the least disabled persons eligible to receive services to increase the number of successfully rehabilitated clients. Although this criticism has been difficult to test, it is known that services do fail to reach many who need them or may benefit from them. Bowe pointed out that of every 11 individuals eligible for vocational rehabilitation by virtue of their disability, only 1 is served (17). The primary reason behind limiting eligibility for services appears to be a lack of enough appropriated funds, both Federal and State.

Vocational rehabilitation services for severely disabled people tend to be provided in programs at work activities centers, developmental centers, other sheltered workshops, or at independent living centers. A sheltered workshop may be defined as a vocationally oriented rehabilitation facility that utilizes work in a structured, controlled environment to provide evaluation, training, and employment and is designed to assist disabled persons to move to their optimum level of production (223). Workshops differ in the type of clientele served, the production-rehabilitation orientation, the placement in competitive industry, the type of goods produced, the consumers to whom goods are sold, and the capital-labor mix used in production. Sheltered workshops that provide services to a number of vocational rehabilitation clients are largely funded with Federal-State vocational rehabilitation moneys. However, many sheltered workshops serve clients considered too severely limited for vocational rehabilitation eligibility (60). Sheltered workshops have been studied extensively. Issues of concern include the dual role of the disabled person as client and employee and the resultant problems, funding for construction and operations, the lack of movement of disabled clients from the workshop to the competitive labor market, the determination of a proper amount of wages to workshop employees, the development of a fair yet little time-consuming process for determining eligibility for the subminimum wage requirement to encourage employment opportunities, and the need to strengthen enforcement of the Fair Labor Standards Act (60,98,223).

The Rehabilitation Act also authorizes formula grants to State vocational rehabilitation agencies to provide comprehensive independent living services to those disabled individuals who do not have present potential for employment. This authority was created in the 1978 amendments to the act in recognition of the needs of many severely disabled people who were unable to qualify for vocational rehabilitation services. "Independent living" is a concept with a variety of definitions, although the following ideas seem to be important generic components: individuals make their own decisions and are responsible for their own lives; individuals are integrated into the community to the maximum extent feasible or desirable; and individuals have access to support services in order to maintain independence. Independent living services are those services that make independent living possible; the kind and amount necessarily vary from person to person. Housing, however, can be viewed as a central theme around which other independent living services and issues resolve (206). It is included as an allowable service under the independent living authority of the Rehabilitation Act. Other allowable services include counseling, modification of existing housing, appropriate job placement services, transportation, attendant care, physical rehabilitation, therapeutic treatment, needed prostheses and other appliances and devices, health maintenance, recreational activities, services to children of preschool age, and appropriate preventive services to decrease the need for future services.

Since the allowable services appear comprehensive enough to permit attainment of independent living, eligibility for services should be the primary issue of concern with respect to the use of technologies. However, the independent living formula grant authority received no appropriation for 1980. There was $15 million appropriated for project grants to vocational rehabilitation agencies to establish and operate centers for independent living which provide or arrange for many of the activities listed above (58). However, this level of funding does not actually pay for the necessary services, and centers for independent living must spend huge amounts of time obtaining other funds. It should also be noted that the Federal policy of deinstitutionalization of mentally retarded persons (as discussed earlier) has increased the need for independent living services (223). Appropriations for this authority may be needed now more than ever.

Nonpublic Programs

Activities concerned with the delivery, use, and financing of technologies for disabled people in the nonprofit and private sectors are numerous and varied. Since the 1930's, developing and assuring the delivery of services has been primarily a public (governmental) sector activity. The availability of public funds in support of public policies has greatly shaped the nonpublic sector. Nonprofit and private agencies and organizations, however, are often the actual service providers under public programs. In addition, they provide services and funding not covered by the public programs.

The major activities in the nonprofit and private sectors are sponsored by volunteer agencies with specialized fundraising activities tied directly to disabling conditions, by fraternal and religious societies, by veterans' groups, and by self-help and consumer organizations (83,201). In addition to service provision, an important function carried out by nonprofit organizations is the coordination of various public sector programs. Disabled individuals are often eligible for more than one public program, yet they do not have the information or the resources to take full advantage of available services. A number of nonprofit organizations serve as information and resource brokers, matching their clients with the appropriate public programs.

Private insurance companies provide income maintenance benefits to certain workers unable to work due to disability. The amount of benefits varies, depending on whether the disability is (in their language) "total" or "partial" and the period of time for which benefits are payable. The duration of benefits usually depends on whether the disability was caused by an accident or by an illness. This feature of private disability income protection insurance differs from the SSDI program under which eligibility does not depend on the cause of disability. Private disability income coverage is either short-term or long-term. Short-term policies provide benefits for up to 2 years, while long-term policies provide benefits for specified periods such as 5 years, 10 years, or to age 65. In 1979, 84 million individuals had some form of disability income coverage. Of these, 66 million had short-term policies, and 20 million had long-term policies. More than 2 million people had both types of coverage (107). (These figures include those covered under public progams.) The total benefits paid under these programs, although substantial, are far less than those paid under the Federal programs. In 1977, insurance companies paid just over $2.2 billion (106). Disabled beneficiaries of private plans often seek coverage under the public programs once benefits run out.

Private and nonprofit insurance companies have traditionally covered disability-related health and medical care; in 1977, Blue Cross-Blue Shield spent an estimated $5.3 billion for those expenses. However, many insurance companies have avoided or limited coverage of preventable or remedial rehabilitation services under their medical care policies. One method used to limit coverage is the exclusion of any education or research costs performed by hospital staff. Often, rehabilitation services fall under one of those categories. Reasons cited for these exclusions include the problem of defining the eligible populations; the difficulty in selecting limits to eligibility on an individual basis once the eligible populations have been defined; the difficulty in determining cost, cost benefit, or cost effectiveness of services; the need for new methods of data collection; the need for an analysis of past experience; and the need for evidence of meaningful utilization review mechanisms (143,201).

In recent years, an increasing number of companies have become involved with rehabilitation services coverage. Part of the increase is due to the efforts of the Insurance Rehabilitation Study Group (IRSG). IRSG, founded in 1965, is a group of 50 insurance company executives who are actively engaged in rehabilitation and medical administration. Activities of the group include maintaining awareness of current rehabilitation principles and practices, developing innovative policies, and providing information to the public (144). Membership is on an individual, not company, basis, but the influence of the members on their parent companies is continuing to be demonstrated.

In contrast to the slower development of rehabilitation coverage by insurance companies, organized labor benefits have been more comprehensive and have been steadily increasing, especially through the larger labor unions (201).

The volunteer agencies have played a significant role in increasing public awareness of the problems of disabled individuals, in raising private funds, in advocating legislation, and in assisting to provide program services (201). Some agencies have started handicap industries that employ severely disabled people. These industries are privately owned companies that compete for profits in the competitive labor market (profits usually accrue to the nonprofit agency that established the company) and that employ disabled and able-bodied workers side by side in the production process (32). An example of a handicap industry is Center Industries Corp., a manufacturing company founded by the Cerebral Palsy Research Foundation of Kansas; this company has often been cited as a model program and company. Furthermore, a study of the economic costs and benefits of employing severely disabled people at Center Industries found the net benefit per worker to be positive (32).

Finally, the university centers that provide services and perform research and training can be considered programs in this sector. These include rehabilitation engineering centers and rehabilitation research and training centers described in chapter 6 as well as the university-affiliated facilities funded under the Developmental Disabilities program. However, the bulk of funding for their activities comes from one or more of the public programs discussed earlier, and, thus, their effect on the delivery and use of technologies by disabled people is largely a function of public policies.

DISCUSSION OF GENERAL ISSUES

In addition to those issues previously discussed, there are several others, not related to particular programs, that affect the use of technologies by disabled people. They may be arbitrarily grouped as follows: 1) the coordination and consistency (or lack thereof) of services and funding, 2) the gaps in enrollment for public and/or nonpublic programs, 3) the difficulty in maintaining medical/rehabilitative device technologies, 4) consumer involvement in service delivery, and 5) the shortage of rehabilitation providers.

Coordination and Consistency of Services and Funding

A common problem, often raised in the literature and in personal interviews, is that services and funding for disabled people come from so many different, often uncoordinated, sources that users and providers are either unable to take advantage of available technologies or must spend enormous amounts of time providing the coordination needed to best assist each individual. This lack of coordination and consistency has meant that resources are often spent inefficiently and sometimes ineffectively. Furthermore, individuals with similar problems do not receive similar amounts or types of assistance (205). The primary underlying reason for this lack of coordination is that the pieces of legislation supporting the various programs were developed separately (usually by groups of advocates). Each advocate group usually had different objectives in mind for what need each program should fill, how it should be administered and funded, how its services should be delivered, and whom it should serve. In addition, Federal policies regarding disabled persons have focused on limited areas of people's lives (e.g., income maintenance or education or work), and laws and regulations stemming from such policies have been drafted without enough analysis of their effects on the other areas (39,217).

The definitions of disability, including age limits used in determining eligibility for services, may foster the lack of coordination. Most laws define eligibility based on determinations that individuals have one or more etiology-specific categories of impairments (e.g., cerebral palsy, mental retardation, or lack of vision). Thus, two individuals with different "categories" of disability but who both need technologies to assist in mobility may be eligible for different programs. A number of steps involving several agencies and providers (and a lack of continuity) may be taken until the individuals' actual needs are met. Some advocates for disabled persons favor changing the definitions in the laws or regulations to reflect functional disabilities (as in the current developmental disabilities legislation) instead of categorical disabilities, in order to remove this barrier to coordination. These advocates maintain that the presence of categorical programs causes duplication of effort and wasting of scarce resources. In addition, it necessitates labeling of disabled people which, because of the stigma associated with being "handicapped," may then cause their exclusion from opportunities necessary for their full development as individuals and in society (110). Furthermore, the existence of categorical legislation helps sustain organizations oriented to one disability that compete for the limited resources and services available to disabled people (19,131).* Advocates for cooperation and coordination believe that such cooperation will assist *all* disabled people receive better services. However, attempts to "decategorize" the definitions in current legislation have been met with resistance from the advocates of particular categorical disabilities who are well served by the legislation and who claim that diversity of self-interest is a productive and efficient approach to obtaining necessary resources (201). Those who have learned to function well within the current system are also reluctant for change (201).

The lack of coordination both causes and is caused by the structure of the service delivery "system." At the overall societal level, separate systems of service delivery have developed in areas pertinent to disabled people, such as health and medical care, education, and social services. Recent legislation (Public Law 94-142, for example) mandates that eligible individuals receive assistance from each of these systems, yet professionals within the systems are unaccustomed to, and thus, reluctant to and/or ineffective in, working together (200,217). At the level of individual providers, the standard behavior of professional autonomy fosters discontinuous care. Individual providers, particularly physicians, know little about other resources within the community with which to assist their clients once their services are no longer needed (154).

Funding for the same or similar technologies is often available under various programs, each with different rules for payment. This inconsistent and confusing situation leads to the expenditure of a great deal of energy and time on locating funding for individual clients or programs. There are numerous examples of manuals developed on how to obtain funding for a particular technology. These are written by researchers, advocates, users, and even manufacturers (47,134,178,192). Similarly, much time may be spent learning how to make the most of funding under one program, given the complexity of the regulations. The title of a manual to assist program administrators, *Roadmap Through Title XX*, provides an illustration of this problem (40).

Services provided, and eligibility for those services, often differ from State to State, even under the same program. This lack of consistency hampers the dissemination of information about technologies and how to gain access to them, because the information is not transferable across State boarders. DeJong and Wenkler (46) illustrate the often confusing differences between States through the example of attendant care services, a technology needed by all quadriplegic and many other individuals who use wheelchairs to live independently. Attendant care services are those

---

*It should be noted, however, that the uni-disability organizations were very influential in the development of the current type of legislation.

tasks performed by an attendant in assisting a severely disabled person with basic activities of daily living. These services are needed by approximately 2.9 million Americans. Yet because of the cost, which runs from minimum wage to $5 to $6 per hour for an average of 6 hours per day, many individuals cannot afford these services without public assistance. A citizen of Massachusetts can receive attendant care services if he or she is over 18, limited in the upper extremities, psychologically and medically stable, and eligible for Medicaid. Medicaid eligibility is determined by the public welfare department, while determination of eligibility specifically for attendant care is made by one of three independent living centers. If, in addition to attendant services, the attendant performs housekeeping services, the time may be billed to Medicaid. If the citizen were in Minnesota, however, the housekeeping services would have to be separately billed to the State's title XX program, if the individual were eligible. In California, all attendant care services, including housekeeping, are funded under title XX; thus, only those eligible for title XX may receive publicly funded attendant care.

Gaps in Enrollment

The Urban Institute study (208) noted that quite a bit is known about those who are served by programs for disabled people, but very little is known about those who do not receive services because they fall through gaps in eligibility for public and nonpublic programs. However, it has been well documented that gaps exist (82,110,201,205,208). Indeed, NIHR has as one of its research issues the development of service delivery techniques to prevent clients from "falling through the cracks" (53). Disabled people who fall into such gaps may be those who are multiply-disabled and as such do not fit neatly into a categorical program (110), as well as those who by some measure fall on the wrong side of the border between "disabled" and "not disabled" under existing program definitions (e.g., those who earn slightly over SGA or those whose vision is bad enough to need special devices and services but who are not quite "legally blind"). In addition to the problem of gaps due to definitions of eligibility, there are gaps in the provision of technologies to unenrolled but eligible individuals. This problem appears to be partly due to a lack of public awareness, partly due to a lack of outreach efforts to correct it, partly due to the lack of systematic method to correct it among uncoordinated programs, and partly due to the system's inability to handle all eligible clients because of a shortage of funds and personnel (154,201).

Maintaining Medical/Rehabilitative Device Technologies

Once disabled individuals obtain needed technologies, maintenance can be a serious problem. The users must be able to obtain parts for their device, locate skilled repair workers, devise a way to function while the device is being repaired, and pay for the whole process. For example, most battery-driven wheelchair users must maintain a second chair for the times when their primary chair is being repaired, because even the simplest repairs can take months. In addition, the average power-chair user spends $900 per year in maintenance and repair fees (141).

Not surprisingly, the difficulty or ease with which these steps are taken varies from device to device. Maintenance costs and availability may depend on whether the device is manufactured by a large company, by a small company, or nearby, so repairs are relatively easy to arrange. However, these devices are generally prototypes and thus, more prone to failure, so repair cost and lack-of-use time may be high. Devices manufactured by small companies often come from far away; repairs may be hard to arrange locally, and shipping the device back to the company is costly and time consuming. Users of devices manufactured by large companies generally have the easiest time with arranging repairs. These companies often establish service centers across the country staffed by personnel trained in fitting the devices as well as personnel trained in servicing them (117). For example, Phonic Ear/Phonic Mirror has more than 75 locations where their devices can be fitted (177). All users, however, face the problem of repair costs. Some insurance companies are concerned about equipment maintenance and repair and cover these services in their policies. These provisions vary from contract to contract. Unfortunately, those with the most comprehensive policies are often those who receive the highest disability income maintenance payments.

Consumer Involvement in Service Delivery

Consumer involvement is as important an issue in the delivery and use portion of the technology lifecycle as it is in the R&D portions, because it is primarily the disabled consumers of technologies who have the level of understanding and experience to ultimately assure appropriate delivery and use.

The term "consumers" may be narrowly defined as the disabled or handicapped individuals who receive a service or commodity from a service program and thus are clients of that program. However, the term may be defined more broadly as those affected directly or indirectly by the rehabilitation system, including disabled clients, families of disabled clients, former and future clients, those who qualify as clients by virtue of their disability but who do not receive services, and persons who represent the interests of the disabled (advocates). Consumer involvement currently occurs both at the individual level (see the narrow definition) and at the program and society levels (see the broad definition). At the individual level, disabled people participate in the creation of IEPs under the Education for All Handicapped Children Act. At the program level, disabled people themselves as well as those affected by the rehabilitation system participate in advisory boards that formulate or affect program policies. Under the Vocational Rehabilitation System, there are statewide advisory boards composed of elected representatives from organizations of disabled persons that review the policies of the State's rehabilitation agency. At the society level, consumers as defined broadly comprise the National Council on the Handicapped. The National Council is mandated to review all policies, programs, and activities concerning disabled persons conducted or assisted by any Federal agency (58).

The preceding examples of consumer involvement were all mandated by legislation passed in the last decade. They are considered positive steps by advocates of disabled people, because they reflect consumer input at a policy level (18).

Previous (and still, in many cases, continuing) approaches to consumer involvement have included newsletters, public hearings, other methods of informing consumers about public program activities, and use of disabled consultants in preparing annual reports and State plans. These approaches have been called inadequate (18). While particular programs for consumer involvement have been neither legislated nor regulated, avoidance of tokenism remains an area on which States must continue to focus in developing programs for policy development consultation by disabled persons.

While current legislation and regulations represent advances in consumer involvement in services delivery, there are several areas that still need improvement. Only half of the State vocational rehabilitation agencies have written plans for consumer involvement. The remaining States need to develop such plans to assure that the legislative requirements are being met. A survey by the American Coalition of Citizens with Disabilities (18) found that consumer advisers were not always representative of rehabilitation agency clients. Mechanisms to assure representation of the clients served in making policies about services must be developed. Finally, the number of areas and activities in which consumers are involved must be constantly assessed and broadened in order that the ultimate goal of consumer involvement—better and more effective services—is achieved.

Shortage of Rehabilitation Providers

It has already been noted that only those providers recognized by law or regulation may prescribe technologies that are paid for by public (and most private) funding and that these providers may not always be the ones best suited to matching particular technologies with individuals. However, another problem is a shortage of these providers, albeit they may not be the desired types.

In the medical area, there are relatively few rehabilitation medicine physician specialists, (physiatrists*), although specialty medical boards have existed in this area since 1948. In 1971, there

---

*This is not a misprint. The term is "physiatrist."

were close to 1,500 rehabilitation specialists, or 0.4 percent of the 334,000 physicians in the United States (150). In 1976, this number increased to 1,715, but the percentage remained approximately the same (181). The Interim Report of the Graduate Medical Education National Advisory Committee (102) predicts that the percentage will be the same in 1990. There have been various estimates of need made (150,181) that differ in terms of assumptions but which all lead to a similar conclusion—there is and will continue to be a substantial shortage of rehabilitation medicine physician specialists through 1990. Estimates for demand in 1990 range from 4,000 to 4,900, while estimates for supply range from 3,380 to 2,900. It should be noted that other physician specialists do provide rehabilitative care, although there are no readily available measures of their numbers. It is usually the rehabilitation physician, however, who is trained to perform the broadest range of rehabilitation services, including providing direct rehabilitative services as well as organizing systems of care in the community, obtaining resources, conducting research, and providing education on disability (181).

One reason for the low number of rehabilitation physician specialists is that the specialty is perceived as one with low status, perhaps in part because of the high proportion of foreign medical graduates who enter it. In 1976, 65 percent of the first year residents in physical medicine and rehabilitation were foreign medical graduates (181). Conversely, it has been suggested that the area has a high proportion of foreign medical graduates because it is a low status specialty for "other reasons," and foreign medical graduates thus find it easier to enter than other areas of medicine.

One of these "other reasons" may be that a physician in rehabilitative medicine has less control than physicians in most other specialties owing to the wide range of other professionals (e.g., vocational rehabilitation counselors, occupational therapists, teachers) who enter into decisions or whose opinion must be taken into account. Second, medicine is a "cure-oriented" profession, and conditions that are stable or deteriorating assault that professional orientation. Third, it may be that rehabilitation medicine receives a low priority in general hospital settings. A study of VA rehabilitation medicine services found that 29 percent of those services were understaffed in support services. The reason proposed was that the support staff (nurses, social workers, psychologists) were under the control of chiefs of service other than the rehabilitation medicine chief, and those chiefs may give the rehabilitation medicine services a lower priority than other services such as medicine or surgery (149). A final reason for the low status of rehabilitation medicine is that professional orientation begins in medical school, where there are few courses on the management of chronic or ongoing disability. Basic physician training does not usually include learning how to refer to available community resource agencies or how to assess the need for such services—skills that every physiatrist uses often.

If the number of rehabilitation physician specialists cannot be increased for the preceding reasons, alternatives might be to increase acute care physicians' skills in rehabilitation or to develop service delivery mechanisms that depend more on related health and disability professionals. Training in these skills is possibly best done during the residency program (because the medical school program is already lengthy); however, it is necessary that orientation toward chronic, ongoing conditions begin in medical school.

There are a number of other types of providers involved in the provision of goods and services to disabled people, including physical therapists, speech therapists, occupational therapists, rehabilitation counselors, vocational educators, rehabilitation engineers, independent living center staff (e.g., peer counselors), orthotic and prosthetic technologists, and social workers. These allied health providers are often paid by institutional providers, including State vocational rehabilitation agencies, education agencies, comprehensive rehabilitation centers, hospitals, etc., recognized under one of the funding authorities. While the number of allied health professionals has increased dramatically over the last 30 years, a shortage remains (60,150). The shortage based on needs as perceived by disabled people is difficult to quantify precisely because demand figures include estimates of demand from individuals who would not be included as "disabled." However, it is predicted that as the implications of legislation such as the Education for All Handicapped Children Act and the Developmental Disabilities Amendments of 1978 become more apparent, the demand for and the shortage of allied health personnel will increase (60).

10.
Developing and Using Technologies: Conclusions From Part Two

Life is the art of drawing sufficient conclusions from insufficient premises.
—*Samuel Butler*

10.
Developing and Using Technologies: Conclusions From Part Two

The preceding chapters have discussed the process of developing and using technologies: A need is recognized or an idea for a technology arises, basic and applied research takes place, testing and evaluation occur, a marketing or distribution plan is developed and implemented, reimbursement or financing methods are determined, use of the technology begins and spreads, widespread use is attained, and eventually (perhaps) obsolescence or disuse sets in. This description of the process, as discussed earlier, is extremely simplistic and idealistic when compared to reality. Nonetheless, it is a useful and important way to examine reality and the performance of the system's actors. The order and the exact content of each of the steps in the process are not as important as the conceptual and practical *connections* between the steps. These connections are as critical in reality as they are in the ideal.

OTA's examination of the current situation leaves little doubt that the disability-related research, development, evaluation, diffusion, and marketing "system" suffers from a number of significant weaknesses. This system is capable of, and has produced, important contributions to disabled and nondisabled people. It definitely has had success stories, stories that frequently have been due to the dedicated efforts of individuals rather than to the thoughtful application of effective governmental or private systems of development and diffusion. Despite these successes, the system is, or could be, capable of a great deal more.

The high level of expectations that has been placed on this collection of public, private, and nonprofit organizations is not unreasonable. This system should be held responsible for reaching the goals that have been set for it. This is an area of high expectations for the simple and obvious reason that the technologies and services are critical to the consumers who use them. Very often, there are few or no alternatives.

OTA finds that there is a crucial lack of attention being paid to the concept of appropriate use of technology. This implies that research and development (R&D) often proceeds without an adequate appreciation of its role in assuring the existence and the diffusion of appropriate technologies. Appropriately used technologies can be simple or complex, manual or electronic, expensive or inexpensive. The key point is that they should be the appropriate technological response to a defined set of needs, desires, and capabilities, taking into account resource constraints. Whether the simple approach to analyzing the appropriateness of technologies as suggested in chapter 5 is the preferable or most effective way to move closer to appropriate development and use of technologies is not important. The critical aspect is that considerable attention needs to be given to the creation of analytical methods for determining and attaining appropriateness. The conclusions that are set out below regarding the more specific problems of the R&D, evaluation, diffusion, use, and financing processes emerge from this concept of appropriate development and use of technology. The discussions and conclusions on resource allocation that follow are similarly dependent on this concept.

The issues and problems discussed in the preceding chapters are not new, nor are they being pointed out for the first time, although the emphasis on a lifecycle approach to appropriate technology has received inadequate attention. In fact, one of the more perplexing and frustrating aspects of a review of the relevant literature is that the same problems reappear year after year in report after report, hearing after hearing, and seminar after seminar. The problems continue to exist despite the efforts of dedicated individuals and organizations and despite government reorganizations, new legislative mandates, new research plans, and the continued expenditure of substantial funds.

Money is, as always, a problem. In real terms, the Federal and State commitment of funds for disability-related R&D has been declining for the last decade. That trend is likely to continue. Funding is and will be an ever present problem. *Increased funding for R&D would definitely help, but at the same time it should be recognized that more money will not in itself solve all problems.*

There are a number of reasons for the above conclusions. As the White House Study has pointed out (226):

> The development of new technology and the adaptation of existing technology for the handicapped have been hampered in the past by inattention to the definition of discrete, project oriented tasks, by the lack of a suitable basic science to support the managerial decision processes required, by a scarcity of people trained and educated in the application of engineering principles to the handicapped, and by the high cost of technical failures induced by non-perception of real needs.

Obviously, few, if any, of the above problems would be totally remedied by the application of increased funds to the existing system. *The nonperception of real needs is a reflection both of low levels of funds available and of a lack of perspective and sensitivity.* In fact, the concept of need could be expanded to a blend of needs, desires, and capabilities. The user, the disabled individual, must be more involved in the defining of those characteristics. Even when addressing only the needs aspect of the three, the "real" needs of users must be distinguished from needs as perceived by researchers or others. The identification of needs, desires, and capabilities has to be strengthened both conceptually and methodologically, as discussed in chapter 5. *When identification and assessment of disabilities and handicaps are performed with the user as a full participant and with the goal of developing effective plans for applying technologies appropriately, one byproduct will be the creation of data that can and should be used in directing future research—especially applied R&D.*

Increasingly, the public is expressing disappointment and dissatisfaction with the rate of *application* of research results. OTA researchers were frequently told that the capability and resources to develop technologies that will benefit disabled people do exist, and further, that there are existing technologies that could be made much more widely available. Yet, currently only a fraction of disabled individuals are adequately benefiting from this capability (123). Much of this capability is in, or has come out of, the federally sponsored disability-related research system. The rapid pace at which the private sector is producing innovations is also adding to the list of technologies that could have significant benefits.

The public, especially those members with disabilities, has been witness to significant accomplishments of the government-private sector relationship, specifically in those instances when public policy has complemented private sector incentives and when actions at each step of the technology's lifecycle have been consistent with actions at the other steps. These have been exceptions. In general, public and private policies are not established with lifecycle consistency in mind.

OTA believes that there has not been a full-scale attempt to address the range of lifecycle issues through an explicit consistency of policy. Certainly, other observers have noted the importance of considering the effects of R&D on marketing or of reimbursement on diffusion. And yet there are only beginning efforts to modify policies in line with a comprehensive perspective. Such efforts do not have to cost large amounts of additional funds. *In this area, foresight is more important than finances.*

There are a number of other issues that need to be resolved concerning Federal agencies' approach to the lifecycle of technologies, especially at the R&D and diffusion stages. There appears to be a historical imbalance between, on the one hand, the emphasis on basic and applied research and, on the other, on the diffusion or marketing of technologies and the dissemination of information. Both the National Institute of Handicapped Research (NIHR) and the Veterans Administration (VA) are moving toward (on paper at least) a greater emphasis on these latter activities. The generation of research reports and the development of prototypes are unacceptable end-points for the federally supported disability-related R&D process. However, efforts to support more information dissemination activities have been slow to catch on and are underfunded. The efforts to enlist more private sector involvement in the transfer of research results into marketable devices have also been sporadic and of mixed results.

There is a need for a strengthened public-private sector partnership in marketing new technologies for disabled people. Companies that are interested in marketing such technologies should be encouraged and assisted to do so. Small private firms often have the capacity for developing innovative technologies yet lack the means to identify and reach those people who might benefit from their products. The cost of performing marketing surveys is usually large when the potential market is small, as it is with many segments of the population of disabled individuals. More importantly, the state-of-the-art of identifying (for marketing purposes or for public policy purposes) disabled individuals and populations is not advanced enough to consistently or even frequently provide valid and usable data.

Another marketing need is research on how technologies for disabled people can assist nondisabled people. Examples of such technologies often cited include ramps and curb cuts designed for wheelchairs that assist senior citizens, bicyclists, and people with baby carriages, and computer-assisted communications devices that may be applied to computer systems used by nondisabled people. A large-scale demonstration program, or even better a series of small-scale programs, on multiple uses of technological developments might help in fulfilling this need.

Public and private agencies involved in the disability-related R&D process have devoted a very small portion of their resources to any type of evaluation or monitoring of research programs or resulting technologies. Performance testing or evaluation is not pursued to any significant degree.

The disability-related R&D system has a tendency to focus its energies and attention on the "gee whiz" technologies. The "sophisticated," and usually very expensive, approaches seem to consume a major portion of both the public and private sectors' efforts. In a recent article announcing the opening of the new VA Rehabilitation Engineering and Development Center at the Palo Alto VA Medical Center, the world was served notice that: "The new center will put 'Star Wars' technology directly into helping the human being" (158). One needs only to open a current periodical or science magazine to discover accounts of "high-technology" innovation related to disabilities. *However, when workshops or surveys of disabled consumers are conducted, a very common and important suggestion is that more emphasis should be put on the development of less sophisticated, more easily repairable, easier to use, cheaper technologies or approaches.* As one professional has commented (147):

> You wouldn't want to spend $1,000 on a piece of equipment that would be used on only 5 percent of the job tasks . . . It would be more practical to see if you could restructure the job tasks.

The same questions need to be raised in other situations. Is it feasible or desirable to spend a certain amount of dollars to achieve 95- to 100-percent efficiency when half or less of that amount would produce 60- to 80-percent efficiency; enough to handle most of a person's needs in a given situation? All too often it appears that the research system becomes infatuated with the most technically sophisticated approach to attaining 100-percent efficiency. *Alternative research strategies and goals need to be seriously considered and supported.*

The need for information dissemination is just as great at the delivery and use stages of the technology lifecycle as it is at the R&D, evaluation, and marketing stages. Only with the best possible information can an individual's needs, desires, and capabilities be appropriately matched with available technologies. Perhaps more important is that only with complete information on what technologies are available (on the market), how they perform, how they may be obtained, and how they may be funded can the best use be made of limited resources. *Yet many of the numerous parties-at-interest, such as users, providers, and third-party payers, who need such information have only small parts of it available. Thus, the decisions made that result in an individual's use or disuse of a particular technology are often desirable only on a short-term basis.*

Much of the dissemination of information on available technologies currently occurs through publicly financed or publicly operated programs for disabled people. One result of this is often that individuals outside of the public service delivery systems, by virtue of their independence or their noneligibility for service programs, lack access to necessary information. A mechanism is needed whereby individuals who are capable of applying their own resources to purchasing technologies can find and use the information that is available. One mechanism is the use of an entry point into service delivery such as the State vocational rehabilitation agency.

Another result of the current method of information dissemination is that the systems for information dissemination that exist are confined to discrete subject areas. This is in part because of the multitude of uncoordinated and overlapping public and private programs. The average consumers and providers of technologies need information in many related subject areas. Currently, either this information is not obtained or substantial resources must be expended to obtain it. OTA believes that *strategies for coordinating information on the delivery and use of technologies for disabled people should be supported.* It is imperative that new policies in this area reflect a coordinated information dissemination effort, regardless of the (often low) degree of coordination in the legislated service programs.

Because most technologies used by disabled people are either paid for, directly provided by, or learned about through public and nonpublic programs and services, those who are *eligible* for the programs and services are generally those who have access to the technologies. *Thus, decisions regarding who should be eligible and how eligibility should be determined are major determinants of the use of technologies.* Boundaries to eligibility and methods for its determination in individual cases differ from program to program. Eligibility is most often determined by establishing the presence of an etiology-specific category of impairment, by finding a mental or physical impairment that results in a functional limitation, or by a combination of both methods. A common result of having a variety of methods is that individuals in similar situations receive different amounts and types of services. *Services that are necessary may not be received, and those that are received are likely to lack continuity.* Increasingly, public programs are moving toward determining eligibility on the basis of evidence of functional manifestations of physical or mental impairments, so that those who most need services may receive them and so that the services they receive are appropriate and provided in a coordinated fashion. Advocates for disabled people with specific categorical impairments who are served well by the earlier type of definition, however, are reluctant for changes to be made. It is unclear which type of definition, if any, can guarantee the most appropriate use of technologies, although ideally one based on function should be preferable.

Providing individuals with technologies requires the resolution of several policy issues. *One issue concerns the type of provider needed to match the technology with the user.* Traditionally, physicians have done most of the prescribing of device technologies, partly because disabled individuals most often receive their first services through the medical system and partly because the major third-party funding programs often will only pay for items that carry a physician's prescription. It is clear that physicians are best qualified to prescribe certain technologies, particularly many of those that are for medical purposes. Many technologies, however, are applied for purposes other than strictly "medical" ones, and there are other providers who are equally or better qualified than physicians to select the best technology for their client. Yet these providers, including rehabilitation engineers, occupational therapists, and special education teachers, as well as users themselves, usually cannot obtain public funding for the technologies. For example, the NIHR-funded rehabilitation research and training centers (RTCs) are designed to develop innovative technological solutions to problems of disabled people. But even if RTCs are able to disseminate this information, those who receive it may be unable to apply it to their clients. Therefore, *strategies for encouraging the use of various types of providers could be developed.* These may include changing reimbursement policies as well as changing licensing laws or physician education curricula. It is important, however, that any provider prescribing technologies have specific training in the relevant disciplines.

Another issue concerns the criteria for selecting a particular technology once the type of technology and its purpose have been decided. Effectiveness and cost have typically been the criteria used in the past. Certainly, they are the ones cited formally most frequently. These criteria are indeed important, yet they are insufficient for selecting technologies for people who will likely need assistance for most of their lives. OTA believes that *users and providers alike must consider obsolescence, maintenance, and actual procurement of devices to be important criteria.* With the rapidly advancing technological capabilities of our society, most technologies developed today will necessarily become obsolete sometime in the future. Providers must assess the predictable rate at which obsolescence will occur and use that information in making their selection. For maintenance, the frequency, the time taken, and the cost must be considered. For actual procurement, the location of the manufacturer in relation to the location of the client must be considered. *Federal policies do not encourage the formal consideration of these criteria. Even though decisions utilizing these criteria may be based on individual preferences (e.g., for easy maintenance over distant obsolescence), there are few mechanisms for allowing individual users' desires to be taken into account.*

A third issue concerns the structure of the systems under which individuals receive technologies. *A common problem, discussed in several sections of this report, is that services and funding for disabled people come from so many different, often uncoordinated sources that both providers and users often are unable to take advantage of available technologies.* Reasons for the lack of coordination include the methods by which existing legislation was developed, the definitions used in determining eligibility, and the fact that disabled people need assistance in so many different areas of their lives—areas that have entire social systems designed specifically for them.

As noted earlier, money is a problem in the technology lifecycle, particularly in the areas of delivery and use. Simply put, there is not enough to provide all technologies to all people who need them, even if need is defined very narrowly. Thus, the way in which money is applied has important consequences for the use of technologies— what is used, how long it is used, where it is used, and for what purpose it is used. Money applied in one area of technologies usually means that less is available for other areas. Decisions on resource allocation are thus perhaps the most important ones that need to be made by society's policymakers. These will be discussed in Part Three. However, decisions on how to allocate resources among programs for disabled people and between programs for disabled people and programs for nondisabled people cannot be made without an explicit understanding of the effect that funding decisions have on individuals. These effects must be clearly described when new programs are developed.

Part Three:
Resource Allocation

11.
Resource Allocation: Issues and Conclusions

Give a man a fish, and he will eat for a day. Teach him how to fish, and he will eat for the rest of his life.

—*Chinese proverb*

Contents

	Page
Patterns and Forces in Resource Allocation	139
Resource Allocation Decisions	141
Levels of Decisionmaking	142
Allocation Versus Spending	142
Substantive Area of Decisions	143
Current Issues in Resource Allocation	143
Eligibility Determinations and the Definition of Disability and Handicap	143
Categorical Orientation of Allocation	145
Issues of Resource Allocation and Independent Living	146
Outcome Measures Used in Resource Allocation	146
Prevention of Impairments and Disabilities	147
Resource Allocation and Elderly People	149
Analytical Methods for Informing Decisionmaking	150
Role of Analytical Techniques	150
Range of Analytical Techniques	151
Principles of Formal Analysis	153
Structuring Resource Allocation Decisions	153
Explicitly Define the Problem	153
State Goals in Measurable or Evaluable Terms	154
Specify the Range of Parties at Interest	154
Identify the Range of Possible Decisions	154
Identify, Measure, and Value Potential Consequences of Decisions	155
Consider the Effects of Time (Discounting) and Uncertainty	155
Consider Ethical and Other "Nonobjective" Factors	157
Provide for Evaluation of the Results of Decisions	157

LIST OF TABLES

Table No.	Page
9. Comparison of Decision Levels and Decision Variables	142
10. Ten Principles of Formal Analysis	153

11.
Resource Allocation: Issues and Conclusions*

The previous chapters have sought to make two critical points: that the development and use of technologies for disabled persons are greatly affected by available resources, and that, in turn the efficient and effective allocation of resources depends on an appreciation of the powerful role played by technological capabilities and limitations. Efforts to improve resource allocation must take into account the controls and incentives currently operating on the development, evaluation, diffusion, and use of technologies.

This chapter focuses on the allocation of resources. It briefly mentions the historical and current forces that have shaped patterns of resource allocation, presents conclusions relating to several key policy issues, and then discusses a method for structuring decisions.

PATTERNS AND FORCES IN RESOURCE ALLOCATION

Current public policy toward disabled persons has evolved over the last several decades in complex and unpredictable ways. At bottom, however, the process of policy formation in this area can be viewed as a long series of decisions concerning the allocation of resources to and among disabled individuals in our society. Frequently, these resource allocation decisions are expressed in laws and regulations governing who should receive what kind of assistance. For the most part, these decisions have been made by nondisabled people, often with little or no input from disabled people. Income subsidies, medical treatment, vocational therapy, affirmative action, special education, and other social services are examples of the kinds of assistance proffered. Such assistance constitutes the *resources* potentially available to disabled individuals. Which individuals actually receive particular resources is the essence of the *allocation decisions* determined by statutes, program regulations, definitions of disability, need standards, and the like. Both the resources available and the allocation decisions are means to accomplish a given purpose intended by a decisionmaker.

In the 19th century, the United States was a rapidly expanding country with an unlimited frontier and a predominantly agricultural economy. The virtually unrestricted opportunities offered by a rapidly growing population, an abundance of rich natural resources, and vast areas of available land helped mold the American tradition that through hard work, initiative, and thrift, each individual should provide for his own needs and the needs of his family. For those individuals incapable of this, the community and philanthropic institutions provided assistance. What little the State governments did involved custodial care of "the poor," "the orphaned," and "the disabled" in asylums. Toward the close of the 19th century, the industrial revolution altered the economy and changed this society forever.

Economic development, labor specialization, and urbanization shifted this country from a predominantly land-based, rural, individualistic society to a highly industrialized and interdependent one whose people depended on a continuing flow of wage income to provide economic security. The extended family and the tightly knit community it fostered largely passed out of existence. Informal structures such as families, community, and philanthropic institutions became incapable of dealing effectively with the problem of economic need and dependency.

---

*Parts of this chapter are based on material prepared for OTA by Tom Joe, Cheryl Rogers, and John Nelson of the Center for the Study of Social Policy, University of Chicago, and by Mark Ozer of the George Washington School of Medicine.

The responsibility for those with special dependency problems gradually passed, in substantial part, to government. In the 20th century, government efforts, largely at the State level, were directed at providing cash relief to various categories of "the poor," "the orphaned," and "the disabled" in their own homes. By the 1920's, a growing number of States created programs to assist elderly and disabled individuals.

This period also marked the emergence of pension plans for several categories of workers to provide economic security in old age and retirement systems for certain groups of Government employees. The Federal Government also accepted responsibility for providing benefits and services for World War I veterans. States also enacted the first workers compensation programs.

The inadequacy of these early government efforts to deal with the problem of economic security became dramatically evident during the great depression of the 1930's. All of the previous State government mechanisms for mitigating the economic hardships of unemployment, old age, and the breadwinner's death or disability proved totally inadequate in the face of a national economic disaster. In the New Deal era, Federal programs were enacted to meet the economic needs of the population. In the 1960's, Congress authorized a vast array of new Federal programs and expanded the old ones to provide for the needs of elderly, poor, unemployed, and disabled people and children.

The development of Federal programs and expenditures for disabled people was thus an outgrowth of a larger movement in government—particularly at the Federal level—that required increasing responsibility for insuring economic security to the Nation. Indeed, within this movement, income maintenance provisions for disabled people came relatively late. While concern for rehabilitation had been expressed in the 1920's, leading to Federal funding of vocational rehabilitation services in education grants, it was not until the 1950's that major attention was focused on income support for disabled people as a separate group. The sole exception was blind persons.

The two largest income support programs for disabled people became law in the 1950s: Aid to the Permanently and Totally Disabled (APTD) in 1950; and Social Security Disability Insurance (SSDI) in 1956, which has already been discussed. APTD arose largely because efforts to expand and systemize the welfare programs of the New Deal encountered political opposition in Congress. In the face of this political inertia, proponents of aid (to "the needy handicapped") as part of a comprehensive assistance program were forced to enact a new program specifically designed for this group. Resource allocation on the basis of *need* (means tested) was to be categorical. States were not required to participate in the program. The Federal matching grant formula was complicated, and definitions of eligibility varied from State to State.

The Great Society programs of the mid-1960's vastly expanded the resources allocated to disabled people—e.g., Congress created the Medicare and Medicaid programs. Originally intended as a health insurance program for short-term illnesses among elderly people, Medicare became a major source of funds for disabled individuals.

The non-Social Security needy population—disabled people in need of assistance and others—was served by Medicaid, which quickly became a mainstay of medical assistance to disabled people outside the Social Security system.

The final block in the Federal income maintenance and medical care structure for disabled people was the Supplemental Security Income (SSI) program, as described in chapter 9.

Throughout this period, all social services available to "needy" persons, including those with disabilities, expanded. Vocational rehabilitation agencies extended services to all disabled individuals and began rehabilitation programs specifically for SSDI and SSI beneficiaries. In 1975, title XX of the Social Security Act provided block grants to States for social services.

Although they represent the largest expenditures for disabled people, the four major Federal programs in place by the mid-1970's were outgrowths of resource allocation decisions directed principally toward elderly people. Disabled people were included when it was recognized that their needs were unmet by existing program structures. With the exception of rehabilitation services, the social service programs also regarded disabled people as merely one of many needy groups. There is, however, another historical movement that arose during this period—that of disabled people themselves asserting their rights.

During the 1960's, attitudes toward disabled people began to change. First, media attention incited public outrage at unnecessary and careless incarceration of disabled individuals in institutions. Court cases and litigation documented widespread abuse of institutionalized persons. As an outgrowth of this protest, disabled persons and their advocates began to question the resource allocation decisions that affected their lives. They demanded greater personal autonomy in these decisions. This questioning spawned the independent living movement, the consumer involvement movement, and the drive to gain legal rights for disabled people. At the heart of the independent living movement is the idea of exercising control over one's life.

The deinstitutionalization movement also stemmed from this widespread criticism of institutions. Those disabled by mental impairments were released from large sterile institutions so they could be served in smaller community-based facilities. This change was in large part one of resource allocation. Moneys spent on institutions were shifted to community facilities in response to the demands of disabled people. With the passage of Medicaid, States began a massive shift from using only their own State moneys to relying largely on Federal funds for skilled nursing and intermediate-care facilities. Through the independent living movement and deinstitutionalization, it became apparent that disabled individuals were capable of assuming far greater responsibilities for their lives and the public resources devoted to them than previously imagined.

Disabled people also began to assert their civil rights to protest denials of access to public facilities and to shed the stigma and stereotypes so long attached to them. In the 1970's, disabled people began demanding—not unlike the civil rights movement of the 1960's—a reallocation of public resources to facilitate their integration into the mainstream of society.

The disability rights movement produced a new type of resource allocation decision unrelated to the traditional areas of income maintenance, rehabilitation, and custodial care: affirmative action and nondiscrimination laws. Rather than allocating Federal resources, Congress created statutes that mandated the allocation of State, local, and private resources to facilitate the "mainstreaming" of disabled individuals.

The Federal resources involved in implementing such statutes are small compared to those for income maintenance and social service programs. The *social cost* of this type of allocation decision, however, can be very high. It is, perhaps, the most direct method of allocating resources in accord with the desires of disabled people. It can also be the most burdensome to the rest of society. When linked with fiscal pressures to stem the rising costs of traditional programs for disabled persons, this type of allocation method can contribute to the resource allocation dilemma that today's policymakers confront: how to achieve effective allocation to match increasing needs and demands while faced with declining resource availability.

RESOURCE ALLOCATION DECISIONS

There are two extremely important background points to be made in regard to the issue of technology and resource allocation. *First, all decisions concerning the development and use of technologies for disabled persons are either directly or indirectly resource allocation decisions.* This statement follows from the general observation that all decisions under circumstances of scarce resources are ones of resource allocation. An example of a direct resource allocation decision would be legislation requiring that all new phone handsets be compatible with the induction setting of hearing aids.* There would also be indirect resource implications of any such legislation. An example of a decision where the indirect impact on resource allocation would be the critical factor might be legislation appropriating substantial funds for a program to develop methods for restructuring jobs and job sites for disabled persons. The direct appropriation for such a program would possibly be small in comparison to the resource implications brought about by the increased numbers of disabled people who could be employed and thus earning a wage, paying taxes, leaving public income maintenance programs, and so on.

The second background point is that *nearly all resource allocation decisions involve a compromise*. There is rarely an obvious choice to be made that every relevant party agrees with and supports. Social, economic, technical, and political considerations must be considered as a mixture of applicable variables. This situation implies that *analysis, especially quantitative analysis, can rarely if ever play the determining role in a policy decision*. Interestingly, this situation also implies that analysis can play an important role: Because there are so many different types of variables to be considered in a resource allocation decision, and because the indirect and often unintended impacts of such a decision can be so important, methods of structuring decisions and forcing explicit consideration of the range of relevant factors are desirable. Analytical techniques will be discussed in a later section of this chapter.

Resource allocation decisions can be as complicated as they are pervasive. There are several ways to characterize them. One is by the level of the decision. It can be a societal-level decision, a program decision, an institutional one, or an individual decision. Another way to distinguish between types of allocation decisions is by whether they are directly *allocation* decisions or whether they are primarily direct *spending* decisions that affect allocation only indirectly. A third way of characterizing these decisions is by the principal substantive areas they address. For example, a decision may be primarily, or directly, oriented to allocating transportation resources.

Levels of Decisionmaking

The importance of distinguishing between various levels of decisionmaking lies in the differing scope of costs and outcomes to be considered, the differing analytical tools available, and the differing parties at interest whose views and desires could be taken into account.

The types of decision variables do not change very much between levels, but their relative importance does. Table 9 shows the type of decision variables that might be considered in any allocation decision. Legal considerations, for example, still play a role but are less important at the individual level. The reverse is true for psychological aspects of a decision. The costs and benefits of any decision follow from the variables listed. Thus, the relative importance of various types of costs or benefits changes depending on the level of decisionmaking.

Allocation Versus Spending

Strictly speaking, a resource allocation decision should be one where a set amount of resources is distributed among programs, people, goals, or some other division of possible recipients. This

Table 9.—Comparison of Decision Levels and Decision Variables

Decision variables	Level of decision			
	Societal	Program	Institutional	Individual
Technical.........	A	A	A	A
Personal gains and biases of decisionmaker .	C/B	B	B/A	A
Social..........	A	A	B	B
Psychological....	C	C	B/A	A
Legal	A	A	B	C
Economic	A	A	A	A
Political.........	A	A	A	C
Ethical	A	B	B	B

A - Critical variable.
B - Moderate variable.
C - Marginal variable.
SOURCE: Office of Technology Assessment.

---

*Most hearing aids have a "telephone" or "induction" setting that allows the aid to pick up the electromagnetic signal produced by most telephone handsets. However, it is estimated that at least 35 million of the 170 million telephones in the United States do not produce an electromagnetic signal that produces compatibility with hearing aids. Hearing-impaired people are thus denied the use of those telephones. Ironically, many of the incompatible sets are located in hospitals.

type of resource allocation is direct. It may have a substantial amount of visibility—as when the Congress allocates the budget between human services and other areas—or may be a more private one—as when a disabled individual decides how to divide a fixed amount of income among competing uses, or a medical devices company allocates its resources between research and development (R&D), sales, production, etc.

A more complicated allocation decision is one in which no direct distribution among competing uses appears to take place. Seemingly, only a spending decision is made. A person decides to buy a power wheelchair, for example. Or the Veterans Administration (VA) decides to include a technology in its package of services. Such decisions may appear to be relatively straightforward questions of expenditures. However, they may involve other, sometimes more important, questions. They may turn out to be allocation decisions in two ways. First, any decision to spend money from a limited budget reduces the amount of funds remaining. Money has been in effect denied to all other possible competing uses. Second, a decision may lead to further nondiscretionary expenditures, further reducing remaining funds. A power wheelchair, for example, may require more maintenance expenses, battery costs, etc. In effect, money has been allocated without the opportunity to explicitly compare the alternative uses for those funds.

Substantive Area of Decisions

This way of characterizing decisions is important because of the nature of decisions and decisionmakers. Many decisionmakers tend to think in categorical, programmatic, or subject-area terms. Medicare officials, for example, make decisions in relation to the effects on the Medicare program and, perhaps secondarily, on the Medicare constituents. This orientation is natural, but, more importantly, it is reinforced by the organization of programs and responsibilities. The number and size of programs and services for disabled people create the conditions for thinking and administering in a relatively narrow manner, and yet at the same time they demand, ideally, a more comprehensive decision orientation. This is especially true at the Federal level.

CURRENT ISSUES IN RESOURCE ALLOCATION

This section includes discussions of several issues related to resource allocation. The issues covered are not the only ones that exist. There are others that are also quite important. "Competition" between programs for mental health, mental disability, and physical disability as an issue of competing values in society is one example. Another is the issue of how best to allocate funds for maternal and child health programs in order to prevent or ameliorate disabilities. Thus, the issues below are meant to illustrate the types of issues that are faced by those people involved in disability policy and programs.

Eligibility Determinations and the Definition of Disability and Handicap

At present, *most resource allocation decisions focus attention on the individual and the disability instead of the context—the social and physical environments of the individual.* For example, in recent debates about the increasing costs of disability, a great deal of attention has been focused on the question of why more and more people are claiming disability, but little attention has been given to the economic situation that may force people with various disabilities out of the work force because their abilities are no longer needed. Solutions to date have largely included intensifying the evidentiary rules for establishing disability, rather than examining what can be done to modify the situation to provide greater opportunities for disabled individuals. The easier course has been to make a particular program's definition of eligibility more restrictive, rather than to reallocate resources in a manner that will allow the abilities of an individual to find productive expression.

The present tendency to define individuals in terms of medical categories fails to take into account wide variations in individual performance due to differences in motivation, native strengths and weaknesses, available technologies, and environment. Many people in the field have long felt that a more useful definition of disability would be based on individuals' functional performance—i.e., upon their abilities. A functional definition of (dis)ability provides a broader view of the individual in his or her environment. It is also crucial to keep in mind the dynamic nature of both abilities and disabilities. They change over time. Services and policies must not be based on a concept of disabilities as static. Resource allocation decisions based on this definition could systematically take into account personal adaptations to the underlying condition; available environmental and technological supports; changes over time in age, attitude, and motivation; and a variety of possible roles that might be filled in a given profession. The focus is then on the circumstances and not the underlying condition.

A disability is currently defined by various medically significant, mental and/or physical conditions. *Categorization based solely on these medical labels reflects a focus almost exclusively on the inability rather than ability.* Often this thinking results in resource allocation decisions that preclude opportunities. Compensatory abilities are neglected, and the (in part thereby) handicapped person may become segregated, frustrated, and economically dependent. Such definitions tend to create the handicap out of the disability. They may skew resource allocations in ineffective directions.

One of the most promising comprehensive definitions is offered by Saad Nagi,* although he uses the term "disability" instead of "handicap," which OTA has chosen.

> .... disability is a form of inability or limitation in performing roles and tasks expected of an individual within a social environment. These tasks and roles are organized in spheres of life activities involved in self-care, education . . . interpersonal relations, recreation, economic life, and employment or vocational concerns . . . .

---

*S. Z. Nagi, "Criteria for Evaluating Disability, Eligibility for Benefits and Needs for Services" (unpublished paper), Ohio State University, 1976.

Thus, disabled persons are those who are limited in their ability to perform certain daily activities. Every disabled individual is, by definition, limited to some extent and therefore will fall along a continuum according to the extent of that limitation. Although one person may have a more severe limitation than another, each requires assistance to overcome or compensate for his or her particular limitations. The focus can then be shifted from the disability per se to what resources an individual requires to overcome the disability and enhance his or her abilities.

If a handicap is viewed as the combination of a disability and other environmental factors, and given that a specific disability does not preclude the existence of other abilities, then the means of alleviating the problems posed by the handicap become quite different. *With a presumption of both disability and ability, the resource allocation decision becomes a task of altering the environment in order to maximize the individual's abilities to perform at levels comparable to the nonhandicapped.* In that event, "nonhandicapped" would include both disabled and nondisabled persons.

The policymaker might use this framework for understanding the context of disability to make more effective resource allocation decisions to accommodate disabled persons. Resources can be allocated to enhance employment and independent living opportunities as well as other programs that seek to maximize the abilities of individuals. The policymaker can also use this framework to allocate resources to modify the physical environment of the disabled person, since it is often the environment that inhibits typical function. One of the most effective ways of doing this is to develop technologies that can assist disabled persons in performing ordinary daily activities.

The voice-controlled wheelchair, for example, uses a voice-command computer to enable a paralyzed person to move about. It also operates an environmental control system installed in an office or home that will open the door, turn on the lights, change television or radio stations, dial a telephone number, operate a page turner, or run a tape recorder on command. The voice-controlled wheelchair can accommodate any language

—even patterns of sounds by persons who cannot vocalize in a language. The allocation of resources for similar independence and ability enhancing technologies should be a prime goal of public policies toward disability.

Development of new technologies is only one example of the directions in resource allocation that policymakers could take if they used comprehensive approaches to the concept of disability. An important effect of such approaches would be to convey to policymakers an understanding that resource allocation decisions must be based on abilities as well as disabilities.

Categorical Orientation of Allocation

A large number of separate constituencies have been supportive of their various program areas and have come into existence as a result of the present organizational structure of programs for disabled people. Despite these factors, there has been considerable movement already towards commonality. One major issue to be considered is the degree to which generic programs, as opposed to ones organized by categories of disability, should be encouraged.

A major step toward integration has occurred in the change in the traditional thrust of rehabilitation services for adults from that of merely employment toward a broader range of goals by including severely disabled individuals in that program area. The developmental disabilities program area, in relating to the most severely disabled individuals, extends its principal services beyond the more traditional school age and educational aspects to those required over the entire life of the individual, including work roles. One other possible need, however, is a greater orientation toward vocational goals at an earlier age. There is at present a discontinuity between educational programs for disabled children and vocational programs.

Reorganization of a generic program for disabled persons could reflect the model already in existence for developmental disabilities, which crosses age boundaries and boundaries of education and work sites. An alternative generic program may continue to recognize age boundaries in terms of delivery of services within the educational system versus outside the system, but some greater integration would be desirable.

The crucial policy issue in any alternative generic program is that of the degree of severity of the problem to be addressed (e.g., the lessening of the effects of disability) and the allocation of Federal funds. An ad hoc decision has already been made in the budgetary process wherein funds are differentially provided to these various program areas. Federal support for educational programs for disabled children, in the range of $1 billion, is roughly comparable to the support provided for rehabilitation; the support for developmental disabilities is in the range of $50 million. Support for education has been mainly provided at the local and State level, with the Federal contribution relatively small and considered supplemental. Federal support for vocational rehabilitation has been a traditionally larger contribution. A major issue currently is the allocation of funds for those individuals who are most severely disabled (for whom funds have not traditionally been made available by the States and localities). A generic program for disabled persons may be organized around the issue of degree of support required rather than existing categories and would make even more critical the need for decisions at the congressional level as to priorities.

Within each of the existing program areas, a similar issue arises when categorical aspects are considered. Considerable movement has already occurred within each of the program areas toward more functional descriptions of those to be considered eligible for services. Although the principle of "impairment" based on medical conditions or diagnostic categories remains, there has been some lessening of its use, particularly in the area of developmental disabilities.

One issue to be resolved, or at least considered, is an organization of services to disabled children that would be based on the degree of severity of the disability rather than on any medical or other category. A cost sharing principle has been in existence for some time in the relationship between the Federal interest and the interest of the States and localities for the increased costs for disabled children. A Federal policy issue is what the distribution of Federal resources should be at different levels of intensity of services. Debate may then focus on the formula for allocation of Federal funds. Some elements in such a review would include methods for the encouragement of integration of disabled children into the mainstream of education and a continued Federal interest in protecting the most severely disabled individuals, as well as the differential costs of various service levels.

A movement toward generic (noncategorical) programs based on the intensity of services required could reduce the amount of inappropriate categorization of individuals in terms of impairments (or diagnostic categories). The focus of such a determination could shift attention from the services provided directly to a specific child to broader programmatic support that would help all children requiring such services within the educational system.

No matter what area of Federal policy is involved—education, vocational rehabilitation, health care, social services, housing, etc.—allocation by program and by geographic or population basis is hampered by the state of data available on the types, amounts, and results of current services and other technologies being delivered and planned for. Current management information systems, as discussed in chapter 3, are not oriented to providing individuals, State governments, or the Federal Government with adequate, functionally based information.

Issues of Resource Allocation and Independent Living

One of the primary directions of the independent living movement is the participation of disabled persons in making decisions about themselves. The implementation of this potentially far-reaching concept has been relatively slow. None of the management information systems in existence or projected in the near future will collect data as to the actual level of participation of the clients. Doing so might help to make the goal of independence more feasible in itself. The issue to be considered is the degree to which it is a Federal resource allocation priority to encourage consumer participation and independent living.

Another goal of the independent living movement concerns the locus of the problem. If, as traditionally thought, the problem is sited in the client, resources are allocated for training and other programs to make the client better able to interact with a given environment. However, if the problem is also in the environment, as mentioned previously, then resources might be differently allocated. A portion of the funds might be allocated for changes in the physical environment for individual persons or for groups. Funds might be allocated preferentially for the development and maintenance of devices that would permit more effective interaction with the environment.

The third issue that arises as a result of the independent living movement is the degree to which the process of rehabilitation can be carried out in independent living centers under the control of disabled persons rather than through more traditional, professionally controlled programs. There may be a potential for less costly and more effective services via this innovation. The significance of this alternative mode of service delivery has been noted in the existing Rehabilitation Act but funded to only a very limited degree. Once again, a decision to encourage such activities would be translated into the percentage of the total budget devoted either directly by the Federal level or by an earmarked component of those funds delegated to the States. The Federal interest in early support for demonstration of effectiveness of innovative alternatives may be seen as a priority which States and localities are generally less likely to support.

Outcome Measures Used in Resource Allocation

The measures of outcome or effectiveness of Federal programs for disabled people are numerous and have changed over the years. "Productivity," however, is still one of the primary outcomes sought. The measure of productivity has been expanded recently beyond earnings in employment to recognize the contributions to productivity made by homemakers and to the community by unpaid volunteers. This measure, however expanded, remains one of the basic measures of outcome.

Another outcome sought by more recent allocation decisions is the degree to which the individual is able to function in the "least restrictive" environment. Like the principle of productivity, this outcome relates to independence and to the degree of support by others. It is important to recognize that less restrictive environments are frequently, but not always, ones in which costs are lessened. The so-called "deinstitutionalization" movement has sought, with some public support of community-based services, to increase the likelihood of disabled persons living independently in their own homes or in group homes. Both the expansion of the principle of productivity outcomes to other than gainful employment and the expansion of the range of options for support for living independently are relatively new concepts expressed in the most recent law.

Underlying these new concepts has been another outcome widely sought by disabled persons themselves: self-determination. This goal is expressed in public policy in the requirement for client participation in the creation of individualized rehabilitation or educational plans. Self-determination implies independence and individual initiative. It is having more control over one's own life than has typically been the case for many disabled people due to the amount of control exercised by physicians and other professionals.

The outcomes may be mutually supportive and should be considered together when allocating resources. Self-determination in terms of clients' participation in planning for themselves is in itself a major outcome and is likely to enhance the other outcomes of productivity and community living. Involvement in the planning process would include not only participation in setting goals, but also contributing to the identification and development of the means by which problems are to solved and goals reached.

The management and administrative skills necessary for "producing" such a blend of outcomes may be somewhat different from those in the "production" of a job placement. One idea to be considered is the use of a management system appropriate for the development of new technology and ideas—the management of an R&D firm rather than an auto factory. The principle is that of resource development rather than simply allocation. Such an approach is highly compatible with, for example, the professional goals of a rehabilitation counselor. However, its actual implementation could require meticulous attention to the attaining of goals through the participation of disabled persons to a much greater degree than at present. This idea is one of the tenets of the independent living movement. The recent funding of programs under title VII of the existing Vocational Rehabilitation Act provides an opportunity for assessing the cost effectiveness of services being provided in this more participatory manner.

Prevention of Impairments and Disabilities

Although prevention is the theoretical ideal, and despite many significant success stories (e.g., polio vaccine), the goal of prevention remains unfulfilled due to a combination of inadequate knowledge, human nature, and finite resources.

Even if resources were unconstrained, it would be difficult to prevent diseases and other disabling conditions whose causes are unknown or for which no effective preventive technologies can be devised with current knowledge. This knowledge constraint underscores one of the aspects of "resource capability:" Resource capability refers not just to the *amount* of resources available but also to the degree of *ability* to use them. Thus, the country cannot spend money administering a vaccine that does not exist, just as it cannot *effectively* spend money persuading people of the risks associated with various behaviors if the knowledge of effective information transfer techniques does not exist. A critical issue of resource allocation related to prevention is what share of its resources a society allocates not just to prevention but also to the search for the ability to prevent disabilities. Basic research on motor function, tissue structure and regeneration, molecular genetics, enzyme function, and cell biology in general are examples of promising areas of basic research. Just as important, however, is research on the development and engineering of technologies that have been made possible through basic research. Similarly, research is needed in services delivery (e.g., how can vaccines be most effectively delivered), in policy and programs (e.g., how can prevention programs be most effectively and efficiently administered), and in demographics and epidemiology (e.g., who is at risk; how can such individuals be identified in advance?).

In discussions of prevention, human nature is sometimes termed "imperfect" or "self-defeating" because humans do not always seem to act in their own, safe, rational best interest. Although the philosophical dimensions of the attitudes behind the use of such terms are not the subject here, it should be noted that seemingly irrational, risk-taking behavior is not necessarily "imperfect" or "improper." It may be a reflection of different individuals placing different values on risk-taking, risk-aversion, probability of negative outcomes, and the meaning of possible outcomes. Whatever the human motives involved, policies toward prevention must take human nature into account. The success of a public health campaign of immunization against childhood diseases, for example, is very much dependent on the willingness of parents and children to comply, to take the vaccine. This may require informing the relevant population of risks and benefits of vaccination; it may require the establishment of various sanctions for failure to comply. Public policy must address a range of attitudes before resources can be successfully devoted to prevention. "Seat belts are inconvenient and uncomfortable." "I like to smoke." Statements such as this may seem mundane and obvious, but the attitudes behind them often reflect strongly held feelings of personal freedom and determination. They must be considered in the allocation of resources for prevention.

This leads to another issue of resource allocation and prevention: *Who in society decides what negative consequences are to be prevented? On what conceptual and pragmatic bases are resources then committed to preventing the identified outcomes?* The answers to those questions illustrate a critical property of prevention of disabilities. Preventive technologies are applied by all individuals and all institutions in society. Individuals apply them when, for example, they seek prenatal care, wear seat belts, stop (or never start) smoking, reduce their use of drugs, and follow safety instructions on the job. Institutions apply them at all levels. The Federal Government devotes resources to auto safety, maternal and child health, immunization campaigns, food and drug safety regulation, basic research on the causes and mechanics of disease, airport safety, and (on a less direct level) a foreign policy that reduces military casualties. States and local governments apply resources to similar activities, including health and safety regulation in the workplace and in public institutions such as schools. Industry and other commercial organizations can apply prevention technologies in workplace safety and in programs for alcoholism and drug abuse. Schools teach driver education. The list could, of course, go on. The point is that prevention is not just a Federal or even a governmental responsibility alone.

Governments, however, and especially the Federal Government, are the institutions of society where responsibility has been placed for much of the generation of knowledge about, and development of more technical approaches to, prevention. Especially when prevention is seen as a common good or a public good, the Federal role has been prominent. This is the case, for example, with respect to the encouragement of vaccine development, the regulation of foods, drugs, and medical devices, the development of (or encouragement or mandating of) technologies for safer highways and automobiles, basic research in most areas, and public information campaigns on hazards or risk-associated behavior.

The above decision has referred to the "who" part of the question about the allocation of resources for prevention. "On what bases" resources are allocated is a much more difficult question to address. At the Federal level, Congress creates and funds prevention technologies and programs. The executive agencies administer the programs and decide the finer distribution of the available resources. In both cases, a mixture of humanitarianism, economics, politics, and scientific capability affect the decisions made. As pointed out in the case study on passive restraint systems (see the background paper on this topic), prevention must compete with cure, reduction of suffering, and rehabilitation for each condition or disability. The aspects of a decision listed above apply to both prevention and treatment. *Because resources are finite, and often quite limited, resources must be distributed between current treatment and rehabilitation of disabilities and the future prevention of them.*

Thus, even if analysis of costs and benefits of prevention versus treatment and rehabilitation indicates that prevention is *economically* and *humanistically* preferable, the existence of people, today, with disabilities means that resources cannot all be allocated to prevention. There is no correct split between prevention and rehabilitation. OTA finds, however, that decisionmakers should more often expand their analysis to include the benefits and costs of devoting somewhat increased portions of resources to prevention, to development of preventive technologies, and to development of effective techniques for delivery of preventive technologies and information on risks.

Further, and very critically, the definitions of disability and handicap gaining prominence in the disability area, and adopted by this report, allow a modified concept of prevention that holds great potential. That is, decisionmakers at the Federal level (indeed, all levels), in addition to allocating resources between prevention of impairments and disabilities and rehabilitation of currently disabled people, could adopt a new, explicit strategy of preventing disabilities from becoming handicaps. The actions embodied in this strategy are not all new, but the idea of seeking opportunities to apply resources consistently and comprehensively to the prevention of *handicaps* is new and could serve as a potentially structuring concept for resource allocation. A disability becomes a handicap when the physical and social environment combines with a disability to prevent the accomplishment of a typical functional task. A physically disabled person who uses a wheelchair will not be handicapped if a prevention strategy has made transportation systems and buildings accessible. A deaf person will not be handicapped in a job or in social functions if telecommunications devices are available and permit the carrying out of the needed functions of communication. Such prevention is not free. In some cases, it may require the allocation of extensive resources. In others, it could be relatively inexpensive—e.g., modifying telephone receivers to make them compatible with hearing aids, or requiring braille markings on elevator buttons. Each possible intervention should be submitted to analysis. The key, however, is viewing the possible technological intervention not simply as an expenditure but rather as an investment in prevention.

Resource Allocation and Elderly People

An increasingly critical resource allocation issue, which will be covered only briefly, is how society and its decisionmakers, *at all levels*, will react to and deal with the changing age distribution of the U. S. population.

Growing old in America has become in some ways less of a threat to one's self-esteem and economic survival than previously. The majority of elderly people are, in fact, self-supporting and relatively healthy. In proportional terms, however, there is a higher incidence of disability among elderly people. The aging process is associated with reduced ability for sight, hearing, and mobility in a higher percentage of elderly people than is found in the general population. The incidence and prevalence of chronic diseases, such as cancers, heart and circulatory conditions, and arthritis, increase with the age of a population. These conditions imply increased need for medical and social services, along with increased costs for those services—and in our society lead to increased dependency.*

The social and financial implications of an elderly segment of the population were serious in the past when about 5 percent of the country's population was age 65 and older. They are critical today: More than 12 percent of the population is age 65 and over, and that percentage may rise to 20 percent or more by 2030. Technological advances in the next 30 years could significantly reduce mortality (death) and morbidity (disease and disability) rates of elderly people, and the proportion of elderly people in the population could rise even more dramatically than anticipated.

Federal decisionmakers make a great many resource allocation decisions that affect and are affected by the population of elderly people. Social Security and Medicare are prime examples of programs involving many billions of dollars.

---

*This discussion is based on ref. 6.

But policies on other matters such as retirement age, tax treatment of retirement accounts, types of technologies and services provided or paid for by medical and social services programs, tax policy related to voluntary work, and actions relative to age discrimination also affect the allocation of resources for and by elderly people.

This OTA report is on disabilities, not on aging. The resource allocation problems associated with an elderly population are an issue, however, because disability among elderly people will be one of the crucial aspects of their need for funds, services, and policies that allow greater independence and self-determination. The key potential problem of resource allocation posed by an elderly population is the disparity between the fiscal and social contributions by elderly people that policies encourage (or allow) and the fiscal and social needs that increased numbers of elderly people will present.

Analytical Methods for Informing Decisionmaking

Finding an appropriate or feasible match between spending goals and resource capabilities requires adequate information relating to both sides of the "fit." Goals must be clear, explicit, and realistically determined. Capabilities must be understood along several dimensions. *Resource capability means more than simply the availability of funds. It also implies an adequate knowledge base*, especially of potential resultant outcomes and of the potential tradeoffs that might be required.

Much of the needed information cannot be provided adequately by formal analytical techniques. Politics, philosophies, concepts of distributive and compensatory justice,* and emotions are intimate aspects of decisions in the disability-related area. But a substantial amount of the needed, and often inadequate, information base can be provided or at least improved by careful use of formal analysis. The danger is inappropriate use: Analysis cannot replace judgment or overrule less objective but more important considerations.

Role of Analytical Techniques

The inherent complexities and uncertainties associated with many decisions make it very difficult to identify and weigh all the possible consequences of those decisions. Often, however, the *process* of analysis can give structure to the problem in question, can allow an open consideration of all the relevant effects of a decision, and can help force the explicit treatment of key assumptions.

The use of formal analysis in the area of disability-related policy has both its enthusiastic proponents and its skeptical detractors. As with the use of technology, however, the most logical position seems to be that analysis can aid in performing the functions mentioned above when it is adequately conceived and designed, conducted properly, and its results are given only an appropriate weight in the process of making the decision. Analysis can illuminate issues and provide synthesis of relevant data. It can provide numbers. But only rarely can those numbers serve as the sole or primary basis for a resource allocation decision.

Analytical techniques are only tools. They can be ignored, abused, or misused. A challenge to analysts, consumers, and policymakers is to use the tools in an appropriate manner, to strive for the ideal uses, but to recognize and be explicit about the limitations. In an ideal world, they could be used to inform and structure the aspects of the decision process that are listed below:

- clarify and force explicit consideration of goals,
- clarify the problem or opportunity to be addressed,
- identify and describe possible decision alternatives: the technical alternatives, or other possible interventions,
- identify the range of parties at interest,
- identify the potential outcomes—positive and negative—of possible decision alternatives

---

*Compensatory justice deals with distribution of resources in consideration of past harms rendered. Although it is at times a significant element in policy discussions about disability, it has been less important and central to policy than has the concept of distributive justice. Distributive justice deals with the distribution of resources in proper share to each party with a legitimate claim to them. Most often, Western culture in theory bases "proper share on the idea of the fundamental equality of individuals, each with an equal right to the resources required for a satisfying quality of life (183).

and the distribution of outcomes among the parties at interest,
- provide a method of considering the potential outcomes together and in relation to the goals,
- provide evaluation of actual v. projected outcomes,
- identify possible changes in interventions based on evaluation results.

These objectives of using analytical techniques are used in a later section as the basis for a suggested approach to a resource allocation framework.

Range of Analytical Techniques

Analytical techniques are often used to provide various types of data used in the lifecycle of technology, as described in parts I and II. Many of these types of analysis are useful for resource allocation in general. Statistical or qualitative *surveys of the needs, desires, and capabilities* of disabled persons are used for planning services and to generate ideas for needed new or modified technologies. Historically, however, such surveys have concentrated on needs, especially as defined by parties other than the disabled persons themselves. Further, they have been subject to the weaknesses of methodology and concept described in chapter 2 for demographic information. *Demographic studies of populations* of handicapped or disabled people are also used to provide information for technology planning and for other resource allocation decisions. Such studies have often concentrated on categories of impairment as opposed to measures of functional limitation.

Economic and fiscal or budgetary analyses are other analytical tools for decisionmakers. Analyses of funds spent by various Federal and State programs for disabled people may provide useful background information, but usually do not yield data helpful for changing the direction, goals, or organization of programs. It is difficult to combine such analyses with analyses of outcomes to produce some measure of efficiency or even effectiveness. "Cost of disability studies," to the extent that they go beyond the preceding type of analysis and include measures of costs other than direct expenditures, can be useful to the setting of goals and decision priorities.

Projections or forecasts of economic or employment conditions help decisionmakers plan for future resource allocation. Obviously, these types of analyses must be used judiciously and with allowance for the inevitable uncertainty of results. Similar caveats are attached to another type of forecasting—that of projections of emerging and future technological developments.

Analyses in the form of *program evaluations and services delivery research and evaluations* are some of the most common information sources used by decisionmakers. These analyses range from sophisticated, large-scale, computer-based studies of program effectiveness to quickly conducted, qualitative studies of, for example, a suggested change in research priorities. There exists no definitive evidence that the usefulness of these techniques is heavily dependent upon their degree of sophistication. A large body of circumstantial evidence that is accumulating, however, indicates analysis should at least follow certain principles of analysis. These principles will be listed at the end of this section.

Most commonly viewed as a technology- or product-specific private sector activity, *market analysis* could actually be helpful in many types of resource allocation decisions by the public sector. Further, improved collection, analysis, and dissemination of some of the above types of analytical data (e.g., demographics, technological forecasts, economic forecasts, disability services R&D) could be of great value to the market analysis efforts of both the public and the private sectors. If a more effective public/private collaboration is desired in regard to disability-related issues, market analysis must no longer be viewed as a tool for use only by profit seekers.

Cost-benefit analysis (CBA) and *cost-effectiveness analysis* (CEA) are relatively common forms of analysis in the disability area. A recent OTA study of the potential usefulness of CEA and CBA included a review and analysis of the health policy and medical literature related to CEA/CBA.* In

---

*This discussion is based on *Background Paper #1: Methodological Issues and Literature Review* of OTA's report *The Implications of Cost-Effectiveness Analysis of Medical Technology*, U.S. Government Printing Office, September 1980.

its analysis of the growth and composition of that literature, OTA found that a considerable number of articles dealt with birth defects, chronic diseases (especially cardiovascular diseases and kidney diseases), mental health services, geriatric care, and rehabilitation technologies and services. Further, interest in these subjects and CEA/CBA is growing.

The principal distinctions between CBA and CEA lie in: 1) the method of valuation of the desirable consequences of a decision (the benefits), and 2) the implications of the different methods of that valuation. Both are formal analytical techniques for comparing the positive and negative consequences of alternative ways to allocate resources. In CBA, all costs and all benefits typically are valued in monetary (or equivalent) terms. The results of analysis are expressed in dollar cost per dollar benefit, yielding a cost-benefit ratio or, sometimes, a measure of net benefit. Conceptually, therefore, CBA can be used to evaluate the "worth" of a project and would allow comparison of projects of different types (e.g., elevators in subways v. passive restraint systems in cars v. the B-1 bomber). In CEA, on the other hand, desirable consequences are measured not in monetary terms, but in some other units. Then, the ratios of desirable consequences to negative consequences for alternative ways of spending are compared. Thus, competing but dissimilar projects (such as dams v. hospitals) may not be able to be compared adequately with standard CEA methods; similar alternatives, however, can be compared without the difficulty or impossibility of valuing outcomes in monetary terms.

Both CEAs and CBAs have been conducted frequently in the disability area. Their existence, however, does not imply the degree to which these techniques have affected policy. Little evidence exists on the extent of their use, but if experience in health policy is typical, it is probable that they have had only minor impact. The reasons for lack of use are numerous and logical. CEA and CBA suffer from a number of serious weaknesses, both of immaturity and of an inherent methodological nature. Some of these, related to the immature state-of-the-art in the disability or general human services area, may diminish as techniques improve. Similarly, as analysts and policymakers gain more experience with them, the usefulness of the techniques may increase. Many of the inherent weaknesses, such as inability to deal with questions of equity and distribution, will continue to affect the usefulness of CEA/CBA.

A substantial degree of effort is being put forth in an attempt to advance the methodology of CEA/CBA in the disability area, principally with the support of the National Institute of Handicapped Research (NIHR). For example, a research resource allocation method developed by the Texas Institute for Rehabilitation Research specifically attempts to address the question of nonmonetary outcomes (27). That method of CBA uses three general classes of outcomes: 1) outcomes of direct benefit to individuals in the target populations for whom the research is directed, 2) outcomes that are of indirect benefit if the research project is successful, and 3) outcomes of indirect benefit but not related to the success of the project. All three of these classes of benefits may have monetary elements, but each may also include nonmonetary benefits. Enhanced quality of services, improved policy bases for rehabilitation, expanded knowledge bases, and enhanced public awareness of an issue are examples of such nonmonetary outcomes. The valuation of the nonmonetary measures is accomplished through a system of ranking and weighting by a peer-review-like group of judges. A comparison is made between the "importance" of the various nonmonetary measures and the monetary ones in order to assign artificial dollar values to the former.

Another example of current attempts to advance CBA methods in the disability area is provided by the more inclusive, more social-outcome oriented model of Dodson and Collignon (73). This model, which is still in development, is designed to identify and measure outcomes other than simply monetary ones related to vocational rehabilitation in its (new) role vis-a-vis severely disabled persons.

The potential usefulness of such methods is still impossible to determine. On the basis of preliminary reviews, however, OTA finds that the models represent legitimate methodological advances and yet still are prey to weaknesses of most CBA/

CEA applications. The assumptions and data employed leave serious questions about the uses to which any results might be applied. The aspect that most deserves critical scrutiny is their traditional orientation to a quantitative bottom-line.

Principles of Formal Analysis

Whatever form of formal analysis the policymaker decides to use to aid in decisionmaking, certain principles of analysis should be followed. Table 10 lists the 10 principles for analysis that OTA identified in its recent review of CEA and CBA (166).

These principles are the basis of the discussion in the following section. Blum has suggested that an additional principle should be added between Nos. 2 and 3 of table 10—Conduct a problem analysis.* Problem analysis consists of four basic steps: preparing for analysis, formulating initial problem, identifying problem precursors, and identifying problem consequences.

Table 10.—Ten Principles of Formal Analysis

1. Define the problem
2. State the objectives
3. Identify the alternatives
4. Analyze the positive consequences
5. Analyze the negative consequences
6. Differentiate the perspective of the analysis
7. Perform discounting
8. Analyze uncertainties
9. Address ethical issues
10. Present and discuss results in a policy context

SOURCE: Office of Technology Assessment, U.S. Congress, *The Implications of Cost-Effectiveness Analysis of Medical Technology*, OTA-H-126 (Washington, D.C.: U.S. Government Printing Office, August 1980).

*H. Blum, University of California, Berkeley, personal communication, Dec. 7, 1981.

STRUCTURING RESOURCE ALLOCATION DECISIONS

The discussion that follows is similar in concept and purpose to the one for appropriate technology decisionmaking in chapter 5. In fact, the framework discussion of chapter 5 should be seen as relating to technology-specific resource allocation. The discussion below is also similar to chapter 5 in that its intent is not to produce a checklist or "cookbook" for decisionmakers, but rather to be a step toward decisionmaking that takes into account the range of relevant variables. The discussion suggests some of the elements that an explicit framework for resource allocation decisions might have. Individual decisionmakers or programs should adopt as much of the material as is helpful. OTA's purpose here is to provide an orderly way to think about the decision process and its structure.

The discussion is based on two sets of guidelines: 1) the 10 principles of formal analysis, and 2) the list of aspects of the role of analysis in decisionmaking. These may help serve as the basis for structuring decisions, because the primary reasons for discussing and using a structuring rationale is to clarify why a decision is to be made and the problem to be addressed, to be sure all assumptions are explicit, and to force consideration of all relevant consequences of alternatives. Thus, the goals of analysis are essentially the goals of the decision *process*. The discussions below will primarily be from the perspective of Federal decisionmakers, but it is important to view them as also applying to other parties, including individuals.

Explicitly Define the Problem

Resources cannot be effectively applied to a problem unless the problem is explicitly stated and adequately understood. *It is not enough merely to specify the goals of resource allocation.* The underlying reason for desiring to reach the goals is an essential part of the policy development process. It will exert tremendous, and often unappreciated, influence on what goals are selected and how those goals are stated. "Development of a portable, lightweight, reliable voice-synthesizing communicator" is of course a goal statement, but unless the organization deciding to devote resources to such development has thoroughly studied the situation that a communicator would be designed to address, it cannot develop more helpful specifications. Similarly, before a portable voice synthesizer becomes the goal statement, the decisionmakers should have considered the functions that are being sought through technological intervention and the alternative technological approaches possible. That is, the function to be addressed must be considered before the form of the solution is decided. "Make subways accessible" is a goal, but the demographic data and human and economic factors that lead to the need for accessibility are critical to the methods and extent of accessibility to be required. In short, *a clear and open examination of the situation or problem to be addressed is a prerequisite to the realistic and effective setting of goals.*

State Goals in Measurable or Evaluable Terms

After the problem is specified, operational goals must be set. These goals must be expressed in measurable terms, not only because evaluation of progress toward the goals can then be assessed, but also because the form in which goals are expressed will affect the manner in which they are approached. If the Federal Government and the States allocate resources for job training and placement programs and express the associated goals in vague terms of increased employment percentages or increased quality of life and self-image, the programs administering the funds will have little guidance as to how to implement the resource allocation decision. They will be free to pursue high percentages of "placement," paying less attention to length of ensuing employment or level of earnings or job satisfaction. This example is merely hypothetical, but Congress or the States might wish to specify, on the basis of thorough analysis of possible goals, that their desire for the resources is such that the goals require subsequent employment of certain lengths or of certain earnings.

Thus, in structuring resource allocation decisions, *decisionmakers should consider the effects that their statements of goals will have on the implementation of programs and on the ability to do subsequent evaluations of outcomes.* In effect, adequate specification of goals is the method for transmitting signals about the importance of various outcomes to be sought.

Specify the Range of Parties at Interest

A "party at interest" is someone with a stake in the outcome of any action taken that distributes resources. Federal decisionmakers must consider the interests and reactions of a wide range of people and institutions—e.g., from taxpayers and constituents of elected officials, to disabled individuals and groups representing disabled people, to industry and other private organizations, to their own and other bureaucratic organizations.

Each decisionmaker must decide which of the many potential parties at interest will be affected by the decisions made—i.e., any decision will distribute costs and benefits to many parties in, usually, an unequal manner. Which of the parties will incur costs and receive benefits to such an extent that the effects on those parties will need to be considered in choosing among alternatives? Not all potential parties at interest will be the subjects of intensive analysis regarding potential positive and negative effects, but one of the crucial aspects of organizing or structuring a resource allocation decision is identifying an initial broad list of possible parties at interest and then narrowing the list to those that can feasibly be studied for purposes of informing the ultimate decision. A desirable, but frequently ignored, aspect of decisionmaking is involving the principal parties at interest in analyzing the potential alternatives and possible methods of implementing any subsequent allocation of resources.

Identify the Range of Possible Decisions

Resource allocation decisions are rarely of the "Do X or do nothing" type. Instead, they most often involve a choice among a series of alternative ways of distributing resources. What is sometimes missing in the allocation of resources for disability-related programs is creativity in identifying the range of possible alternatives. In the past, most allocation decisions were made on behalf of disabled people with little input from disabled people on possible ways to accomplish the goals addressed. Thus, a source of ideas was not exploited fully. Another factor limiting the range of alternatives has been the categorical nature of Federal programs. Medicare, for example, is a medically oriented program. Because of its tradition, perceived and actual mandate, the orientation of its employees, and perhaps its desire not to trespass on areas seen as the responsibility of other agencies, the Medicare program—and the Department of Health and Human Services, and Congress—may see the program's possible range as being limited to primarily medical interventions. This situation may hold even though alternatives that are closer to social services may have a greater potential to improve the "health" of disabled people. This does not imply that the Medicare program is at fault, merely that the categorical structure of organizations restricts a comprehensive consideration of the full range of possible alternatives that might address a particular problem or goal.

The observation above implies two important points for decisionmakers. First, *decisionmakers should consult with disabled persons and other sources of ideas in putting together a list of possible alternatives*. And second, *in the initial analysis of potential options, decisionmakers should not confine themselves to only those types of options that are strictly within their mandate*. Even when legal, programmatic, or budgetary constraints do not allow the realistic consideration of these additional alternatives, they may be of use to other agencies or other decisionmakers who have a relevant mandate.

Identify, Measure, and Value Potential Consequences of Decisions

Once goals have been set and the range of alternatives, along with the potentially affected parties for each, has been identified, the estimation of "costs and benefits" must take place. Quotation marks have been used to highlight the fact that OTA is *not* simply referring to the results of a traditional CBA. The shortcomings of a simplistic (not a simple) CBA have been discussed above. *It is critical that—for each alternative method of allocating resources—the positive and negative consequences for all significant parties at interest be identified, measured, and (where possible) valued*. This is obviously not a simple task, but it is one for which effort expended can pay large dividends in improved decisions.

The identification-measurement-valuation sequence is especially important. Identification must take place first, obviously, but in addition, it is important that decisionmakers not confine identification to only those items that are quantifiable. Similarly, measurement should not be limited to only those items to which dollar amounts can be assigned or to those with absolute figures as opposed to relative rankings or estimates of magnitude or subjective descriptors. The consequences of encouraging (and allocating resources for) increased participation of disabled people in R&D as scientists and engineers and as consumer representatives will not all be expressed in numbers of placements or numbers of advisory panels served on or numbers of technologies designed or developed with the involvement of disabled persons. Subtle or hard to "measure" improvement in the appropriateness of technologies developed may be a very important outcome. OTA finds that simply their lack of amenability to objective measurement and valuation should not preclude the consideration of such outcomes as an important aspect of allocation decisions.

Consider the Effects of Time (Discounting) and Uncertainty

It is very important for analysts and decisionmakers to be aware that time and uncertainty will affect the estimates of potential outcomes of any resource allocation alternatives. The three key questions that should be explicitly asked and considered before a decision is made are as follows. First, has the analysis of potential outcomes considered the effects of time on the values of future costs and benefits? Second, are the analysis and the decision to be made oriented to short-term outcomes, to long-range outcomes, or to both? And third, have the uncertainties of assumptions, data, future states, and possible outcomes been accounted for in deliberations about the desirability of various alternatives?

Because this is not solely a discussion of resource allocation decisionmaking through the use of formal, quantitative analysis, no definite guidelines for the manner in which time should be taken into account can be given. In formal analysis, a process known as *discounting* is used when some of the measured positive and negative consequences (benefits and costs) of the alternatives occur at different times. In fact, in most allocation decisions, costs and benefits will occur in a staggered fashion, with costs commonly being incurred in advance of benefits. "Discounting" is in a way similar to applying a reverse interest rate. It is a technique for transforming future amounts (of dollars, for example) to their "present value." Thus, all costs and benefits can be analyzed using their values today.

The rationale behind discounting is a belief that certain properties of resources and time must be taken into account. One is that resources can be invested and earn future gains ("opportunity cost of capital"). The other is that people prefer benefits today rather than tomorrow and expect to be rewarded for postponing gratification ("social rate of time preference"). Both these properties, in effect, mean that a dollar invested in a program today is a dollar foregone from an alternative use (investment or consumption), and therefore it must appreciate to more than a dollar in the future for the investment to be accepted.

Even when a formal and quantitative analysis is not conducted in support of a decision, it is possible (and desirable) for some informal consideration to be given to the effects of time on the value of the future stream of costs and benefits.

Posing the question of *short- versus long-term outcome orientation* is much simpler than providing answers as to how to maintain an appropriate balance between the present and the future. This balance, in fact, is one of the hardest and yet most crucial objectives of effective resource allocation. The dilemma can be seen in debates about the proper emphasis placed on basic research versus support of technology adoption, or on prevention versus rehabilitation. Competing but equally critical needs combined with limited resources form the dilemma. Even though this may be obvious, the issue should always be raised and discussed because otherwise the pressures of the present may exert undue influence over decisions.

The importance of considering both present and long range implications can be illustrated by an issue mentioned earlier. That issue is the preventing of disabilities from becoming handicaps through alterations to the physical and social environments of the disabled person. It may seem more pressing to allocate the limited resources available to specific individuals for personal-assist technologies (e.g., subsidies for closed captioning devices for the television sets of hearing-impaired persons), and yet investment in a more environmentally oriented technological approach may yield higher benefit for greater numbers of people in the future. OTA is not suggesting this is necessarily true, only that current resource allocation does not address such possibilities to an adequate extent.

Every decision to allocate resources is made with some degree of *uncertainty*. Just as examples, uncertainties exist in regard to the cause of diseases, the distribution of disabilities in populations, the efficacy and costs of diagnostic, preventive, and treatment or rehabilitative technologies, the desires of consumers, future economic indicators, potential effect of education or vocational training, personal habits and needs, and future technological "breakthroughs." These and the many other possible uncertainties will affect the desirability of decision alternatives and the ultimate success of the decisions made. Complete accommodation of uncertainty is never possible. Decisionmakers should, however, identify which sources of uncertainty might strongly affect outcomes and make some effort to consider the changes in predicted outcomes that might accompany incorrect assumptions.

What is suggested here is that such uncertainties be acknowledged and analyzed instead of ignored or hidden. In formal analysis, there is a technique known as "sensitivity analysis" that can be used to vary assumptions about the values of uncertain variables and test changes in values for their effects on predicted outcomes. Sensitivity analysis can often be used to identify which uncertain variables have a substantial effect on outcomes, which variables do not affect outcomes (and whose uncertainty therefore can be ignored), and minimum and maximum values that a variable can take on without changing the desirability of an alternative decision possibility. Sensitivity analysis does not make decisions, but it can increase confidence in estimates of outcomes.

Accounting for uncertainty is just as important when no formal analysis accompanies the resource allocation decision. Although a statistical test of uncertainty might not take place, the decisionmaker can informally and subjectively apply tests of reason to the assumptions being used in the decision. This may lead to a decision to postpone a decision until data can be gathered on some assumption, or to a decision to implement the decision on a pilot or demonstration basis, or to a decision to fund two or more programs to accomplish the same purpose, with provision for review of outcomes and subsequent reevaluation of the decision.

Consider Ethical and Other "Nonobjective" Factors

Ethical factors are highlighted for two reasons. First, issues of ethics, values, human dignity, personal worth, justice, compassion, and so on are often central aspects of policy formulation and debate in the disability area. The goals of, for example, independence and civil rights are not ones for which most of the important variables can be expressed in quantifiable terms. This does not mean that such goals or the attendant variables should not occupy a prominent place in decisionmaking. Resources are not allocated strictly or solely on the basis of expected net return on dollars invested.

The second reason for highlighting ethical and other subjective factors is that, despite their often critical importance, they are frequently omitted or given low weight in policy formulation, either because they are not quantifiable or because they are difficult to deal with. There are no magical solutions to the problem of taking into account subjective and emotionally laden aspects of the allocation of resources. By definition, there is no formula for their inclusion. But, the ethical and other value dimensions of a resource allocation decision can be identified openly to a greater extent than they are at present. And, very importantly, *any formal analyses of the consequences of decision alternatives can be made more amenable to the consideration of ethical and other subjective factors by a purposeful decision not to seek a single, bottom-line estimation of outcomes.*

Other techniques, such as arraying (listing in perhaps order of importance) the potential results, could be used instead of, for example, a traditional CBA that results in a cost-benefit ratio. That is, the analyst would identify all the relevant potential consequences, measure and value them quantitatively when possible and appropriate, and list those consequences that are not quantifiable in descriptive terms, with some estimate of importance or magnitude if possible. The key, however, is that the analyst would make no attempt to unrealistically quantify or artificially combine factors in order to yield a "clean" answer.

Provide for Evaluation of the Results of Decisions

Providing for evaluation of the results of decisions is a seemingly obvious but frequently undervalued aspect of decisionmaking. As stated above, decisionmaking takes place under conditions of uncertainty. This fact of life must be taken into account by the analyst and the decisionmaker. If the problem to be addressed, the goals to be sought, and the assumptions about consequences have all been specified clearly and in measurable terms, the basis for design of an evaluation component has been established.

Very often, evaluation of past resource allocation decisions has been the responsibility of people or organizations other than those who made the decisions. This situation implies that evaluation will be an "after the fact" activity. Data that readily or effectively support or even allow evaluation efforts will usually not have been collected over the course of implementing the decision. The objectives of the original decisionmakers may not be adequately known by or taken into account by subsequent evaluators. For these reasons, it is important for those individuals or organizations who are making resource allocation decisions (indeed, any decisions) to plan for the evaluation of their decisions. The objectives being sought can be specified in evaluable terms, data systems can be designed into the decision itself, records can be kept on populations and effects, and the timing and criteria for evaluation can be set. "Course correction" possibilities can be examined and set forth during the process of making the allocation decision.

If Congress is the decisionmaker, it can provide for evaluation directly in legislation or it can less formally plan for it by including a discussion of anticipated evaluation needs and goals in hearings and bill reports. Whether formal or informal, planning for evaluation should include at least the following:

- explicit statement of the problem being addressed, outcomes sought, and assumptions about potential consequences and any other uncertainties;
- highlighting of especially critical uncertainties to be examined during evaluation;
- specification of criteria against which evaluation should take place;
- design of an information system to track variables to be used during subsequent evaluations;
- specification of who is to do such tracking and how the tracking will be funded;
- recommendations or specification of times for evaluation, organization to do the evaluation, form of the evaluation; and
- any specification or suggestions of possible changes in policy as a result of evaluation information.

Even if fully considered and dealt with by those allocating resources, the eight elements of a resource allocation decision, from explicitly defining the problem to providing for evaluation of the results will not result in obvious or perfect decisions. The goal of presenting them in this report is simply to help make the process of allocating resources more sensitive to uncertainty and to a broader range of interests and possibilities. The list is to serve as a reminder to decisionmakers to explicitly ask themselves: What do I hope to accomplish? Why? Who will be affected in what ways? What assumptions am I making? Am I avoiding the trap of numbers? And have I planned for a test of my decision? These simple questions may require more than simple answers, but they are worth answering.

Part Four:
Policy Options

12.
Policy Options

> Refusal to accept the inevitable shortcomings of any society is responsible for a good deal of what is best in political life.
> —*Peter F. Drucker*

Contents

	Page
Production, Marketing, and Diffusion of Technologies	163
Involvement of Disabled People and Other Consumers	169
Research, Development, and Evaluation of Technologies	172
Financial Barriers to the Use of Technology	177
Personnel Issues	179

12. Policy Options

A large number of factors affect the success of technological applications in the area of disabilities. Among the most influential factors are Federal policies. This chapter discusses possible changes in those policies. Some involve legislative changes. Others are oriented to actions of the executive branch, but would involve congressional oversight or encouragement. None of them are recommendations: OTA does not recommend any particular course of action. They are options for congressional consideration. The options are not, for the most part, mutually exclusive. The adoption of one option within a category does not necessarily mean that the others are inapplicable. On the contrary, better effect can often be had by a careful combination of options.

Many of the generic problems that exist in this area range from a lack of financial incentives for manufacturers to produce devices for disabled people, to a lack of evaluation and evaluation criteria, to inadequate information transfer systems. These types of problems could be alleviated by a concerted effort involving public agencies, private organizations, and consumer and citizen participation. However, many of the other problems are so deeply rooted in complex financial circumstances that it might take substantial changes in reimbursement policies and in the public-private sector relationship to bring about significant improvements.

Some of the problems are based in social and psychological attitudes that cannot be changed simply by appropriating more money or by reorganizing Federal agencies. Federal policies can have some effect in changing attitudes, but any substantial change may depend as much or more on disabled persons themselves. Opportunities for changing attitudes, however, can be enhanced by Federal policies and administration that assure employment and education activities, thus changing the amount of interaction that takes place between disabled people and nondisabled persons.

The options below are presented by issue areas. Despite this division, which is for the purposes of presentation, it is important to bear in mind the extremely important interactions that occur both among the stages in the lifecycle of technology and between technical issues and resource or social issues.

PRODUCTION, MARKETING, AND DIFFUSION OF DISABILITY-RELATED TECHNOLOGIES

ISSUE 1

How can the Federal Government increase the probability that technologies will reach the people who need and desire them?

In as many cases as possible, commercial viability should be one of the goals sought in technology developed using Federal funds. A critical issue is how to alter the currently inadequate state of marketing efforts and processes.

As discussed in chapters 8 and 9, one of the most critical and yet currently inadequate stages in the lifecycle of technologies for disabled people is the movement of technologies from development to use. Production and distribution are weak links in the process of technology development and diffusion. *The production, marketing, and diffusion of technologies are steps that are most often appropriate private sector activities, and yet a number of factors work against that sector's willingness and ability to engage in those activities.* Research and development (R&D) organizations have typically placed a low priority on production, marketing, and diffusion activities. The National Aeronautics and Space Administration's (NASA's) activities in technology transfer illustrate an exception. In general, however, the ultimate commercial production and distribution of technologies being developed with Federal funds have not been given sufficient attention.

There are several market-oriented factors that work against the involvement of the private sector. The difficulty in projecting the markets for disability-related technologies increases the risks of a commercial venture, as do the often small populations in question. Also, disabled individuals traditionally have had low average earnings or funds at their disposal.* The financing and reimbursement policies of the Federal Government and the States also contribute to the uncertainties of the marketplace for a firm considering the production of a technology. (this problem is covered under the option area below on financial barriers to the acquisition of technology.)

OTA finds that the key problems in the production and marketing area are the following: 1) lack of attention to production and marketing during the R&D and evaluation stages (this is covered under the option area below on research, development, and evaluation of technologies); 2) absence of adequate data on potential markets and on the needs, desires, and capabilities of people in those markets; 3) lack of organizations that could provide such data in the form needed by potential production and marketing firms; 4) greater than average risks related to entering the disability market; 5) Federal fiscal and regulatory policies that do little to reduce such risks; and 6) inadequate mechanisms for funding the purchase of devices (especially those seen as "not medically necessary").

OPTION 1A

Congress could amend current legislation to create a consistent and comprehensive set of fiscal and regulatory incentives encouraging private industry to invest in the production and marketing of disability-related technologies.

This option would require a substantial effort on the part of Congress to identify and review relevant sections of many statutes and regulations. Amending fiscal, monetary, and regulatory policy to create a consistent package of incentives will not be an easy task, nor, perhaps, one that can be accomplished without much compromise.

Nevertheless, this option recognizes the current confusing and often detrimental collection of competing incentives set up by such laws. It implicitly is based on several ideas: 1) that a great many technologies, though certainly not all, could be serving far more people than currently; 2) that some, perhaps many, technologies' development and subsequent distribution depends less on further research than on the willingness and ability of private industry to develop, produce, and market them; 3) that policies of the Government greatly affect private industry's willingness and ability to produce and market these technologies; and 4) that current legislation and regulations do not create adequate positive incentives for those firms to do so.

This option is more applicable to hard technologies such as devices than to soft technologies such as counseling methods, planning or educational techniques, or service delivery systems. Nevertheless, firms or other organizations that might potentially develop and market soft technologies should also benefit from any changes in fiscal or regulatory incentives.

Fiscal incentives are created by policies that reduce the financial uncertainties associated with risk-taking in the disability field. Their objective would be to allow private investors and firms to make more reliable estimates of potential returns on investment *and* to increase the probability of a satisfactory return on investment. The principal type of policy that creates fiscal incentives is taxation policy.

Regulatory incentives seek to accomplish the same objectives as fiscal incentives but do so through methods less directly connected to financial factors. Patent and licensing policies are ex-

---

*As indicated earlier, figures on the average earnings of disabled people may be deceptively low due to the fact that many such estimates are derived from people in assistance programs. Disabled people who are not enrolled in such programs are often not counted, and, presumably, these people have higher earnings than the estimates for the average disabled person. The perception of earnings levels of disabled people, however, are still based on such possibly deceptive average estimates and therefore may negatively affect the willingness of firms to take marketing risks.

amples of areas where regulatory incentives might be created. Another example would be changes in the penalties for noncompliance with Federal regulations regarding the hiring of disabled people or the provision of appropriate technologies to disabled people. This type of incentive would increase the demand—and therefore the potential market—for technologies, as well as more fully utilize the skills of professionals and technicians who happen to have disabilities.

A full study of the possible incentives and their potential interactions and results might be necessary before this option could be implemented. The following potential fiscal and regulatory mechanisms for creating incentives should be included in such a study:

- accelerated tax writeoff of equipment and other capital investments;
- allow individual tax deductions for devices that are not covered by insurance or other payment programs;
- expanded efforts in guaranteeing markets to potential producers of a technology (e.g., through the Veteran's Administration (VA), vocational rehabilitation programs, or education assistance programs);
- modified capital gains taxes on investments in firms designated as producers of disability-related technologies;
- extended carryover of losses for designated firms;
- tax credits against profits for designated small businesses for a specified number of years;
- other tax reduction policies for investors or firms engaging in the production or delivery of relevant technologies;
- strengthening and clarifying of rules for compliance with Federal laws concerning nondiscrimination in hiring, employment, etc., and concerning the reasonable accommodations that must be made by employers, schools, etc., to allow the participation of disabled people (this mechanism acts to increase the productivity and well-being of disabled people and to increase their ability to afford technologies, thereby increasing potential markets);
- facilitating the awarding of grants and contracts to small, profit-seeking businesses for the development and testing of relevant technologies;
- cooperation with State and local governments in providing low-interest-rate loans, direct subsidies, or guaranteed markets/purchases for small firms;
- expanded coverage under Federal health insurance and service provision programs to include those technologies which, though not viewed as strictly "medically necessary," increase the capacity of disabled persons to function more independently and productively;
- modification of the present patent system to allow small firms (which make up the majority of firms in this area) to secure patents in less time and at less expense (e.g., through Federal subsidies for patent expenses);and
- clarification and greater standardization of Federal policies in regard to the granting (to firms that might produce needed technologies) of exclusive or nonexclusive licenses to Federal patents.

In designing a package of fiscal and regulatory incentives, Congress should consider a range of factors that play an important role in the willingness and ability of organizations to produce and market technologies. Some of these factors are:

- the difficulty of obtaining venture or risk capital for the production of a technology whose future success is subject to the higher than average uncertainties of the disability-related market;
- uncertainty about patent rights for products developed with Government funds;
- uncertainty about whether the technology will be covered by insurance companies or Government programs;
- the possibility of product liability costs;
- the difficulties of "selling" the merits of a product to intermediaries (e.g., insurance companies, the VA school districts, Medicare) as well as direct users; and
- the need to spend more time and funds than the average on market analysis, prototype development and testing, and training of

consumers and others in the maintenance and use of the product.

The implementation of this option would have both benefits and costs, all of which would share some of the uncertainty inherent in this area. On the benefit side, revenues to the Federal Government might be increased as a result of the larger corporate taxes paid by firms and the increased taxes paid by disabled people who would receive technologies that allow them to lead more productive lives. Revenues would be reduced by the amounts of any tax reductions embodied in the fiscal incentive structure. Federal costs would be diminished by the reduction in funds spent on income transfer, health insurance payments, etc., due to disabled people's being able to leave Federal and State programs. A prime social benefit of changes in incentives, however, is one that would be very difficult (perhaps impossible) to put into dollar terms—i.e., the increases in well-being (psychological and economic) of the disabled people who would benefit from the distribution of helpful technologies.

OPTION 1B

Congress could legislatively charter a private organization to provide marketing and production-related services to both the private and the public sectors.*

The Federal Government, through Congress, has occasionally granted an official Federal charter to an organization when Congress has felt that such an organization would serve the public welfare. An example is the charter granted to the National Academy of Sciences. Chartering can be accomplished by an act of incorporation passed by Congress and signed by the President. A federally chartered organization, though not a Federal agency, is or may be considered a public organization for such things as compliance with civil rights legislation.

The initial funds and the operating expenses for such an organization would come from the nonpublic sector, with perhaps a small startup grant

---
*Much of the discussion under options 1B and 1C were suggested by and drawn from a paper by Tom Joe, "The Application of Technology for the Disabled: A Joint Public-Private Venture" (Center for the Study of Social Policy, University of Chicago, 1981).

from the Government. After startup, however, the organization would be expected to operate on its own revenues. For purposes of taxation, it would be considered a nonprofit organization. An organization of this type would be eligible to receive funds from any source, including Government agencies, philanthropic foundations, voluntary agencies, industry, estates, and gifts or donations.

The goal of the organization would be to provide technical assistance, analysis, and other services related to the production, marketing, and diffusion of disability-related technologies. In return for fees, it could perform marketing surveys and help put together market strategies for private firms who are considering entering a new product on the market. It could serve as a liaison between firms or Government agencies and ultimate consumers. It could develop and manage demographic and product data sets.

The success of this type of organization might depend on three items: the quality and reputation of its staff, its ability to deliver helpful services, and its ability to cope with what might be a large demand for its services while it is still young and growing. One of the goals of a Federal charter, in fact, would be to give the organization the prestige to attract qualified staff members. The organization would be eligible to receive Federal and other governmental grants and contracts. The National Institute of Handicapped Research (NIHR), its rehabilitation engineering centers, the Rehabilitation Services Administration (RSA), VA, NASA, the National Science Foundation, the National Institutes of Health (NIH), and other agencies should be encouraged to use the organization *as appropriate.* An organization of this type must be very careful to represent itself as being able to deliver only those services that it can (which will change as the organization grows and builds expertise and data) and only within the time frame that it can handle.

The proposed organization might be able to do technology evaluations, either directly or by managing evaluation projects that others are actually carrying out. However, this function should be added to the list of the organization's activities only if it can be clearly and cleanly separated from the functions of assisting the marketing of products. Conflicts of interest could prove very harmful to the organization and its goals.

One potential advantage of the proposed organization is that it is designed to carry out an important and currently inadequately performed function; another is that it is located in the nonpublic sector. Potential disadvantages lie in the possibility of conflict of interest and in the nature of the tasks assigned to the organization. In order to consistently attract private and public funds, the organization would have to deliver valuable but extremely difficult services.

One crucial point is that the proposed organization should have broad representation of many different groups and constituencies. Consumers and marketing and production experts would be essential. Demographers, taxation and fiscal experts, the general public, analytical experts, technologists and researchers would also be very important to the organization's success.

Canada has an organization similar to the one of this option. Technical Aids and Systems for the Handicapped, Inc. (TASH) was established as a nonprofit corporation by the Canadian National Research Council and the Canadian Rehabilitation Council for the Disabled. It provides marketing, supply, and maintenance services, especially for devices that are not widely available. The experience of TASH should be examined closely before any decision about establishing a similar domestic organization is made.

OPTION 1C

Congress could establish a joint public-private corporation to provide marketing and production-related services to both the private and the public sectors.

This option has goals similar to those of the previous option and seeks to accomplish them through somewhat similar means. The principal difference between the two options is the legal authority under which the proposed organization would operate. The organization proposed in the previous option would be considered a private corporation for most purposes; that proposed in this option would be as quasi-governmental entity. the entity could be a nonprofit corporation existing to serve the public good by acting much as a private sector organization. Analogous organizations are the Overseas Private Investment Corporation, the Tennessee Valley Authority, and the Federal National Mortgage Association.

An example of a similar organization is the Communications Satellite Corp. (COMSAT). COMSAT is a private firm, owned by its shareholders, with a board of directors who are not officials of the Government. It is not a public corporation, nor has it been granted a Federal charter of incorporation. Three of COMSAT's directors, however, are nominated by the President and confirmed by the Senate. Even though COMSAT is a wholly private organization, it is considered to be performing a service that is in the best interests of the public and has therefore been given special status (e.g., it is by Federal statute designated the organization that represents the United States in the International Telecommunication Satellite Organization). COMSAT, therefore, illustrates another possible method of aiding the establishment of an organization to provide needed services.

The goal of setting up a public-private corporation such as that proposed in this option is to support the performance of services deemed to be in the broad public interest through the use of primarily private funding and private sector managerial techniques. One possible and potentially very important element of such a corporation's mandate could be the inclusion of a formal requirement that the corporation subcontract with consumer groups or a single consumer organization for the testing and evaluation of technologies. The consumer groups could be chosen competitively, on the basis of criteria established by, for example, the board of directors of the corporation. The corporation need not be limited to consumer groups for its subcontracting, but such groups should play a significant role in its operations. As in the previous option, the corporation should only be allowed to perform evaluation services where no conflicts of interest exist.

Because of the possibility of conflicts of interest, Congress may wish to establish two separate public-private corporations (or two separate chartered organizations) to perform the two functions of providing marketing and production-related services, and evaluating technologies and disseminating the results. If so, it would be desirable to have some mechanism to coordinate the activities of the two organizations (e.g., a joint board of directors). It might also be desirable for the two to share a data system, both to ensure compatibility and standardization of information and to avoid much potential duplication.

OPTION 1D

Congress could mandate the collection of market-related demographic data by an interagency group led by the Bureau of the Census.

This option would be an attempt to reduce some of the uncertainty that accompanies decisions to develop or market products to be used by disabled people. It would also be useful to the public sector, because the data generated might be very helpful in the setting of research priorities and the allocation of funds for the applied engineering and diffusion stages of technology's lifecycle.

Current activities of Federal agencies are primarily oriented to the collection of data by etiological categories of impairments (and sometimes by disabilities). Less frequently do agencies collect data concerning limitations on functional abilities. The information that might be gathered from individualized plans (see ch. 3) is not seen as a source of raw material for the development of marketing-related data bases. Especially absent in data collection efforts are data on handicaps—i.e., disabilities turned into handicaps by an interaction of the disability and the physical and social environments. If data were available on the demographics (e.g., age, income, sex, other characteristics) of populations divided by types of functional limitations, the task of projecting the needed characteristics of technologies and the potential market for them would be made somewhat, perhaps considerably, easier. Such an outcome might be beneficial not only to the economic health of the private sector, but also to the public sector and the Nation as a whole.

Chapters 2, 3, and 11 discuss the issue of data based on functional limitations in more detail.

One important point in regard to the collection of such data by the Bureau of the Census is that the design and testing of the surveys should be done with the substantial advice of disabled people, Government program administrators (especially of R&D activities), other data collection agencies and experts (e.g., the National Center for Health Statistics (NCHS)), and industry representatives. Alternatively, an agency with more experience in the disability field, such as NIHR, might coordinate the data collection and analysis efforts with the assistance of the Bureau of the Census and NCHS. The key point here is that one agency should have the responsibility for national data on disabilities in order to achieve uniformity of definitions and measurements, but that agency must draw on the pertinent technical resources of other agencies. Although it might be possible for a private organization to perform these functions, an advantage of using a Federal agency is the ability of the Government to access the medical and other records from which many of the data would come.

The Federal Government recently conducted a substantial planning effort for a very similar data collection activity. An interagency committee (including, NCHS, the Bureau of the Census, and NIHR) was established and pretested a survey instrument for the Census Disability Survey. That survey, using 100,000 disabled people and designed to collect information on functional abilities and disabilities, was to be a follow-on to the 1980 census. If the survey had been funded, and if it had been successful, it would have provided a substantial portion of the information needed by Government agencies, industry, and other groups. Lack of funds was cited as the reason for the project's not taking place.

The costs of option 1D would vary considerably, depending on how extensively the current survey techniques and activities of the Bureau of the Census would have to be modified or expanded. It might be possible to create a mechanism whereby the private sector, including industry, advocacy groups, and foundations, could contribute funds to the effort. Another dimension along which costs would vary is the extent to which new data are collected as opposed to old data analyzed to provide new answers. A recent study of national sources of data by the Bureau of Social Science Research (BSSR) concluded that the current sources in regard to disability data do not lend themselves to making national estimates. According to BSSR, the data from these sources exhibit numerous inconsistencies. However, because of the cost of designing and implementing new surveys, a second best alternative to gathering new data might be to establish an adequately funded effort to reevaluate existing data to get more accurate and more useful information. This alternative might be a fiscally easier first step.

A critical aspect of the success of this option would be the effectiveness of the dissemination of the generated data. Methods would have to be developed to allow all relevant parties to easily learn what would be available and how to gain access to it.

INVOLVEMENT OF DISABLED PEOPLE AND OTHER CONSUMERS

ISSUE 2

> How can policies and programs be designed to encourage or assure the effective involvement of disabled people and other consumers in the development and delivery of technologies? In addition to providing information, consumers should themselves be part of advisory and policymaking bodies to the maximum extent feasible.

In theory, assuring maximum effectiveness, efficiency, and relevance in the development and application of technologies requires the extensive involvement of those who will use the technologies—the consumers. In practice, however, there is fairly little involvement.

There is no "correct" amount of consumer involvement, and there is no easy way to achieve *effective* involvement. OTA found the area of consumer involvement to be one filled with much irony. Consumer involvement is one of the most talked about aspects of the disability-related policy area—and everyone seems to believe in the concept—but few satisfactory schemes to improve the situation were suggested to OTA and few people or agencies appear to be taking aggressive steps to put the concept into practice.

OTA found a number of reasons for inadequate consumer involvement. One major reason is attitude. Although it is possible that, as a group, people working in the disability area are less prejudiced against disabled people than are other people, it appears that prejudice still plays a significant role in the willingness and desire of people in this area to interact with disabled people.

Another major reason is simply a bureaucratic one. Program administrators or service delivery individuals naturally seek to simplify their functions; adding another source of review, oversight, or advice is not usually compatible with the bureaucratic outlook.

A third reason for lack of involvement is the outlook of disabled people and handicapped people themselves. Despite dramatic changes in their view of themselves and their abilities, many people still are reluctant to consult to, or get involved in the administration of, programs addressing disabilities. When people do not see themselves as having something to contribute, they are less likely to be asked to do so.

A fourth reason is the difficulty of identifying "consumers." Should a program seek any disabled person? A "representative" person? A representative from a consumer organization? From a coalition of organizations? How handicapped or disabled does the person have to be? One irony in this area is that the more articulate and mobile a disabled person is, the less *handicapped* (as defined in ch. 2) he or she likely is. Some people with disabilities may not be "handicapped," since they can perform life's functions substantially as well as a "nonhandicapped" person. Does this make them less representative? Not necessarily, but it makes the selection of consumers more difficult. Furthermore, consumers can include parents of disabled children, physicians and other providers, bus riders (both disabled and nondisabled), etc. Do parents always represent the needs and desires of their children and others' children?

Another, very critical, reason for the inadequacy of consumer involvement is a lack of knowledge about how to design the advisory mechanisms that consumers would fit into in order to ensure effective involvement. In equal opportunity programs, in urban renewal, in education, and in many other policy areas, the country has sought to use consumer (affected party) involvement. Many of these efforts have been less than successful. That does not mean that they accomplished nothing, merely that they did not come close to meeting expectations or their potential contribution to policy formulation or implementation.

The tactical goal of consumer involvement is *realism.* Consumers and the groups or organizations they interact with should gain a more realistic appreciation of the others' needs and capabilities. Designing a subway system that will handicap many disabled people is perhaps worse than designing a system with a plan for handling disabled people in a particular way, without the initial and continuing involvement of disabled people. Even so, the latter approach may not be the most effective or efficient way to make the system accessible and may also generate a priori resistance on the part of disabled people. Early, extensive involvement of potential disabled riders in planning for a new system might inject an element of realism: Subway designers and financers, may gain a more realistic idea of the needs, desires, and capabilities of disabled people and be made aware of alternatives to their plan; *and* disabled people may gain a more realistic idea of

Photo credit: Association of Handicapped Artists

Confined to a wheelchair by cerebral palsy, Neita May Kimmel of Catawissa, Pa., has appeared before high school, college, church, and club audiences to show and tell of her work and that of the Association of Handicapped Artists. She has written a book, "Reaching for the Stars," in collaboration with Dr. Raymond Treon

the design and financial constraints operating on the subway builders, thus allowing them to suggest possible alternatives within the constraints.

OTA found that R&D of technologies often proceeds with little input from potential users. When involvement is sought, it may be perfunctory. The everyday, realistic needs of users very often do not find expression in the funding of R&D by the Federal Government. Nor are consumers represented very often on the groups that perform evaluations of technologies. (These shortcomings are addressed under the option area below on the research, development, and evaluation of technologies.

Consumer involvement is critical at each stage in the lifecycle of technologies. If Federal programs change their orientation from one of concern with simply the *needs* of consumers to concern with a mix of *needs, desires, and capabilities* (see ch. 2), the lack of consumer involvement will become even more critical. Besides R&D and evaluation activities, marketing, delivery, and financing programs need information that can best be provided by those directly affected.

The options provided below for the issue area of consumer involvement are organized by the degree of formality involved. This does not mean that they are necessarily mutually exclusive. More formal action may be desired in one area of policy (e.g., research project review, or consumer review of technologies for coverage under Medicare) and less formal actions in others (e.g., oversight hearings on compliance with individual education program (IEP) preparation and use).

OPTION 2A

Congress could mandate formal consumer involvement in any or all Federal programs or federally funded programs related to the development and use of disability-related technologies.

As mentioned above and in other parts of this report, Congress has already mandated consumer ("handicapped persons") involvement through several Federal laws. The National Council on the Handicapped, for example, must have consumer representation, and the individualized educational program, individualized written rehabilitation program, and individual habilitation plan processes are designed to involve disabled people or their parents or other representatives in decisions about education or rehabilitation.

Under this option, Congress could expand the formal, statutorily based, requirements for the participation of disabled people in the policy development and implementation processes. Numerous agencies, including the Department of Health and Human Services (DHHS), the Department of Education, VA, the Department of Labor, and the Small Business Administration, could be required both to involve disabled people directly and to support consumer activities.

Direct involvement of consumers could be mandated in the process of R&D. (Option 3A also attempts to accomplish this.) Consumers would provide valuable advice to the process of setting research priorities, evaluating grant and contract proposals, and evaluating reports of progress on existing grants and contracts. The process of peer review would thus be expanded to include a more realistic appreciation of research needs and the usefulness of results.

Agencies that finance the use of technologies or that directly provide technologies to people with impairments and disabilities (e.g., VA) could set up panels, composed wholly or partially of consumers, to review technologies that might be included in reimbursement schedules or purchase lists. Alternatively, the Health Care Financing Administration (HCFA), NIHR, and VA could jointly fund a private nonprofit organization of consumers to review proposed technologies.

In general, this option could involve a program-by-program review to determine which programs could use the various mechanisms for establishing or expanding consumer involvement. As discussed above, *effective* consumer involvement is difficult to achieve. Thus, consideration should be given wherever possible to the use of flexible mechanisms—e.g., combinations of advisory panels, staff hiring, and contracts with consumer groups.

OPTION 2B

Congress could mandate an office of consumer involvement to monitor and provide assistance to other offices dealing with technologies, and Congress could encourage all relevant agencies to expand consumer involvement.

Instead of legislatively mandating consumer involvement in specific instances, Congress could clearly encourage various agencies to expand their consumer involvement activities. This option provides the advantage of flexibility—flexibility to change as conditions change over time and as data on the performance of involvement methods become available. Congress could encourage specific actions through oversight hearings, committee reports, and other means.

The obvious disadvantage of this option relative to the previous one is the difficulty of gaining voluntary compliance by the agencies. That disadvantage is part of the rationale behind the creation of an office of consumer involvement to coordinate, monitor, and provide technical assistance regarding the involvement of disabled people. The legislative record, including hearings, committee reports, and the law itself, would serve as mechanisms for signaling the intent of Congress to encourage involvement. Further, the office could be required to submit annually to Congress a report on all relevant executive branch activities.

Another reason for the creation of an office of consumer involvement coordination and technical assistance is the desirability of *effective* consumer involvement. Achieving effective participation will not be easy; thus, providing agencies with an office that possesses expertise and experience in techniques to encourage such participation could be very helpful. It would be a small office with a modest funding level.

The proposed office, perhaps with the assistance of an interagency advisory or coordinating committee, could monitor all consumer involvement activities, keep standardized records of these activities and any evaluations of their outcomes, maintain lists of consumer organizations and individuals who may be called upon, advise agencies on methods of increasing consumer activities, evaluate agency activities, and report on its own and other agencies' activities to Congress, the President, the National Council on the Handicapped, and any other designated groups.

The office could also be responsible for testing the feasibility of, and perhaps eventually implementing, a management information system based on data from individualized plans (as described in ch. 3) in order to evaluate and support involvement of consumers and consumer-generated information.

OPTION 2C

Congress could encourage agencies to increase consumer involvement activities.

If Congress wishes to signal a concern about the inadequate amount and quality of consumer involvement activities, it could do so through mechanisms less formal than legislation. These mechanisms include, as noted above, oversight hearings and records of hearings, and language in committee reports accompanying related legislation. Such informal, though official, encouragement has some potential to effect change. However, in view of tight agency budgets, bureaucratic inertia, and the difficulties inherent in attempts to achieve fully useful consumer participation, it is likely that this option possesses substantial disadvantages.

RESEARCH, DEVELOPMENT, AND EVALUATION OF TECHNOLOGIES

ISSUE 3

How can R&D activities be organized and funded to produce knowledge, techniques, or devices that serve the needs of disabled people and relevant providers in accordance with the magnitude of various problem areas and opportunities? How can evaluation of present and emerging technologies be organized to provide consumers, providers, and policymakers with adequate information?

R&D activities and related evaluations must be adequately funded, their potential contribution to the ultimate goals of technology application must be recognized, and their organization be such that it support the attainment of those goals. In the area of disability-related technology, however, as discussed in chapters 6, 7, and 10, these needs for R&D and evaluation activities fall short of being realized.

Excluding the general health research of NIH, the amount of Federal funds spent on R&D related to disabilities is approximately $66 million. (This figure includes education and vocational-related R&D, but not R&D in areas such as transportation or housing; even if these other areas were included, it is unlikely that the figure would be substantially increased.) In contrast, transfer payments alone to disabled people from Government programs total $36 billion. Thus, *R&D expenditures represent about one-fifth of 1 percent of the transfer payments. If the other public and private sector expenditures for services to disabled individuals were added to the transfer payments, the R&D budget would be an even smaller percentage.* These comparisons are not meant to suggest that there is any way to identify a "correct" amount to spend on disability- or handicap-related R&D. (Total Federal health R&D is about 2 percent of total national personal health care expenditures—a figure that, at a minimum, is 10 times greater than that for disability R&D.)

Similarly, the level of evaluation activities is extremely low. No figures for the total effort in evaluation of disability-related technologies are available. However, it is clear that relatively little formal clinical or life-use testing takes place (see ch. 7). The reality of competition for funds certainly affects the levels of both R&D and evaluation activities. For evaluation, though, a perhaps equal factor is the lack of recognition given to the potential contribution of evaluation to decisions about the appropriate application of technologies.

The organization and directions of R&D and evaluation also contribute to the inadequate number of useful technologies from these activities. The peer review systems in effect at the start of the OTA study were not well organized (see ch. 6), although that situation appears to be changing. *Inadequate attention is paid to what will happen to the results of R&D once development is completed. The constraints and demands of marketing, production, and consumer acceptance and preferences continue to play a relatively small part in the R&D process, though that situation also seems to be changing—slowly.*

Methods of evaluation and analysis remain underdeveloped. Recent work of NIHR and RSA seems to be moving in promising directions, but such work may not be a priority item for those agencies. Cost-benefit and cost-effectiveness techniques and modified forms of comprehensive technology assessment show potential in this area, but these methods are not being investigated thoroughly.

Complex, expensive technologies continue to recieve a large share of NIHR's and other agencies' R&D funding. Complex, expensive technologies are not inherently more or less appropriate to concentrate on than simpler, inexpensive ones. R&D and evaluation funding should be apportioned among different technologies according to their potential for appropriate applications to the needs of consumers; such funding should not be apportioned on the basis of investigator interest or how fascinating or futuristic a technology may appear. The R&D process should be organized according to the needs it is designed to satisfy. More attention could be given to the apportioning of R&D funds by the potential payoff of various efforts in various technological areas. Some areas need more basic research, others need development funds, and others have technologies that need diffusion assistance. In short, attention should be divided according to the state of maturity—"readiness"—of the technologies and the nature of the population in need. NIHR and other agencies already have the authority to take many of the needed actions; they do not have to wait for legislative change. Agencies could, for example, allocate increased funds for low- or middle-technology fairs and contests. (Such fairs or contests should not become ends in themselves, but should be followed by publicity and publications summarizing the ideas generated.) Also, agencies could devote resources and attention to development and testing of methods of evaluation.

OPTION 3A

Congress could mandate that consumers and production and marketing experts be represented on R&D panels and evaluation panels.

This option explicitly recognizes that considerable involvement of the people and organizations who will play a major role in the subsequent usefulness and diffusion of technologies should take place early in the processes of R&D and evaluation. The objective of this option is the improvement of systems for conceiving new technologies, adapting existing ones to new applications, allocating R&D funds, and evaluating the results of current or past R&D. Congress has already indicated its desire that consumers and other groups be represented on the National Council on the Handicapped. The council is involved in setting or recommending directions and policy for NIHR. This body, however, cannot play a role in each R&D allocation decision; nor can it serve as the only source of consumer, production, and marketing input to the entire R&D and evaluation process. Further, its influence is far less extensive in agencies other than NIHR.

Implementing this option would require extensive thought on the most effective ways of avoiding tokenism and conflict-of-interest situations for private industry. Effective consumer involvement has often been a goal of many public policy areas, yet that goal is difficult to achieve. Questions have been raised, for example, about the effectiveness of consumer representation on the Food and Drug Administration's medical device classification panels. However, the addition of consumer, production, and marketing experts to disability-related R&D peer review and other groups may be somewhat more effective. Many aspects of the R&D process for technologies that will be used by disabled people are amenable to experienced consumer input. Consumers might inject a degree of realism to the setting of R&D goals and priorities; evaluation criteria might be set to more closely resemble the list of factors that lead to a technology's successful application. A consumer does not have to be a mechanical engineer to know that wheelchairs must fit through doors.

Production and marketing experts could help the R&D process in several ways. For example, the simple presence of such people on panels could remind researchers and policymakers that the end result of R&D is supposed to be (in most cases) useful and cost-effective techniques and devices. Also, their experience and expertise would allow them to make suggestions concerning the evaluations that are necessary and the technological characteristics (reliability, cost to produce, ease of repairs, potential demand, flexibility) that should be sought. Such experts might help in the process of considering potential technologies, whether complex or simple, in relation to their eventual application and distribution.

Theoretically, no congressional actions are necessary for the adoption of this option. The executive branch agencies could implement it by themselves. If Congress finds that it is a desirable option, however, and agencies do not implement it on their own, Congress could amend relevant laws to mandate that R&D-related peer review and other advisory groups have such representation.

OPTION 3B

Congress could mandate demonstration projects for the awarding of "production stage" grants or contracts early in the R&D process.

The objective of this option is similar to that of the previous one. The ultimate goal of most R&D efforts is the development of technologies or techniques that will be effective *and* will be distributed—i.e., successfully reach their market. Small grants or contracts to nonprofit or profit-seeking organizations to analyze the potential market and to develop plans for the efficient production and diffusion of specific technologies *may* help. This option is oriented to only a demonstration effort because of the many questions that exist concerning the effectiveness of such a mechanism. Enough potential exists for the idea to be given consideration by Congress, however, and, if Congress believes it is warranted, for the idea's trial through pilot projects.

Congress could specify, either in renewal legislation or in appropriations language, its desire that NIHR (and perhaps NASA and VA) develop such a demonstration program.

One method of implementing the demonstration would be to select through a competitive process a firm that is interested in the marketing rights, for a specified time or area, for a particular technology. That firm would use the contract funds to examine the most efficient ways to produce the technology under development. It could suggest changes in the technology or the populations for which the technology is being designed. It could aid in any evaluations of the technology. Essentially, this option is designed to set up a strong positive incentive for organizations to produce and market technologies.

The grants or contracts should not be so large that organizations would seek them without a real desire to eventually market the technology. The funds should be set at an amount that covers part or most of the cost of the activities in conjunction with the R&D process, as listed above. The hope for this option is that it will reduce the risk and the cost of deciding to market the technology, thus allowing a more intensive look at the appropriate potential applications of that technology.

OPTION 3C

Congress could appropriate specific increased funds for evaluation of technologies.

This option follows from the discussion of the relatively low level of funds and activities currently existing in the disability area. Although current economic realities naturally affect the viability of this option, it is important to remember that the current level of funding for evaluation is extremely low and that the number of technologies in need of clinical and other forms of evaluation is increasing constantly (see ch. 7). Especially pertinent is the probability of an acceleration of the number of technologies being developed. Many observers speak of the "explosion" in technologies for disabilities. Although the term "explosion" is a dramatic one, it is clear that advances in solid-state electronics, other communications developments, new alloys, and medical advances are producing numerous new technologies. Some of these may produce dramatic effects, others may turn out to be useless, but most will produce benefit under certain conditions—i.e., when applied appropriately in relation to their costs and risks. An increased amount of funds will be needed to adequately assess these new technologies as well as existing ones. The money, attention, and personnel will have to come from existing resources, which are already scarce in the disability-related R&D area, or from new funds specifically indicated for evaluation. Further, in the absence of increased funding—from whatever source—of evaluation, it is likely that program funds will not be spent in as efficient a manner as might be possible.

One drawback to this option is the immaturity of analytical techniques for comparing costs, risks, benefits, and social implications of disability-related technologies. The direct health-related benefits and risks can be estimated through relatively sophisticated techniques (using controls and statistical methods), but other effects are less amenable to current methods of evaluation. Thus, selection and implementation of this option may require that some initial attention and resources be devoted to the development of methods of analysis. Additionally, if this option is adopted, the very fact that increased funding, and therefore researcher attention, will be devoted to the area may mean that more work will be done on methods.

OPTION 3D

Congress could conduct oversight hearings with the Department of Education to determine why the dissemination of information on technologies remains inadequate.

OTA finds that the amount, usefulness, and accessibility of information on the characteristics, availability, and performance of technologies are not meeting the needs of users or potential users. Interviews with researchers, administrators, and consumers and with disabled people and nondisabled people; a review of the literature; and the results of OTA's public outreach survey all reveal that dissemination of information is inadequate.

There are many partial explanations of the inadequate state of information flow that exists. One, for example, is that the National Rehabilitation Information Center (NARIC) is relatively new, and its ABLEDATA system is even newer. Also, these activities have not had significant amounts of funds appropriated. Thus, while ABLEDATA appears to be a potentially model system for disseminating information on assistive devices, the number of devices about which information has been entered into the ABLEDATA system and the amount of data on each such device are still quite limited because of the small size of the staff. Another reason is the generally low level of information that exists. It is difficult to disseminate what is not available or is of poor quality, low relevance, or nonstandardized. This is one reason that option 3C would assist in improving the performance of information dissemination activities, particularly for evaluation information.

Furthermore, experts in the field disagree on the best way to approach the collection and dissemination of data on disabilities and technologies. Some people believe that a large, centralized data system for the collection of masses of data is not the most effective or efficient method. However, others believe that such a single standardized system is necessary. The evidence available to OTA indicates that one system is not the answer, given the nature of disabilities and the disability field. There is a wide variety of parties who have a number of differing information needs. Disabled people themselves represent one of the largest groups of potential users of information. Yet the data needs of disabled people are as varied as the disabilities, desires, and capabilities they possess. Still, questions remain about the alternatives to a single system.

Before any specific legislative actions are taken, a number of questions could be addressed in oversight hearings. Such hearings could be designed to bring out more clearly the reasons for the current situation and the administrative reactions to that situation. Examples of questions that could be explored in oversight are the following: Why have agencies, especially in the Department of

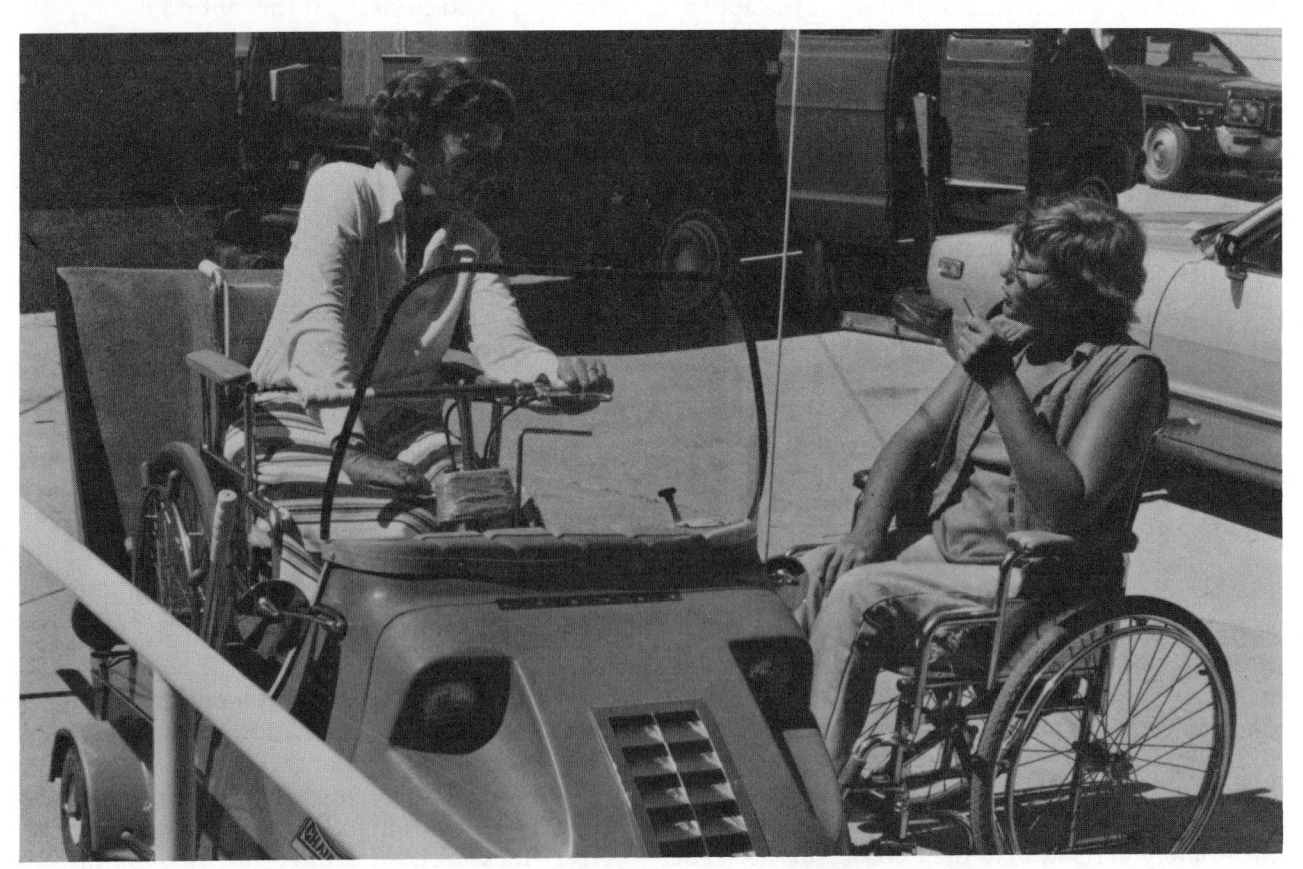

Photo credit: Barry Corbet. Courtesy of North American Reinsurance Corp.

Imogene Dickey of Buffalo, Wyo., uses a wheelchair for mobility. She and the chair ride on a Chair-E-Yacht or, for longer distances, a ramp-equipped van

Education, oriented their dissemination activities to professional research institutions and similar clients? What is being done to establish the criteria for the design of a system to make information available to disabled people directly? What effects might be expected from an increase in the funding levels for NARIC and, especially, ABLEDATA? Why has little effort gone into the standardization of evaluation and performance data on technologies? How will disabled persons not enrolled in public programs have access to information on technologies? Do agencies plan to expand their evaluation activities in regard to the performance of any existing systems for disseminating information, including NARIC (and specifically ABLEDATA) and any non-Federal systems?

Oversight questions could also address the factors cited above that make dissemination difficult and explore what the agencies are doing to minimize the difficulties, or to compound them.

Depending on the results of any oversight hearings, Congress may then decide to take substantive legislative action or to encourage specific actions by the agencies.

FINANCIAL BARRIERS TO THE USE OF TECHNOLOGY

ISSUE 4

How can financial barriers to the acquisition of technologies by disabled people be reduced, within reasonable constraints? Can the levels and distribution of available funding be made more appropriate in relation to the level of the problems addressed?

Imperfections in the structure of delivery systems need to be minimized. Inadequate and sometimes illogical criteria for reimbursement or payment for technologies should be reviewed and where appropriate changed.

Despite eligibility for the public and nonpublic programs that may pay for technologies to assist them to function more independently and productively, *a number of disabled people are denied funding for particular technologies that are clearly appropriate.* As discussed in chapter 9, a primary reason for the denial of funding—especially under Medicare and Medicaid, but also under other programs—is that the technologies in question are not strictly "medical" in nature and are therefore not considered "necessary." A connection needs to be made in these programs between paying for these technologies and the potential independence or productivity of disabled people. Another finding is that when device technologies *are* funded, services necessary to their proper use (e.g., fitting, training in correct usage, and maintenance) are often not included in the funding. Furthermore, OTA finds that decisions to fund certain technologies are sometimes based on the criterion of low initial, short-term cost. Use of such a criterion may fail to identify instances when a greater initial investment might result in decreased long-term costs and greater functional ability for the individuals involved.

While most indigent disabled persons are eventually able to receive *some* assistance towards meeting their needs, OTA finds that *acquisition of technologies in the period immediately following the onset of their impairment presents particular financial hardships.* Those individuals who must leave their employment because of their disability often lose the insurance coverage that would have funded the technologies. Eligibility for a Federal program may be established, but benefits are provided only after a number of months have elapsed. Earlier intervention through funded technology would often serve to reduce or ameliorate disabilities during the early stages and thus lessen the long-term disability.

OTA finds that disabled people with enough resources to prevent their participation in programs that pay for technologies also face serious financial barriers to technology acquisition. *There are few available methods for financing the capital outlays that are often necessary, and those few that exist are available only in selected parts of the country.* Additionally, there is a need to expand the use of innovative ways to eliminate financial barriers to the use of technologies. One such method that shows promise is pooling of devices by schools, voluntary health or disability organizations, hospitals, or similar organizations. This approach should be taken only with great care, however, since pooling of obsolete or simply "left over" technologies from other users could lead to inappropriate matches between the new user's needs and the available pooled technologies.

OPTION 4A

Congress could establish a loan guarantee program with low interest financing (on an income-related sliding scale) to assist disabled people in device purchases.

This option would reduce or eliminate financial barriers to acquiring devices for individuals who have the capability to generate the funds to pay for the devices but who do not have the recources for the initial capital outlay. Either the amount of money available for the loan or its interest rate, or both, would vary according to the financial need of the individual beneficiaries. The rationale for such a program is straightforward—the loans would assist in the purchases of devices which, in turn, would assist the individuals directly or indirectly to function independently, work, and pay back the loan.

Pursuit of this option would likely involve a minimum of Federal dollars. The program could be State-administered, as is the program of federally guaranteed student loans for higher education. Adding this new program to a similar one for administrative purposes would minimize the funds spent on administration. The interest subsidies could be provided either by the Federal Government directly or by the lending institutions with tax incentives to do so. The actual Federal funds necessary for coverage of defaulted loans could be kept at a minimum as long as the beneficiaries of the program are selected to fulfill criteria that would increase the likelihood of their ability to repay the loans.

A significant implication of this option is the public-private partnership likely to occur if it were implemented. Such a partnership might be an important advantage in an era of pressures to constrain expenditures of public dollars.

OPTION 4B

Congress could conduct oversight hearings on ways to change criteria for reimbursement under the Federal health insurance programs with respect to technologies for disabled people.

This option is developed from OTA's finding that disabled people eligible for coverage under one of the Federal health insurance programs are often denied payment for technologies that are not considered strictly medical in nature, although the technologies would improve the ability of the individuals involved to lead more independent, productive lives. The current patterns of reimbursement exist largely because of the history of these programs as assistance for acute medical problems rather than for the chronic problems faced by disabled people. The legislation for the programs does not expressly prohibit payment for "nonmedical" technologies such as communication, education, and rehabilitative aids. Instead, the denials usually occur at the State or regional level through regulation.

A significant effect of the current "system" is that in the short term, funds may be saved, while in the long term, a greater amount of total funds is expended in, for example, income maintenance payments or institutionalization expenses. In addition to the cost-related effects, there are psychological effects on the individuals involved—the current system provides incentives for the dependence of disabled people on public programs. Changes enacted should provide incentives for independence.

Hearings on methods to change reimbursement criteria to foster independence and productivity would focus attention on the need to consider the implications of policies in one area on other related areas. Such hearings, if pursued, could include testimony by consumers and providers of disability-related nonmedical technologies as well as by representatives of HCFA, the State Medicaid offices, and the contractors. Theoretically, the hearings should provide alternative criteria for expanded reimbursement and suggested regulatory changes to accomplish that objective which HCFA and the States could then adopt. Congress could then hold oversight hearings at a later date to determine the effects of any adopted changes. However, it is possible that legislative action may be required to assure expanded reimbursement. In that case, the actual law should include safeguards against abuse of the expanded opportunities for reimbursement. One method would be to detail the criteria for payment in the law directly.

Finally, OTA finds that reimbursement for an expanded variety of technologies should not be pursued without accompanying reimbursement for the services of those who select the technologies, those who fit them, and those who train the users in their proper use. A portion of the oversight hearings could address various criteria for assuring that these essential related services will be provided.

OPTION 4C

Congress could conduct oversight hearings on methods to improve health insurance coverage for persons leaving employment as a result of disability.

The objective of this option is to reduce the financial barriers to the acquisition of technologies during the period immediately following termination from employment due to disability. The option stems from OTA's finding that the systems for assistance are least able to assist disabled people during that time, although some form of early assistance may prevent or reduce assistance at a later time. Most people who leave employment lose health and medical insurance coverage formerly provided by their employers. Even if they are eligible for public or private disability income maintenance payments, they often do not have the funds to purchase private individual coverage. Since health and medical insurance programs are a primary source of funding for technologies for disabled people, Congress could investigate ways to close these gaps and examine the resultant benefits and costs to society of any administrative or legislative action implemented.

One method that might be covered in oversight hearings is the provision of Medicare coverage during the 29-month period that individuals must wait for Federal disability insurance. This method should be used only for those people who do not have private insurance or other financial resources readily available to them. Criteria for providing Medicare coverage (e.g., a likelihood of having the severity of the disability reduced as a result of early medical intervention), or methods for measuring fulfillment of the criteria could be topics for testimony. Another method that might be covered is the provision of incentives to employers to provide health and medical insurance coverage to their terminated employees for 12 to 29 months following termination for disability-related reasons.

It is likely that legislative action will be necessary to implement any of the methods presented. Such action could range from changes in the Social Security Act to minor changes in tax deductions. The amount of Federal dollars will vary according to the source of the coverage (Federal or private), the amount of coverage extended, and the number of new beneficiaries. A potential drawback to this option is that it is not designed to improve coverage for those disabled from birth or those disabled later in life who are not working at the time of disability onset. Furthermore, unless changes in the criteria for reimbursement under the Federal health insurance programs are pursued as discussed in the previous option, there is likely to be an inefficient expenditure of dollars under any program arising from these hearings as long as appropriate technologies are not covered.

PERSONNEL ISSUES

ISSUE 5

How can Federal policies assure an adequate number of well-trained personnel at all stages of the development and use of technologies? Systems for R&D as well as delivery of services should provide incentives for the cost-effective use of these personnel.

Although the actual number of professionals (disabled and nondisabled) working to develop and apply technologies to disabled people has increased dramatically over the last 40 years, there remains a shortage in a number of key areas. First, there are too few rehabilitation researchers and rehabilitation engineers. Although difficult to quantify, this shortage can be described by the primary reasons behind it. One, as discussed in chapters 6 and 10, is the relatively low level of funds spent on disability-related research in relation to the amount spent on general health-related research. Another reason, as discussed in chapter 9, is a lack of reimbursement for the skills of these professionals, particularly rehabilitation engineers. Together these reasons result in an unfavorable job market that may discourage prospective students from entering those fields. Second, there are too few allied health professionals, including physical therapists, occupational therapists, orthotic and prosthetic technologists, speech therapists, vocational educators, and rehabilitation counselors. As in the case of rehabilitation engineers, the size of the shortage is difficult to quantify, primarily because demand figures for these professionals usually include the needs of nondisabled clients as well as disabled persons. It is clear, though, that legislation such as the Education for All Handicapped Children Act, as amended, has served to increase the demand for allied health professionals. Furthermore, there is a shortage in these areas of professionals who are disabled themselves.

Finally, there is a shortage of rehabilitation physician specialists, although the specialty has been in existence since 1948. Under the current reimbursement system, this shortage is often a key one, because it is often the physician who must prescribe a technology for it to be funded. OTA explored the reasons behind this shortage and found them to include a perception of the specialty as one with low status, a relative lack of control over the client's treatment due to the wide range of other professionals whose opinions must be considered, a lack of professional orientation towards the treatment of stable or deteriorating conditions, and a lack of training in the undergraduate medical education on the management of chronic disability.

Another key finding with respect to personnel is that *those providers who are permitted by the structure of the delivery and funding systems to select or prescribe technologies for disabled users may not be the most appropriate ones to do so.* Traditionally, physicians have prescribed most of the device technologies, partly because disabled people often receive their first services through the medical system and partly because the major third-party payers will pay only for items that carry a physician's prescription. For certain technologies, physicians are the most appropriate providers to make the best selection for their clients. However, for other technologies, particularly those that are not medical in nature, other providers are equally or better qualified to make the best selection. Yet if these other providers, including rehabilitation engineers, occupational therapists, and special education teachers, as well as users themselves, cannot obtain funding, their skills may not be fully utilized, and the overall costs to society may be greater. Changes in physician curricula as well as in reimbursement policies might alleviate this problem.

OPTION 5A

Congress could appropriate funds for the training of increased numbers of disability-related personnel, including rehabilitation engineers, rehabilitation medicine physician specialists, and allied health professionals.

The objective of this option is to alleviate the shortage of providers in the development and use of technology. The option is weighted toward the application end of the technology lifecycle, since it is likely that researchers trained in related fields could apply their basic skills to the disability field if funds were available for new projects. Schools eligible to receive the funds under this option would include schools of engineering with specific programs for rehabilitation engineering, medical schools that sponsor residency programs in rehabilitation medicine, and schools for allied health professionals. As under the existing programs for training assistance (including public health, nursing, and physician traineeships), the funds could be awarded directly to recognized programs but applied to educate specific individuals. This mechanism allows nationally determined priorities to affect the selection of both the educational programs and the individuals in them. Funds appropriated for these programs might come from funds curently appropriated for physician training in specialties for which there is likely to be an excess according to the recent report of the Graduate Medical Education National Advisory Committee (102).

A corollary objective of this option is to encourage disabled individuals to become rehabilitation professionals, particularly rehabilitation engineers. As noted throughout this report, the appropriate application of technologies to disabled people requires input from consumers at every phase of the technology lifecycle. Because rehabilitation engineering is a blend of technology development and application, it is a key field in which to focus Federal efforts to encourage the training of disabled professionals. Mechanisms to encourage an increase in the number of disabled professionals trained include requiring or creating incentives for programs that receive Federal assistance to implement affirmative action programs.

This option will not be effective unless mechanisms for improving criteria for reimbursement for nonmedical technologies are developed, as discussed under options 4B and 5C. Currently, a lack of funding for nonmedical personnel who assist disabled people to function independently has made the job market undesirable for prospective students. Training more professionals for these positions would probably be an inefficient use of scarce resources.

Finally, an alternative to training more rehabilitation medicine specialists is training physicians in other specialties to become "managers" of the rehabilitation and habilitation of their chronically disabled clients. This alternative recognizes that physicians are likely to influence delivery and payment systems for at least the short-term future. Funding courses in medical schools or residency programs might assist other physicians to better help their disabled clients.

An additional need in this area is for the training of existing disability-related and general health professionals in the specialized skills necessary for the appropriate use of technologies.

OPTION 5B

Congress could encourage volunteer participation in assisting disabled people by modifying tax incentives related to volunteer expenses and charitable contributions.

As with the previous option, the objective of this option is to alleviate the personnel shortage in various parts of the technology lifecycle. This option suggests the use of volunteers to perform some of the functions normally provided by professionals, to enhance the services provided by professionals and to assist in implementing existing legislation that has, to date, not been appropriated enough funds for full implementation (e.g., the Education for All Handicapped Children Act). Although "volunteer participation" suggests that no compensation is provided, the incentive of reduced taxes is known as a relatively inexpensive method of providing compensation. This option assumes that the provision of such "compensation" will increase the supply of volunteers. Although tax provisions currently exist both for deduction of charitable contributions and volunteer expenses, strengthening these provisions might increase volunteer participation. For example, the current deduction of 9 cents per mile of volunteer travel by automobile might be increased (for business travel, the current deduction is 20 cents).

Specific examples of possible volunteer assistance are: serving as information resources and referral persons (a function often performed by several types of allied health professionals); assisting in planning and conducting education and training programs on the application of existing and emerging technologies (a function performed by allied health professionals when performed at all); assisting in the evaluation of new products and services (a function often neglected); conducting self-help groups for peer counseling (an activity best performed by disabled volunteers); and donating money or goods. Possible strengthened tax incentives are: tax credits (instead of deductions) for some portion of charitable contributions; deductions for more than 100 percent of expenses incurred in providing services that otherwise would not be provided because of budget cuts; deductions for expenses incurred by families who provide services to disabled members of the family who would otherwise be served under a publicly funded program; and deductions for activities which might affect the environment of disabled and handicapped people in a positive way (e.g., an attitudes awareness campaign by a television station).

Because the expenses incurred under this option, if adopted by Congress, would be primarily in the form of lost tax revenues rather than direct outlays, few Federal dollars would be expended if volunteer activity were not increased. A potential drawback to this "solution" to provider shortages, however, is the lack of quality control over volunteer activities.

OPTION 5C

Congress could mandate the funding of demonstration projects to test reimbursement for technologies under Federal health insurance programs by the types of skills provided rather than by the types of providers.

This option is in response to OTA's finding that those providers who are permitted by the structure of delivery and reimbursement systems to prescribe technologies for disabled people may not always be the most appropriate ones to do so. In some instances, therefore, a client may not receive the proper assistance, or the skills of several providers (those able to prescribe and those unable to) may be employed at more expense and loss of efficiency than necessary or desirable. Another problem is that services necessary for the proper use of prescribed technologies are often not reimbursed under the Federal health insurance programs (see option 4B) if they are not provided by a physician and are therefore not provided. So far, there has been no proven method established to solve these problems, although numerous suggestions have been made. A program of demonstration projects mandated by Congress is proposed under this option in recognition of the untested status of this potentially helpful solution.

Because reimbursement experiments are common under the Medicaid and Medicare programs, it would be logical that HCFA administer this demonstration program. Congress could provide the Secretary of Health and Human Services with the authority to issue waivers from current Medicare and Medicaid rules to demonstration project participants when it next amends titles XVIII and XIX of the Social Security Act.

In order to meet the objectives of providing more appropriate, cost-effective services and assuring that services are of an acceptable quality, Congress might want to limit the types of services eligible for the program in its authorization of the project. Alternatively, each pilot project might limit the types of services reimbursed by service to an area in which the project's sponsors had already demonstrated quality and effectiveness. The funds appropriated for the demonstrations should be sufficient to assure quality; the limits should be placed on the number of projects.

Appendixes

Appendixes

Appendix A.—Method of the Study

This assessment of "Technology and Handicapped People" was preceded by a 3-month planning effort that identified areas to concentrate on and established a tentative study approach for the full study. The planning phase took place from July to September of 1980, and resulted in a study proposal for the full assessment. That proposal described the plan to examine the processes of research and development, evaluation, diffusion and marketing, and delivery and use of technologies for disabilities and to develop a conceptual framework for decisions made regarding these processes. The proposal also presented examples of possible case studies.

The full assessment began on October 1, 1980. One of the first tasks undertaken was the selection of the advisory panel. Most of the studies undertaken at OTA rely on the advice and assistance of an advisory panel of experts. The advisory panel for a particular assessment suggests source materials, subject areas, case studies, and perspectives to consider; assists in interpreting information and points of view that are assembled by OTA staff; and suggests possible findings conclusions based on the accumulation of information produced by the study. The panel members review staff and contract materials for accuracy and validity, discuss policy options of the study, and present arguments for and against the options and conclusions. They do not, however, determine the report's final form and are not responsible for its content, direction, or conclusions.

The advisory panel for the current assessment consisted of 18 experts with backgrounds in rehabilitation medicine, sociology, innovation, economics, industry, ethics, law, health policy, rehabilitation engineering, psychiatry, consumer advocacy, and state level disability program administration. The panel was chaired by Daisy Tagliacozzo of the University of Massachusetts. One member of the OTA Health Program Advisory Committee, Melvin Glasser, also served on the advisory panel.

The first panel meeting was held on January 14, 1981, in Washington, D.C. (the site of all three panel meetings). Panel members discussed the overall study plan of the assessment and helped OTA staff refine the goals for the project. The panel examined the project boundaries and definitional issues and was key in sharpening the study's focus. The panel was also helpful in reviewing the primary issue areas to be covered and in providing suggestions of individuals and organizations to contact for information and assistance. Case studies of specific technologies or disabling conditions were discussed, and the panel provided ideas of possible cases as well as criteria for final case study selection. The case study approach was intended to illustrate problems and opportunities found in the various stages of the development and use of technologies for disabilities or impairments.

Following the panel meeting, a draft of a status report was prepared. This draft was distributed to panel members and to over 50 additional reviewers who provided comments. The status report contained only descriptive information; analysis and policy options were not included.

The second panel meeting was held on May 1, 1981. At that meeting, the panel provided comments on the revised draft status report and reviewed the progress of the study. Considerable time was spent discussing ways to analyze and synthesize the material that had been collected and to develop policy options. In addition, the panel identified strengths, weaknesses, and omissions in the work to that point. Finally, the panel explored modifications in the emerging conceptual approach of the project. The final version of the status report was issued in June 1981 to the Labor and Human Resources Committee and other selected Members of Congress.

Two subprojects were conducted during the spring of 1981: 1) a public outreach effort, and 2) a workshop on "Attitudes, Handicapped People, and Public Policy." The public outreach effort, which is described in appendix D, was undertaken during April and May.

The workshop on attitudes and public policy was held in Washington, D.C., on May 11 and 12. The goal of the workshop was to explore the ways in which the attitudes of and toward disabled people affect public policy on resource allocation and technology development and use. There were more than 70 participants from the academic, legislative, and program implementation communities. The workshop provided OTA with a number of specific options for changes in programs and policies affecting disabled people.

Two preliminary workshops were held in preparation for the May 11 and 12 workshop. One was a general strategy or planning session and one was on legislative issues and disabled people, attended by lawyers specializing in civil rights. Also in preparation for the workshop, several background papers were written by experts in different fields relating to attitudes of and towards disabled individuals. Proceedings of the May workshop, including the papers and a summary of conclusions reached by participants, will be available through the National Technical Information Service. Copies for congressional use will be available from OTA. Authors of the papers are listed at the end of this appendix.

The initial, partial drafts of the main report were

reviewed by OTA staff, special consultants, and advisory panel members. In certain instances, outside reviewers were also asked to provide comments. The first complete draft of the report was then sent to the advisory panel.

The final meeting of the advisory panel occurred on October 2, 1981. The entire meeting was spent reviewing the first complete draft on the main report. The primary focus of the review was on the policy options for congressional consideration.

The draft was then revised by OTA staff based on the suggestions and comments of the advisory panel. This second draft was then sent for a further round of review by a much broader range of experts in a diversity of settings: Federal agencies, private and nonprofit organizations, academic institutions, practicing health professionals, consumer groups, and other selected individuals. Altogether, more than 180 individuals or organizations were asked to comment on drafts of the main volume or individual case studies of this assessment. The final draft of the main volume of the report, containing the policy options, was reviewed by approximately 50 individuals. After appropriate revisions were made based on comments received, the report was submitted to the Technology Assessment Board.

The project resulted in a number of documents: the main report, of which this appendix is a part; a booklet that summarizes the main report; a status report to Congress on the project, issued in June of 1981 and fully encompassed by this main report; a series of background papers of individual case studies and issue papers; a background paper containing the proceedings of the workshop on technology, attitudes, and public policy; and a xeroxed bibliography (prepared for the workshop, by the Institute for New Challenges) on attitudes toward and of disabled people, which is available for inspection at the OTA offices.

The background papers containing the case studies and issue papers were prepared both to provide information and ideas for the main report and to serve as individual analyses of particular issues and technologies. The case studies, as well as the issues papers, were selected according to several criteria:

- *Area of policy covered.* Cases were selected to cover more than just health-related disability policy.
- Several *functional types of disability* should be represented, e.g., deafness, mobility limitations, speech impairment, and learning disability. In addition, there should be cases or papers which address issues generic to all or many forms of disability.
- *Physical form of technology.* Physical technologies (such as joint implants) should be included, as well as process technologies.
- *Complexity of technology.* Both complex and simple technologies should be represented.
- *Purpose of technology.* Prevention, treatment, diagnosis, and rehabilitation should be represented.
- *State of knowledge.* There must be sufficient data or information available for analysis.
- *Policy relevance.* There must be significant policy questions involved in the cases selected.

The case studies and issue papers commissioned by OTA are listed below with their authors. As mentioned, they are being issued in separate volumes and will be available through either the Government Printing Office or the National Technical Information Service (or both):

- "Passive Restraint Systems in Automobiles" by Kenneth Warner.
- "The Technology of Joint Implantation" by Dan Lawson.
- "Sheltered Workshops as an Employment Technology" by Jeffrey Rubin.
- "Learning Disabilities" by Candis Cousins and Leonard Duhl.
- "Telecommunications Devices for Deaf People" by Virginia Stern and Martha Reddan.
- "Assistive Communication Devices for Severe Speech Impairments" by Judith Randal.
- "Mainstreaming in Education" by Nancy Carlson.
- "Congress, the Courts, and Civil Rights for Disabled Persons" by Stephen Chitwood.
- "Technology and Disability Programs and Rights: A State Perspective" by Kent Hull.
- "Techniques for Resource Allocation Decisions" by Mark Ozer.

An additional background Paper, as mentioned above, will include the papers presented at, or included in the proceedings of, the May 1981 workshop on attitudes and technology. The topics of the papers and their authors are:

- "Cultural and Societal Views of Handicapped Individuals" by John Gliedman and William Roth.
- "Denial of Emotional Needs to People with Handicaps" by Irving Zola.
- "Communications Barriers Between 'The Able-Bodied' and 'The Handicapped' " by Irving Zola.
- "Values Informing U.S. Attitudes Toward Disabled Persons" by Ruth Purtilo.
- "Disability: The Policymaker's Dilemma" by Tom Joe and Cheryl Rogers.
- "Changing Structures in Society and Handicapped People" by Joan Costello.
- "The Media and Attitudes Toward Disabled Persons" by Harold Yuker.

Appendix B.—Legislative Overview

There is legislation, at both the State and Federal levels, that pertains to most, if not all, aspects of the disabled individual's existence. Much of the legislation is broadly drawn to include a range of policies that go beyond affecting only disabled people. A significant part of this body of law, however, is aimed directly and solely at issues of specific relevance to the disabled people. To list or even summarize completely the myriad laws, related regulations, administrative actions, or pertinent court decisions is beyond the scope of this overview.

According to a series of studies prepared for the Office of Handicapped Individuals (OHI), there are 11 general policy areas that encompass 52 specific legislative categories (58,62).* Those general policy areas are:
- education;
- health;
- income maintenance;
- rights;
- transportation;
- miscellaneous (Internal Revenue Code, Copyright Act, etc.);
- employment;
- housing;
- nutrition;
- social services; and
- vocational rehabilitation.

Many of the laws contained in these policy areas are only peripherally related to the needs of disabled people. A few of the laws, though, are directly concerned with major issues that dramatically affect the lives of the disabled people. Examples of these laws are:
- Developmental Disabilities Assistance and Bill of Rights Act—Public Law 88-164; Public Law 91-517; Public Law 94-103; and Public Law 95-602.
- Vocational Education Act of 1963—Public Law 88-210; Public Law 90-576; Public Law 94-482; and Public Law 95-40.
- The Rehabilitation Act of 1973—amended by Public Law 93-516; Public Law 94-230; and Public Law 95-602 (the Rehabilitation, Comprehensive Services and Developmental Disability Amendments of 1978).**

- The Architectural Barriers Act and Amendments—Public Law 90-480 and Public Law 90-480 and Public Law 91-205.
- The Housing and Community Development Amendments—Public Law 95-128 and Public Law 95-557.
- The Education of the Handicapped Act and Amendments—Public Law 94-142; Public Law 95-49; and Public Law 95-561.
- The Comprehensive Employment and Training Act Amendments—Public Law 95-44 and Public Law 95-524.
- The Social Security Act Amendments—Public Law 95-171; Public Law 95-216; Public Law 95-291; Public Law 95-600; and Public Law 96-265.

OHI points out that the numerous legislative initiatives summarized in its reports represent "only the most salient regulation (legislation) with the broadest implications for [disabled] children and adults" (62). It goes on to point out that "this summary is intended to offer a brief overview of Federal policies affecting [disabled] citizens issued during 1977 and 1978" (62). One must keep in mind that there is an equal, if not greater, body of law at the State and local levels that relates to disabled persons. The sheer volume of legislation in this area is awesome. Not only is the amount formidable, but the laws can vary from State to State and may be similar or contradictory to the Federal initiatives. Increasingly though, the States are trying to become synchronized with the Federal legislation in order to qualify for Federal moneys. This tendency might be decreased if programs for disabled persons are decentralized or converted to block grants (whereby the individual States would be far less limited in how the funds are used). An example of an area where this bilevel approach to legislation has resulted in unclear program definitions and goals are the programs serving disabled children. In other areas, such as due process procedures and the administration of the Rehabilitation Act, the Federal-State relationship is fairly consistent.

Charles Bubany of Texas Tech Law School has described the Federal and State laws as falling into three general categories (21):
- special protective legislation and programs provided by law to compensate persons for disability;

---

*The three studies prepared for OHI that are relied on for this discussion are: "Key Federal Regulations Affecting the Handicapped, 1977-78," "A Summary of Selected Legislation Relating to the Handicapped, 1977-78," and "Summary of Existing Legislation Relating to the Handicapped." Any of these studies, especially the last, will provide a much more thorough account of the relevant legislation or regulations involved in this area.

**Public Law 95-602 is especially noteworthy and relevant to this study. Among the many areas of rehabilitation policy and administrative focus that

it reaffirmed and initiated are: the creation of the National Institute of Handicapped Research; establishment of the National Council on the Handicapped; the 501, 502, 503, and 504 sections under title V that established and confirmed a number of civil rights for disabled people; the creation of the independent living centers grant programs; and the employment provisions of title VI (214).

- restrictions imposed either directly or indirectly by law which discourage participation of the disabled in "normal" community life [quotation marks added]; and
- affirmative action to provide the opportunity or encouragement for full participation in community life.

The rehabilitation system has had an inconsistent, overlapping, and piecemeal collection of programmatic goals grafted on to it over the years. Traditionally, most rehabilitation programs are directed towards serving those who were thought to be most readily employable. The remainder of the disabled population was largely ignored. The broadening of definitions and goals by the recent legislation in the independent living area has expanded the scope of the habilitation system to include a wider range of disabled people. However, these changed definitions have largely applied only to the independent living programs. The bulk of the legislation though still serves specified categories of individuals. It is too early to tell whether these remaining categories and areas of legislation will also be broadened in scope and definitional boundaries.

The relationship of the disabled population, in all its variations, to society in general is changing in numerous ways. Public policy is shifting away from the paternalistic "taking care of" approach to addressing handicap-related issues. Increasingly, the country is moving towards an approach where assistance or protection (in the civil rights sense) is provided to individuals in an effort to equip them with the necessary tools to move into a more independent environment. These general policy directions are fairly clear, yet the supporting systems to assure their implementation are still being formed. However, it is possible to provide a sense of where and how Federal legislation will affect the disabled population and the rehabilitation system. A good place to start is with the "civil rights" sections of the Rehabilitation Act of 1973 and its 1978 amendments.*

Section 504 of the Rehabilitation Act, as amended, contains an explicit provision protecting the rights of persons with disabilities in this country. The purpose of this section is to (113):

> ... prevent discrimination against all disabled individuals ... in relation to Federal assistance in employment, housing, transportation, education, health services, or any other federally-aided programs....

The foundation of section 504 is almost identical to the antidiscrimination language of section 601 of the Civil Rights Act of 1964 and section 901 of the Education Amendments of 1972 (113). Section 503 of the same law requires affirmative action in the employment and advancement of qualified disabled individuals by many federally funded contractors. For the definitional purposes of section 504, a "handicapped" person is anyone who:

- has a physical or mental impairment that substantially limits one or more major life activities;
- has a record of such an impairment; or
- is regarded as having such an impairment.

The dark side of this legislative progress is the slowness and confusion that has characterized the Federal Government's efforts at implementing these provisions. Each Federal department is responsible for carrying out the responsibilities included in these laws. It took the Department of Health, Education, and Welfare (now Health and Human Services) 4 years (1973-77) to announce regulations for its programs. It also had responsibility for the development of guidelines for other departments in their implementation of section 504 requirements. It took 5 years (1973-78) to announce guidelines for *the process of developing regulations* for the other departments and agencies (113). It should be mentioned, however, that no funds were authorized or appropriated for the implementation of section 504. And the Department of Health, Education, and Welfare is not an isolated example of the problems and delays involved in implementing the goals and programs required by these provisions.

A piece of legislation that preceded the Rehabilitation Act is the Architectural Barriers Act of 1968 (amended in 1976). Without the implementation of the goals set out in this legislation, subsequent civil rights measures, employment acts, or transportation laws lose their effectiveness very quickly. One of the most fundamental barriers to disabled individuals' full participation in society is accessibility or the lack thereof to the buildings and facilities they must use. Without access, they are in effect subjected to the most severe form of discrimination. The mandate of the Architectural Barriers Act was to ensure that (113):

> Every building designed, constructed, or altered after the effective date of a standard issued under this chapter which is applicable to such building, shall be designed, constructed, or altered in accordance with such standards.

In essence, the general goal of the legislation was to open up federally owned or operated buildings and facilities to disabled people. The law excluded privately owned buildings or facilities unless they were related to a federally funded operation. The direction and general administration of this act comes from the General Services Administration, the Department of Health and Human Services, the Department of Hous-

---

*Kent Hull, in his book *The Rights of Physically Handicapped People*, is the source of a significant portion of the discussion related to the specific legislative initiatives in this area (113). This book provides an extensive and illuminating analysis of the legislative, administrative, and judicial issues involved.

ing and Urban Development, the Postal Service, and the Department of Defense. Each has various jurisdictional concerns for which it is responsible. The legislation in this area receives much of its criticism over three general points: definitional issues, uneven interpretation and use of discretionary powers, and implementation efforts that proceed at glacial speeds.

Education, transportation, and employment are also areas of intense concern that have been addressed by Congress. The focus on education of disabled children dates back many years. The most recent initiatives are updates and summaries of those previous efforts. The Education for All Handicapped Children Act of 1975 and its amendments, Public Law 95-49 and Public Law 95-561, are the primary sources of Federal aid to State and local school systems for instructional and support services to disabled children. This legislation has stimulated the debate over what should be the "least restrictive environment" for disabled children in school systems.

In the area of transportation, a number of amendments to the Urban Mass Transportation Act of 1974 (Public Law 91-453, Public Law 93-87, Public Law 93-503, and the most recent—Public Law 95-599) have provided authorization to eligible local jurisdictions to plan and design mass transportation facilities to serve, or be usable, by the elderly or the disabled. These authorizations did not mandate action, but the arrival of section 504 of the Rehabilitation Act of 1973 did so. Dramatic battles have been in progress since that date. The employment picture is similar. There are the Comprehensive Employment and Training Act of 1973 (CETA) provisions that classify disabilities in the eligible column for CETA training programs—job corps, Employment Demonstration Programs, etc. There are also provisions in the Small Business Act of 1953 (amended by Public Law 92-595 and Public Law 95-89) that award assistance to nonprofit sheltered workshops and that assist disabled individuals who want to set up businesses, if such funds are not available from other sources. There is an extensive Federal-State system of vocational rehabilitation that is designed to provide disabled persons the appropriate training, support services, etc., and help place them into remunerative employment. Other than vocational rehabilitation programs, the remainder of the Federal efforts are fairly passive. Once again, sections 501, 503, and 504 of the Rehabilitation Act of 1973 changed the Federal Government's relationship to the disabled population. These sections continue to be instrumental in moving the Federal Government and a portion of the private sector towards ending discriminatory employment practices in this area. These sections also mandate an affirmative hiring approach in the employment areas covered by the legislation.

The changes in the law and in society over the last decade have been many and significant. Actions have been taken at the local, State, and Federal levels. But there is still a long distance to travel before the country even approaches the goals established by these various pieces of legislation. The political, hence societal, policy agenda has been established for bringing the population with disabilities into the flow of American society. Putting in place adequate mechanisms and systems to implement the legislation, however, is a task that remains.

Appendix C.—Glossary of Acronyms, Glossary of Terms, Acknowledgments, Health Program Advisory Committee Members

Glossary of Acronyms

ADAMHA	Alcohol, Drug Abuse, and Mental Health Administration (PHS)
AIS	abbreviated injury scale
APTD	Aid to the Permanently and Totally Disabled Program
ATCB	Architectural and Transportation Compliance Board
BRP	Beneficiary Rehabilitation Program (SSDI)
BSSR	Bureau of Social Science Research, Inc.
CBA	cost-benefit analysis
CBO	Congressional Budget Office (U.S. Congress)
CEA	cost-effectiveness analysis
CETA	Comprehensive Employment and Training Act
CIL	center for independent living (also can be ILC)
COMSAT	Communications Satellite Corp.
CRS	Congressional Research Service (Library of Congress)
DD	developmental disability(ies)
DHEW	Department of Health, Education, and Welfare (now DHHS)
DHHS	Department of Health and Human Services
DME	durable medical equipment
DOD	Department of Defense
DOE	Department of Education
DOL	Department of Labor
DOT	Department of Transportation
FAI	functional assessment inventory
FDA	Food and Drug Administration (PHS)
GAO	General Accounting Office (U.S. Congress)
GMENAC	Graduate Medical Education National Advisory Committee
HCFA	Health Care Financing Administration (DHHS)
HEW	See DHEW
HHS	See DHHS
HP	habilitation plan (developmental disabilities)
HRA	Health Resources Administration (PHS)
HSA	Health Services Administration (PHS)
HSQB	Health Standards and Quality Bureau (HCFA)
HUD	Department of Housing and Urban Development
ICF/MR	Intermediate Care Facilities for the Mentally Retarded
IDE	investigational device exemption
IEP	individualized educational program
IHP	individualized habilitation plan
ILC	independent living center (also see CIL)
IRSG	Insurance Rehabilitation Study Group
IWRP	individualized written rehabilitation program
LRE	least restrictive environment
NARF	National Association of Rehabilitation Facilities
NARIC	National Rehabilitation Information Center
NAS	National Academy of Sciences
NASA	National Aeronautics and Space Administration
NBS	National Bureau of Standards
NCHCT	National Center for Health Care Technology (OASH)
NCHS	National Center for Health Statistics (OASH)
NCHSR	National Center for Health Services Research (OASH)
NEI	National Eye Institute (NIH)
NHTSC	National Highway Traffic Safety Administration
NIA	National Institute on Aging (NIH)
NIADDK	National Institute of Arthritis, Diabetes, and Digestive and Kidney Diseases
NICHD	National Institute of Child Health and Human Development (NIH)
NIH	National Institutes of Health (PHS)
NIHR	National Institute of Handicapped Research (DOE)
NINCDS	National Institute of Neurological and Communicative Disorders and Stroke (NIH)
NSC	National Safety Council
NSF	National Science Foundation

OASH	Office of the Assistant Secretary for Health (DHHS)
OHDS	Office of Human Development Services (DHHS)
OHI	Office for Handicapped Individuals (DOE)
OHRST	Office of Health Research, Statistics and Technology (OASH)
OPPR	Office of Policy Planning and Research (HCFA)
OSE	Office of Special Education (Department of Education)
OSMA	Office of Small Manufacturers' Assistance (FDA)
OTA	Office of Technology Assessment (U.S. Congress)
PHS	Public Health Service (DHHS)
R&D	research and development
REC	rehabilitation engineering center (NIHR)
RER&D	Rehabilitation Engineering Research and Development Program (VA)
RI	rehabilitation indicators
RSA	Rehabilitation Services Administration (DOE)
RTC	research and training center (NIHR); sometimes seen as R&TC
SBA	Small Business Administration
SGA	substantial gainful activity
SSA	Social Security Administration (DHHS)
SSDI	Social Security Disability Insurance Program (SSA)
SSI	Supplemental Security Income Program (SSA)
SSI-VR	Supplemental Security Income-Vocational Rehabilitation Program (SSA)
TASH	Technical Aids and Systems for the Handicapped, Inc.
VA	Veterans Administration
VDI	vehicle deformation index
VR	vocational rehabilitation

Glossary of Terms*

Allied health provider: A specially trained and licensed (when necessary) health worker who provides direct services to clients which supplement, complement, or support the professional functions of physicians, dentists, podiatrists, or nurses. Types of allied health providers include physical therapists, speech therapists, occupational therapists, rehabilitation counselors, rehabilitation engineers, orthotic and prosthetic technologists, and social workers.

Appropriate technology: A term used in this report to mean the appropriate development and, especially, *application* of technology to eliminate or reduce an impairment, disabling condition, or a handicapping condition. It does not refer to the intermediate- or low-capital technology movement.

Attendant care services: Services that are provided by an attendant in assisting a severely disabled person, usually a person needing a wheelchair for mobility, with basic activities of daily living so that the disabled person may live more independently.

Comprehensive technology assessment: See "technology assessment."

Cost-benefit analysis (CBA): An analytical technique that compares the costs of a project or technological application to the resultant benefits, with both costs and benefits expressed by the same measure. This measure is nearly always monetary.

Cost-effectiveness analysis (CEA): An analytical technique that compares the costs of a project or of alternative projects to the resultant benefits, with cost and benefits/effectiveness not expressed by the same measure. Costs are usually expressed in dollars, but benefits/effectiveness are ordinarily expressed in terms such as "lives saved," "disability avoided," "quality-adjusted life years (QALYs) saved," or any other relevant objectives. Also, when benefits/effectiveness are difficult to express in a common metric, they may be presented as an "array."

Development disability (DD): A severe, chronic disability that is attributable to mental or physical impairments that are manifested before the person reaches age 22, which is likely to continue indefinitely, and which results in substantial functional limitations in three or more of the following categories: self care, receptive and expressive language, learning, mobility, self-direction, capacity for independent living, and economic sufficiency.

Device (medical): Any physical item, excluding drugs, used in medical care (including instruments, apparatus, machines, implants, and reagents).

Disability: A term used to denote the presence of one or more functional limitations. A person with a disability has a limited ability or an inability to perform one or more basic life functions (e.g., walking) at a level considered "typical."

Drug: Any chemical or biological substance that may be applied to, ingested by, or injected into humans in order to prevent, treat, or diagnose disease or other medical conditions.

---
*OTA would like to thank Marvin Kornbluh of the Congressional Research Service for sharing his glossary of disability-related terms with us.

Durable medical equipment (DME): A category for reimbursement under Medicare, part B, which refers to equipment that: 1) can withstand repeated use, 2) serves primarily a medical purpose, 3) is not generally useful in the absence of an illness or an injury, and 4) is appropriate for use in the home. Examples of DME include hospital beds and accessories, wheelchairs and accessories, canes and crutches.

Efficacy: The probability of benefit to individuals in a defined population from a medical technology applied for a given medical problem under ideal conditions of use.

Functional limitation: An inability to perform some basic life activity (e.g., walking, grasping, or speaking) at a "typical" level due to an underlying physical or medical condition.

Habilitation: The process of the combined and coordinated use of medical, social, educational, and vocational services for training individuals born with limited functional ability to attain the highest possible level of functional ability. Also called "rehabilitation."

Handicap: Inability to perform one or more life functions (e.g., eating, conversing, working) at a "typical" level, caused by the interaction of an individual's disability with the physical and social environments in which that person is functioning or expected to function.

Impairment: A physiological, anatomical, or mental loss or "abnormality" caused by accident, disease, or congenital condition. An impairment may be the underlying cause of a disability.

Incidence: In epidemiology, the number of cases of disease, infection, or some other event having their onset during a prescribed period of time in relation to the unit of population in which they occur. It measures morbidity or other events as they happen over a period of time.

Independent living center (ILC): A program that provides or organizes services to assist disabled individuals experience independent living (the ability to make one's own decisions and assume responsibility for one's own life), including integration into the community to the maximum extent feasible or desirable, and access to support services in order to maintain independence.

Least restrictive environment (LRE): A concept incorporated into the Education For All Handicapped Children Act that means that handicapped children must be educated to the maximum extent appropriate with nonhandicapped children. Appropriateness is the factor that determines whether a child will be educated in the regular classroom or in another setting such as a special classroom, a special (separate) school, at home, or in a hospital or other institution.

Mainstreaming: A process that assists or enables disabled persons to live, work, and learn in the same settings as nondisabled persons. The term is often used to refer to the process of educating disabled children with nondisabled ones in the same classrooms and schools. A more accurate term might be "integration."

Medicaid: A Federal program that is administered and operated individually by each participating State government that provides medical benefits to certain low-income persons in need of health and medical care. Disabled individuals who receive Supplemental Security Income (SSI) payments (see SSI) also receive Medicaid benefits.

Medical technology: The drugs, devices, and medical and surgical procedures used in medical care, and the organizational and support systems within which such care is provided.

Medicare: A nationwide, federally administered health insurance program authorized in 1965 to cover the cost of hospitalization, medical care, and some related services for eligible persons over age 65, persons receiving Social Security Disability Insurance (SSDI) payments for 2 years (see SSDI), and persons with end-stage renal disease. Medicare consists of two separate but coordinated programs—hospital insurance (part A) and supplementary medical insurance (part B). Health insurance protection is available to insured persons without regard to income.

Morbidity: A measure of illness, injury, or disability in a defined population. It is usually expressed in general or specific rates of incidence or prevalence. Sometimes used to refer to any episode of disease. See also "mortality (death)."

Mortality (death): A measure of deaths, used to describe the relation of deaths to the population in which they occur. The mortality rate (death rate) expresses the number of deaths in a unit of population within a prescribed time.

Prevalence: In epidemiology, the number of cases of disease, infected persons, or persons with disabilities or some other condition, present at a particular time and in relation to the size of the population. It is a measure of morbidity at a point in time.

Procedure (medical or surgical): A medical technology involving any combination of drugs, devices, and provider skills and abilities. For example, an appendectomy may involve at least drugs (for anesthesia), monitoring devices, surgical devices, and physicians', nurses', and support staffs' skilled actions.

Rehabilitation: The process of the combined and coordinated use of medical, social, educational, and vocational services for training or retraining individuals, who have become disabled, to the highest possible level of functional ability. Also called "habilitation."

Rehabilitation engineer: A professional who coordinates various concepts, techniques, and developments in engineering, psychology, systems information, medical and rehabilitation practice, and information regarding diseases or handicaps, to assist disabled persons in the rehabilitation process by providing specific solutions to problems these individuals face in utilizing their abilities.

Rehabilitation engineering center (REC): A research center devoted to research in specific rehabilitation engineering topics funded by the National Institute of Handicapped Research. Since 1971, 12 RECs have been established in the United States, with 3 collaborating centers overseas.

Rehabilitation physician specialist (physiatrist): A physician who has completed postgraduate medical education in the specialty of rehabilitation medicine and who provides medical rehabilitative services and organizes systems of care in the community, obtains resources for clients and programs, conducts research, and provides education on disability.

Research and training center (RTC): A university-based research center funded by the National Institute of Handicapped Research that performs research in one of the following areas of the rehabilitation field—medical rehabilitation, mental retardation rehabilitation, vocational rehabilitation, deafness rehabilitation, blindness rehabilitation, and mental health rehabilitation—and conducts training programs for rehabilitation and health care professionals in the specialty area.

Related services: An entitlement under the Education for All Handicapped Children Act to available technologies in the form of aids and services that are necessary for educating a disabled child in the least restrictive environment (LRE). (See LRE.)

Risk: A measure of the probability of an adverse or untoward outcome's occurring and the severity of the resultant harm to health of individuals in a defined population associated with use of a medical technology applied for a given medical problem under specified conditions of use.

Risk-benefit analysis: The formal comparison of the probability and level of adverse or untoward outcomes versus positive outcomes for any given action. The comparison of outcomes does not take into consideration the resource costs involved in the intended action.

Safety: A judgment of the acceptability of risk (see above) in a specified situation.

Special education: The process of teaching children with disabilities, particularly children who have emotional illness, specific learning disabilities, or mental retardation. Also refers to the process of teaching children with unusually high intellectual potential.

Social Security Disability Insurance (SSDI): A Federal social insurance program for workers who have contributed to the social security retirement program and become disabled before retirement age. Beneficiaries receive monthly cash payments.

Substantial gainful activity (SGA): An earnings test used in the determination of eligibility for the Social Security Disability Insurance or Supplemental Security Income programs. In order to be considered disabled under either program, an individual must have a severe impairment and cannot be engaging in SGA, or earning more than $300 per month. Earnings above the SGA limit automatically cause a determination of "not disabled."

Supplemental Security Income (SSI): A Federal income support program for low-income disabled, aged, and blind persons. Eligibility for the monthly cash payments is based on the individual's current status without regard to previous work or contributions to a trust fund. Some States supplement the Federal benefit.

Technology: The application of organized knowledge to practical ends.

Technology assessment: A comprehensive form of policy research that examines the technical, economic, and social consequences of technological applications. It is especially concerned with unintended, indirect, or delayed social impacts. In health policy, the term has also come to mean any form of policy analysis concerned with medical technology, especially the evaluation of efficacy and safety. The comprehensive form of technology assessment is then termed "comprehensive technology assessment."

Vocational rehabilitation: In general, the process of utilizing services and assistive devices to enable a disabled individual to enter or return to gainful employment. Specifically, vocational rehabilitation refers to the program authorized by the Rehabilitation Act of 1973, as amended, which provides Federal grants to State rehabilitation agencies to provide vocational rehabilitation services. The Vocational Rehabilitation program is administered at the Federal level by the Rehabilitation Services Administration.

Acknowledgments

This project has benefited from the advice of a great many people in addition to the Advisory Panel, the Health Program Advisory Committee, special consultants, and contractors. The staff would like to especially thank the following individuals for their assistance and support.

Bruce Archambault, Council of State Administrators of Vocational Rehabilitation
Association of Handicapped Artists, Inc.
Robert L. Beadles, Research Triangle Institute
Pat Berilgen, Great Oaks Center
Carol Berman, Department of Education
Harold Buzzell, Department of Education
David Campbell, DC+ - Designs in Sound
Jeffrey Cohn, Washington, D.C.
Frank Coombs, Veterans Administration
Barry Corbet, Golden, Colorado
Joan Costello, University of Chicago
Thomas Cowley, Phonic Ear, Inc.
W. Palmer Dearing, Blue Cross and Blue Shield Associations
Thomas Drury, National Center for Health Statistics
George Engstrom, National Institute of Handicapped Research
Barbara Finberg, Carnegie Corp.
Richard Flaherty, Health Industry Manufacturers Association
Donald Galvin, Michigan State University
Margaret Giannini, Veterans Administration
John Gliedman, New York City
Anna C. Hofmann, Phonic Ear, Inc.
John Kal, Federal Aviation Administration
Richard LeClair, National Institute of Handicapped Research
Harriet Loeb, Washington, D.C.
David Martin, Health and Welfare Canada
Howard Matthews, Senate Committee on Labor and Human Resources
Richard Melia, National Institute of Handicapped Research
Michael Mittelmann, Aetna Life & Casualty
Danny Naylor, Great Oaks Center
Seymour Perry, National Institutes of Health
Roger Peterson, Institute for Economic Development
Ronald Philips, National Aeronautics and Space Administration
Margaret Porter, Department of Health and Human Services
Ruth Purtilo, Massachusetts General Hospital
James Reswick, National Institute of Handicapped Research
Reese Robrahn, American Coalition of Citizens With Disabilities
Cheryl Rogers, University of Chicago
David Saks, Organization for the Use of the Telephone
I. Richard Savage, Yale University
Eugene Schneller, Union College
Edward Sontag, Department of Education
Joseph Traub, National Institute of Handicapped Research
Donald Vargo, National Aeronautics and Space Administration
Claude Whitehead, New Jersey Association of Rehabilitation Facilities
George Willingmyre, Health Industry Manufacturers Association
Ronald Wilson, National Center for Health Statistics
Harold Yuker, Hofstra University
Irving Zola, Brandeis University

Health Program Advisory Committee Members

Sidney S. Lee, *Chairman*
  Vice President, Michael Reese Hospital and Medical Center
Stuart H. Altman
  Dean, Florence Heller School
  Brandeis University
Robert M. Ball
  Institute of Medicine
  National Academy of Sciences
Lewis H. Butler
  Health Policy Program, School of Medicine
  University of California, San Francisco
Kurt Deuschle
  Mount Sinai School of Medicine
Zita Fearon
  Consumer Commission on the Accreditation of Health Services, Inc.
Rashi Fein
  Center for Community Health and Medical Care
  Harvard Medical School
Melvin A. Glasser
  Committee for National Health Insurance
Patricia King
  Georgetown Law Center
Joyce C. Lashof
  Dean, School of Public Health
  University of California, Berkeley
Mark Lepper
  Vice President for Inter-Institutional Affairs
  Rush-Presbyterian-St. Luke's Medical Center

Margaret Mahoney
    President, The Commonwealth Fund
Frederick Mosteller
    Department of Health Policy and Management
    Harvard School of Public Health
Beverlee Myers
    Director, Department of Health Services
    State of California
Mitchell Rabkin
    General Director
    Beth Israel Hospital

Frederick C. Robbins
    President, Institute of Medicine
    National Academy of Sciences
Rosemary Stevens
    Department of History and Sociology of Science
    University of Pennsylvania
Kerr White
    Rockefeller Foundation

Appendix D.—OTA Public Outreach Survey

Introduction

Effective development and use of technologies for disabled people require the extensive involvement of disabled people themselves, as well as others who research, develop, produce, provide, and pay for the technologies. In practice, however, such involvement does not always occur. This finding became clear early in the OTA study and was refined and confirmed throughout the course of the project.

Similarly, it is generally recognized that the identification and analysis of problems and opportunities related to Federal policies that affect the development and use of technologies require input from those directly using, marketing, and providing the technologies—the "public." This principle is particularly salient when applied to areas related to disabled people. The need for public input is primarily due to the great influence of technology in nearly every aspect, from personal to societal, of the lives of disabled people and those around them. A complete understanding of issues which shape and, in turn, are affected by policies can occur only when personal experiences are examined.

Thus, from the beginning of this assessment, OTA sought to involve the broad public interested in issues relating to technology and disabled or handicapped people. The objective was to reach beyond the world of the *experts on making policy* affecting disabled persons to the world of *experts on experiencing the effects of the policies.* OTA hoped to learn more about the real problems and opportunities which currently exist and obtain suggestions for policy options to present to Congress.

Methods

After determining the objective of the public outreach effort, the next step was defining the "public" to be reached. As established in the objective, the public did *not* include disabled or nondisabled public policymakers, practitioners, or academic experts on disability-related technology development and use.* It *did* include disabled people not in those categories. However, as noted throughout the assessment, there is an enormous variety of disabled individuals, with differing needs, desires, impairments, disabilities, handicaps, abilities, attitudes, and resources. True representation, therefore, was beyond the capabilities of the project.

A feasible alternative for the outreach survey was determined to be contacting as many organizations dedicated to assisting different "types" of disabled people as practical.

The remainder of the public consisted of people directly involved with some stage of technology development and use. As does the group of disabled individuals, this group includes individuals and organizations with a wide range of functions and a wide range of attitudes and perspectives. It includes parents, teachers, researchers, manufacturers, physicians, allied health professionals, rehabilitation counselors, institutional providers, State agencies, third-party payers, and many others. Again, true representation was beyond the capabilities of the project. However, OTA hoped that by contacting professional associations, rehabilitation facilities, manufacturers of devices, and insurance companies, input could be obtained from many of the key perspectives of this sector of the public.

The third step was developing a method to obtain the public input. Although several forms of personal contact were seriously considered (e.g., a national public forum or a series of public meetings across the country), a mail effort was selected because of time and financial constraints. First, a concise description of the entire assessment was developed; this description is attached as addendum A to this appendix.

Next a survey method was selected. In order to avoid limiting or steering responses to particular categories of problem statements or options for change, OTA decided against the use of a questionnaire. Instead, a request for *specific* informaton on *problems* and *missed or potential opportunities* was presented in a general letter that stated the purpose of the assessment and of the outreach effort. This general letter, attached as addendum B, was modified according to the type of recipient.

The third step was compiling the actual list to which the request letter and project description were to be sent. Four categories were selected to encompass the public as previously defined. The first and largest included "advocacy groups." OTA defined advocacy groups broadly to include organizations devoted to the various interests of different disabled people as well as associations of and for parents, teachers, providers (e.g., physicians and allied health professionals), program administrators and others who affect and are affected by the lives of disabled people. A list of 197 organizations and associations was compiled; the two sources which provided the bulk of the list were the 1980-81 edition of *Directory of Organizations Interested in the Handicapped* (176) and the *Directory*

---

*It is standard policy at OTA for these type of individuals to provide input to assessments by serving on the study advisory panel, by providing information for staff analysis, and by reviewing drafts of the report. This process is further described in app. A.

of *National Information Sources on Handicapping Conditions and Related Services* (61).

The second category included medical rehabilitation facilities. From the 1980 membership directory of the National Association of Rehabilitation Facilities (NARF) (155), the alphabetically first facility offering medical rehabilitation services listed under each State was selected. Not all States had such a facility. While it was understood that the sample was not representative of all facilities in the country,* it was hoped that geographic variation allowed a wider range of perspectives to be represented. The final list of 41 also included several facilities that had heard about the assessment and contacted OTA. The third category included companies that manufacture devices for disabled persons. This list of 36 companies was not designed to be even loosely representative of all product manufacturers. Instead, it was compiled by using names of companies participating in seminars and workshops attended by OTA project staff members. Finally, the fourth category included 10 insurance companies whose benefits include coverage of some technologies for disabilities. The companies and people within them who were contacted were suggested by a member of the Insurance Rehabilitation Study Group, a group of 50 insurance company executives who are actively engaged in rehabilitation and medical administration.

The letters to the advocacy groups were mailed at the beginning of April 1981, and the letters to the other three groups were sent out in groups at weekly intervals. Recipients were requested to respond within 3 weeks so that their views could be fully considered. However, although many of the responses arrived between 2 to 4 weeks later than the requested deadlines, all responses were utilized in the preparation of the draft and final reports.

---
*The membership of NARF is not necessarily representative of rehabilitation facilities in the country. Furthermore, the code used in classifying the services offered were likely to be used to mean different services by different institutions. OTA proceeded, however, as though "medical rehabilitation" meant the same services for each facility.

Once received, the written responses and notes on telephone responses were circulated among the staff. A summary of issues, problems, and suggestions for change was prepared for internal use; each staff member received a copy. This summary was used in drafting the body of the report and in the revision process. Perhaps equally important, though, the summary was carefully reviewed as the findings and policy options were developed. In a number of cases, the respondents were contacted for followup information.

Response

Of 283 requests sent, 8 were returned unopened, and 61 responses were received. Table D-1 presents the response rates by group. The overall and individual response rates were surprisingly low, particularly for the advocacy groups at 18.2 percent. Because issues relating to disabled people have become increasingly visible in part because of publicity developed by advocacy groups, OTA had anticipated a greater response. As noted earlier, true representation of the "public" was not an objective of the outreach effort, although the low response rate diminished the amount of representation that would have been possible. An examination of the respondents produced no pattern in the type of organization responding. A possible exception to this was the multiplicity of responses from organizations concerned with visually impaired persons and with hearing-impaired persons, although there are more of these organizations than those with other concerns.

Despite the low response rate, the responses received were generally quite helpful to OTA. Most appeared to have been carefully considered. As a whole, the responses served several important purposes. They confirmed problems described in the literature relating to all stages of the technology lifecycle, including research and development (R&D), evaluation, marketing and production, and delivery, use, and financing. Perhaps more important, though, they provided spe-

Table D-1.—Response Rates of Public Outreach Survey

Category	Number sent	Number returned unopened	Number responses received	Percent responses received of requests reaching destination
Advocacy group	196	4	35	18.2%
Medical rehabilitation facilities	41	1	11	27.5
Product companies	36	3	11	33.3
Insurance companies	10	0	4	40.0
Totals	283	8	61	21.2%

SOURCE: Office of Technology Assessment.

cific examples of problems found in the process of technology development and use. Often, these examples were of actual experiences at the local level. Furthermore, while there were no *policy* alternatives provided, there were several examples of changes that might be made at various points in the technology process. Several of these were used at appropriate points in the report. Finally, the responses helped to emphasize the importance of certain problems over others because of the frequency with which they appeared. Owing to the lack of a representative sample, the frequency of problems was used only as a rough guide of their prominence.

An examination of the responses by category—advocacy groups, medical rehabilitation facilities, product companies, and insurance companies—revealed more similarities than differences in the problems that were stated most frequently and in the areas of the technology lifecycle that were discussed. For example, inadequate and inappropriate *funding* of technologies, particularly devices, was the most frequent problem cited in each group. And, in each group, with the exception of the insurance companies where there were the fewest responses, there were problems cited with research, evaluation, production, marketing, delivery and use of technologies. Also, while most organizations discussed only device technologies, several respondents specifically utilized OTA's broader definition of technology in their discussions.

As noted previously, the responses were used in all stages of the preparation of the report. Presenting them separately in great detail would involve unnecessary repetition of the report. In addition, as noted above, the responses differed little by category. Still, in order to illustrate the results of the public outreach effort, highlights of problem statements and suggestions found in each category will be listed below. The order is not significant.

Advocacy Groups

- Support for programs employing disabled people or enhancing their opportunities for employment is an essential expenditure of funds and should not be decreased even in this era of budget cuts.
- There is a lack of adequate and appropriate funding for technologies for disabled people.
- Information developed by researchers, which could assist disabled people, does not reach them often or systematically. It is essential that this gap be eliminated.
- There needs to be more input by disabled people in research and services delivery in order that they may determine the course of their own lives. In addition, consumers of technologies, particularly devices, need to be actively involved in evaluation and testing of new technologies.
- There is a lack of coordination among public and nonpublic programs, causing a waste of resources to society and a lack of necessary services to some individuals.
- Policymakers need more and better data on disabilities and handicaps.
- There is a lack of trained personnel to apply technologies to disabled people.
- Research funding is often for complex devices, and there is too little for necessary, but less complex, ones.
- Federal research funds are generally awarded to established researchers. Thus, the "basement" researcher with ideas developed from experience is often unable to receive support.
- The existence of different definitions of disability for program eligibility impedes coordination of services and may cause families to undergo multiple assessments.
- Groups supporting people with particular disabilities (e.g., visual impairments, hearing impairments, or certain diseases) urged an appropriate focus on their constituents.

Medical Rehabilitation Facilities

- Although deinstitutionalization is a stated policy under several programs, the services and funding available often do not support it.
- The research performed is not always appropriate; there is a need for many more functional devices.
- There is a need for uniform standards to assist in client evaluation of products.
- Programs that pay for technologies often do not cover technologies that might cost more in the short run but cost less in the long run. The total amount of funding is inadequate.
- The type of personnel licensed to prescribe technologies is not always appropriate. Further, there is a shortage of all trained personnel.
- Rehabilitation centers have particular difficulty in obtaining funds for the R&D of new technologies.
- There is a need for better organization of services to assist disabled people.
- There is a need for more centers to evaluate and train clients in the use of devices.
- Regulations governing institutional providers are often unclear.

Product Companies

- Too few large firms produce technologies for disabled people. The small firms that do are often created out of the founder's personal involvement with disability. Small companies need relief from regulation.
- There is a great need for data on the disabled population to assist in research as well as marketing.
- Information transfer between researchers and companies and between companies and users about devices is often a problem.
- Medical and social service personnel are often resistive to new technologies. In addition, there are too few well-trained people to prescribe the technologies.
- Federal money goes into R&D but not beyond. The risks of production of technologies for a small, undefined market are often too great for the private sector.
- It is difficult to move technologies from the R&D stage to the market.
- There is a need for marketing/sales-oriented people to be involved in the peer review process of awarding research grants.
- There is inadequate third-party funding of devices.

Insurance Companies

- The availability of funding for technologies influences their availability to disabled individuals.
- There is a lack of information on the availability of specialized equipment.
- There is a lack of general information on centers that apply specialized equipment for disabled people.
- It is essential that the needs and desires of disabled individuals be balanced against the economic costs and benefits of those needs and desires.
- There is often a lack of adequate information for users on the upkeep and available service for many of the complex pieces of equipment funded by insurance companies.

Addendum A

Project On

TECHNOLOGY AND HANDICAPPED PEOPLE

Office of Technology Assessment
Congress of the United States

At the request of the Senate Committee on Labor and Human Resources, the Office of Technology Assessment (OTA) is conducting a comprehensive assessment on "Technology and Handicapped People." One purpose of the project is to examine the policies and specific processes through which technologies are developed, evaluated, diffused, delivered, and used. Another purpose is to examine the broader issues related to providing an appropriate fiscal and technical fit between technologies and users.

<u>Project Focus</u>. Policies concerning technologies and handicapped people must take into account a large number of technological possibilities, organizational factors, resource allocation demands and complexities, individual and societal attitudes, and various (and often competing) levels of decisionmaking. OTA believes that a unifying framework for analysis is needed in order to develop and evaluate policies that might fulfill the goal of an appropriate match between the needs, desires, and capabilities of handicapped people and the nation's ability to develop and deliver the needed technology. This concept of <u>appropriate development and use of technology</u> will guide the study.

Appropriate technology implies an organized way of matching resources to problems or opportunities. Appropriateness cannot be defined unless its context is specified, and that context will always involve social values as well as technical considerations. Thus, OTA is tentatively defining a technology as appropriate when its development and use: 1) are in anticipation of or reaction to handicap-related problems or opportunities, 2) are compatible with resource constraints and occur in an efficient manner, and 3) result in a favorable or acceptable ratio of desirable outcomes to negative effects and resources consumed. In the above, problems, opportunities, resource constraints, desirable outcomes, and acceptable ratios must be defined and valued by appropriate parties-at-interest.

Policies, processes, problems, and opportunities associated with elements of the technology life cycle will be examined from the perspective outlined above. In particular, OTA is developing or synthesizing specific information regarding: 1) research and development of technologies, including identification of needs and priority-setting; 2) evaluation of the effects of technologies, including performance, efficacy, safety, economic and social consequences; 3) diffusion and marketing of technologies, including incentives for private sector involvement; and 4) delivery and use of technologies, including methods of payment or financing.

<u>Definitions and Boundaries</u>. It is necessary to decide on study boundaries while remaining aware that many distinctions will be drawn artificially. Throughout the study, decisions on scope and boundaries -- in effect, decisions on whether to include or exclude specific types of handicaps, technologies, or policy issues -- will have to be dictated by pragmatism.

Much work has been done by others on the definition of a "handicap" or "disability" and on estimating the numbers of handicapped individuals in this country. Despite this prior work, the situation is confused. By one estimate, there are at least 41 definitions of "disability" or "handicap" used by federal programs. Similarly, many estimates of the number of handicapped people suffer from various deficiencies such as lack of measures of severity, double-counting, or under-reporting. However, the OTA study is not intended to identify populations to receive entitlements or other services. Therefore, it will not attempt to develop a preferred or recommended definition, nor will it focus on the development of estimates of the numbers of handicapped people. Instead, it will cover the importance and the implications for policy of methods by which the functional limitations of individuals are identified.

OTA defines technology broadly, as the application of an organized body of knowledge to practical purposes. Under this definition, technologies include physical objects, such as voice synthesizers, as well as processes, such as vocational rehabilitation or reimbursement systems. As a practical matter, the study will focus on those technologies designed for and used directly by individuals (as opposed to populations) with the intent of eliminating, bypassing, or reducing one or more of the individuals' functional limitations. Thus, for example, medical devices, prostheses, modifications of automobiles, and techniques or programs for vocational training are within the study's focus. Technologies designed to address and be applied to population-oriented needs, such as transportation systems or educational systems as a whole, are generally considered outside of the study's focus.

Other Elements of the Project. To support the core elements of the project, several additional activities are taking place. An analysis of the role of the courts and the judiciary in the implementation of federal legislation relating to handicaps is being conducted. This analysis will also cover the general issues of rights and entitlements and the potential for proposed legislative initiatives to effect change in the present situation. OTA is also developing information about the attitudes (of society and of both handicapped and able-bodied individuals) that affect processes and policies relating to the development and use of technology. This issue will be examined in a workshop to be held in May 1981. A third additional activity is the examination of methods for developing individualized rehabilitation or education "plans."

Several case studies will be conducted. Case studies are designed to provide both specific information about the technologies or areas of disability being studied as well as information that informs the more general issues being examined. Ones in progress include: techniques for "mainstreaming" in early childhood and elementary school; employment technologies (techniques); technologies for severe speech impairments; the impact of federal legislation on a state government; knee and hip implants; and learning disabilities. Ones under consideration include: individually scheduled van service for handicapped individuals; rocker shoes; incontinence; and toys.

The assessment began in October of 1980 and is scheduled for completion at the end of 1981. It is being conducted by the Health Program of OTA. If you have any questions, or would like to contribute information or suggestions, please call the Project Director, Clyde Behney, on (202) 226-2070, or write to:

Office of Technology Assessment
U.S. Congress
Washington, D.C. 20510

Addendum B

March 27, 1981

%

Dear %:

As you may know, the Office of Technology Assessment is conducting a comprehensive study on "Technology and the Handicapped" for the Senate Committee on Labor and Human Resources. A brief narrative description of the project is attached.

The purpose of the assessment is to examine the specific problems and opportunities found in the development, evaluation, and use of technologies. Its purpose is also to examine the broader issues associated with providing an appropriate match between the technology needs, desires, and capabilities of users and the fiscal and technical ability to develop and deliver the technologies. The assessment will present policy options for Congressional consideration. These options may cover all aspects of the research, development, evaluation, diffusion and marketing, delivery, and use of technologies.

While the responsibility for the project rests with OTA staff, the advice of our advisory panel and numerous other individuals and groups in the private and public sectors is essential. We know that you and your organization have a particular perspective that would be helpful to us in our investigation of technology-related problems and opportunities. Could you review the attached description of our project and suggest, from your perspective, specific information on problems and missed or potential opportunities? We request and welcome your ideas. As mentioned, the final report of the OTA project will include a series of policy options for the Congress. If you have suggestions for needed actions, we would appreciate seeing them.

We have purposely avoided the use of a questionnaire in our request because we do not want to encourage or discourage particular categories of problem statements or options. Indeed, we hope that your response is constrained only by the boundaries of your expertise in this area. Please do not restrict suggestions for solutions to those that require legislative change or even to those involving the public sector.

We ask that your response be sent to us by April 22nd in order to lessen the possibility of omitting key issues from consideration. Please send it to me at the following address:

>Health Program
>Office of Technology Assessment
>Congress of the United States
>Washington, D.C. 20510

We look forward to receiving your response and thank you in advance for your time. If you have any questions, please do not hesitate to call me or Anne Kesselman Burns at (202) 226-2070.

Sincerely,

Clyde J. Behney
Project Director

References

1. Abt Associates, Inc., "Cost-Benefit Analysis," in *The Program Services and Support System of the Rehabilitation Services Administration: Final Report* (Cambridge, Mass.: Abt Associates, Inc., 1974).
2. Allard, M. A., and Toff, G., *Current and Future Development of Intermediate Care Facilities for the Mentally Retarded* (Washington, D.C.: Intergovernmental Health Policy Project, George Washington University, August 1980).
3. American Association of Fund Raising Counsel, Inc., *Giving U.S.A.: 1980 Annual Report* (New York: American Association of Fund Raising Counsel, Inc., 1980).
4. Bagnato, S. J., "The Efficacy of Diagnostic Reports as Individualized Guides to Prescriptive Goal Planning," *Exceptional Child.* 46:554, 1980.
5. Bailey, D. R., and Harbin, G. L., "Non-Discriminatory Evaluation," *Exceptional Child.* 46:590, 1980.
6. Behney, C., "Health Policy and an Aging Population," paper presented to the Consumer Commission for the Accreditation of Health Services, New York City, Nov. 18, 1978.
7. Berkeley Planning Associates, *VR Program Evaluation Standards: Final Report* (Berkeley, Calif.: Berkeley Planning Associates, 1978).
8. Berkowitz, M., "Social Policy and the Disabled," paper presented at the Conference on the Implications for Social Security of Research on Invalidity, Vienna, Austria, Apr. 1-3, 1981.
9. Berkowitz, M., et al., *An Evaluation of Policy-Related Rehabilitation Research* (New York: Praeger, 1975).
10. Berman, C., Office of Special Education and Rehabilitative Services, Department of Education, Washington, D.C., "A First Report of the National Council on the Handicapped," unpublished paper, March 1981.
11. Bersoff, D. N., "The Psychological Evaluation of Children: A Manual of Report Writing for Psychologists Who Work With Children in an Educational Setting," unpublished manuscript, 1973.
12. Better, S., et al., "Disability Benefits as Disincentives to Rehabilitation," *Milbank Mem. Fund Q./Health and Society* 57(3):412, 1979.
13. Bisbee, G. E., Jr., et al., *Musculo-Skeletal Disorders: Their Frequency of Occurrence and Their Impact on the Population of the United States* (New York: Prodist, 1978).
14. Blum, R., and Minkler, M., "Toward a Continuum of Caring Alternatives: Community Based Care For the Elderly," *J. Social Issues* 36(2):133, 1980.
15. Booz, Allen, & Hamilton, Inc., *Management of New Products*, 4th ed. (New York: Booz, Allen, & Hamilton, Inc., 1981).
16. Bowe, F., *Handicapping America: Barriers to Disabled People* (New York: Harper & Row, 1978).
17. _____, *Rehabilitating America: Toward Independence for Disabled and Elderly People* (New York: Harper & Row, 1980).
18. Bowe, F., et al., "Consumer Involvement in Rehabilitation," in *Annual Review of Rehabilitation: Volume One*, E. Pan, et al. (eds.) (New York: Springer Publishing Co., 1980).
19. _____, *Executive Summary of Coalition Building: A Report on Feasibility Study To Develop a National Model for Cross-Disability Communication and Cooperation* (Washington, D.C.: American Coalition of Citizens With Disabilities, Jan. 30, 1978).
20. Brown, H. W., and Redden, M. R., *A Research Agenda on Science and Technology for the Handicapped* (Washington, D.C.: American Association for the Advancement of Science, 1979).
21. Bubany, C. D., "Legal Status of the Disabled" in *Human Rehabilitation Techniques, A Technology Assessment, Volume III, Part A, Supplemental Reports: Contract Papers* (Lubbock, Tex.: Texas Tech University, 1977).
22. Bunker, J. P., Professor of Anesthesia and Family, Community, and Preventive Medicine, Stanford University, Stanford, Calif., personal communication, June 16, 1981.
23. Bunten-Mines, E., *Planning Report: Measurement Standards for the Handicapped* (Washington, D.C.: National Bureau of Standards, U.S. Department of Commerce, November 1980).
24. *Business Week*, "A Miniaturized Typewriter," Sept. 25, 1978, p. 87.
25. *Business Week*, "Technology's New Promise for the Handicapped," Sept. 22, 1980, pp. 46B-46P.
26. Butler, J., et al., Institute for Health Policy Studies, U.C.S.F., "Health Care Expenditures for Children With Chronic Disabilities," unpublished paper, October 1981.
27. Cardus, D., et al., *A Benefit-Cost Approach to the Prioritization of Rehabilitation Research* (Houston: T.I.R.R., 1980).
28. _____, "Quality of Life in Benefit-Cost Analyses of Rehabilitation Research," *Arch. Phys. Med. Rehab.* 62:290, 1981.

29. _____, *Relationship Between the Survey of RSA Program Benefits and the Management Information System* (Houston: T.I.R.R., 1981).
30. _____, *Relationship Between the Survey of RSA Program Benefits and the Management Information System: Interim Report* (Houston: T.I.R.R., March 1981).
31. _____, *Some Features of Benefit-Cost Modeling for the RSA State-Federal Vocational Rehabilitation Program: Interim Report* (Houston: T.I.R.R., July 1981).
32. Cho, D. W., and Schuermann, A. C., "Economic Costs and Benefits of Private Gainful Employment of the Severely Handicapped," *J. Rehabilitation* 46:28, 1980.
33. Ciutat, V., and Flick, G., "Examiner Differences Among Stanford-Binet Items," *Psych. Rpt.* 21:613, 1967.
34. Clearfield, D., *Medical Devices and Equipment for the Disabled: An Examination* (Washington, D.C.: Disability Rights Center, Inc., 1976).
35. Cole, C. B., *Comprehensive Management Information System for the State/Federal Vocational Rehabilitation Program* (Cambridge, Mass.: Abt Associates, Inc., 1980).
36. Conley, R. W., *The Economics of Vocational Rehabilitation* (Baltimore: Johns Hopkins Press, 1975).
37. Coombs, F., Program Manager, Veterans Administration, Washington, D.C., "RER&D Program Analysis," internal memorandum, 1980.
38. Coop, R. H., and Sigel, I. E., "Cognitive Style: Implications for Learning and Instruction," *Psychol. Schools* 8:152, 1971.
39. Copeland, W. C., and Iverson, I. A., HHH Institute of Public Affairs, University of Minnesota, "Not Just the Aged, Not Just Health Care, and Not Just Nursing Homes: Some Proposals for Policy and Legislative Changes in Long-Term Care," unpublished paper, Jan. 14, 1981.
40. _____, *Roadmap Through Title XX* (New York: Child Welfare League of America, 1978).
41. Cowley, T. J., President, Phonic Ear, Inc., Mill Valley, Calif., personal communication, Aug. 7, 1981.
42. Crewe, N., and Athelstan, G. T., *Functional Assessment Inventory* (Minneapolis, Minn.: University of Minnesota, 1980).
43. Crewe, N., et al., "Vocational Diagnosis Through Assessment of Functional Limitations," *Arch. Phys. Med. Rehabil.* 56:513, 1975.
44. Curtis, W. S., *The Development and Application of Intelligence Tests for the Blind: A Research Utilization Conference* (Athens, Ga.: University of Georgia, 1972).
45. DeJong, G., "What's Different About Functional Assessment in Independent Living?" in *Symposium on Functional Limitations*, R. Turner (ed.) (Cambridge, Mass.: Abt Associates, Inc., 1980).
46. DeJong, G., and Wenker, T., "Attendant Care as a Prototype Independent Living Service," *Arch. Phys. Med. Rehabil.* 60L:477, 1979.
47. DePape, J., and Krause, L. A., Trace Research & Development Center, Madison Wis., "Guidelines for Seeking Funding for Communication Aids," unpublished paper, 1980.
48. Department of Education, National Institute of Education, *The Vocational Education Study: The Interim Report*, September 1980.
49. Department of Education, Office of Special Education and Rehabilitative Services, *Second Annual Report to Congress on the Implementation of Public Law 94-142, The Education for All Handicapped Children Act*, 1980.
50. Department of Education, Office of Special Education and Rehabilitative Services, National Institute of Handicapped Research, *Informer*, 1980-81.
51. _____, *Long-Range Plan*, n.d.
52. _____, "Long-Range Plan: Executive Summary," November 1980.
53. _____, *Long-Range Plan, Technology for Handicapped Individuals: 1981-1985*, vol. III, August 1980.
54. _____, "REC Coverage of NIHR Long-Range Plan Initiatives," 1980.
55. _____, *Research Directory of the Rehabilitation Research and Training Centers, Fiscal Year 1979*, December 1979).
56. Department of Education, Office of Special Education and Rehabilitative Services, Office for Handicapped Individuals, *Rehabilitation Engineering and Product Information*, DE publication No. E-80-22015, 1980.
57. _____, *Selected Federal Publications Concerning the Handicapped*, DE publication No. 80-22005, 1980.
58. _____, *Summary of Existing Legislation Relating to the Handicapped*, publication No. E-80-22014 (Washington, D.C.: U.S. Government Printing Office, August 1980).
59. Department of Education, Office of Special Education and Rehabilitative Services, Rehabilitation Services Administration, *American Rehabilitation*, 1980-81.
60. Department of Health, Education, and Welfare,

Office of the Assistant Secretary for Planning and Evaluation, *Training and Employment Services Policy Analysis: First Year Progress Report*, September 1979.
61. Department of Health, Education, and Welfare, Office of Human Development Services, Office for Handicapped Individuals, *Directory of National Information Sources on Handicapping Conditions and Related Services*, DHEW publication No. (OHDS) 80-22007, May 1980.
62. _____, "Key Federal Regulations Affecting the Handicapped, 1977-1978," HEW publication No. (OHDS) 80-22008, November 1979.
63. _____, "A Summary of Selected Legislation Relating to the Handicapped, 1977-1978," publication No. (OHDS) 79-22003, May 1979.
64. _____, *Digest of Data on Persons with Disabilities*, May 1979.
65. Department of Health, Education, and Welfare, Office of Human Development Services, Rehabilitation Services Administration, and the Veterans Administration, *Rehabilitation Engineering: A Plan for Continued Progress* (Charlottesville, Va.: Rehabilitation Engineering Center, University of Virginia, 1978).
66. Department of Health and Human Services, Health Care Financing Administration, *Long-Term Care: Background and Future Directions*, HCFA publication No. 81-20047, January 1981.
67. Department of Health and Human Services, Public Health Service, National Institutes of Health, "Tailor-Made Verbalizer Machine Helps Handicapped To Communicate Independently," *The NIH Record* 33(11), 1981.
68. Department of Health and Human Services, Social Security Administration, "Social Security Disability Amendments of 1980: Legislative History and Summary of Provisions," *Soc. Sec. Bull.* 44(4):14, 1981.
69. _____, "Table M-3—Selected Insurance and Related Programs: Beneficiaries of Cash Payments, 1940-1980," *Soc. Sec. Bull.* 44(2):32, 1981.
70. Department of Health and Human Services, Social Security Administration, Office of Policy, *Work Disability in the United States: A Chartbook*, SSA publication No. 13-11978 (Washington, D.C.: U.S. Government Printing Office, Dec. 1, 1980).
71. Diller, L., et al., *Rehabilitation Indicators* (New York: Institute of Rehabilitation Medicine, 1979).
72. _____, *Rehabilitation Indicators Update* (New York: Institute of Rehabilitation Medicine, April 1979).
73. Dodson, R., and Collignon, F. C., *Benefit-Cost Analysis of Vocational Rehabilitation Services Provided to Individuals Most Severely Handicapped* (Berkeley, Calif.: Berkeley Planning Associates, April 1975).
74. Dodson, R., et al., *An Evaluation of the Costs and Effectiveness of Vocational Rehabilitation Service Strategies for Individuals Most Severely Handicapped* (Berkeley, Calif.: Berkeley Planning Associates, May 1975).
75. Doucette, J., and Freedman, R., *Progress Tests for the Developmentally Disabled: An Evaluation* (Cambridge, Mass.: Abt Books, 1980).
76. Dudek, R. A., *Human Rehabilitation Techniques: A Technology Assessment* (Lubbock, Tex.: Texas Tech University, 1977).
77. Education Advocates Coalition, Washington, D.C., "Federal Compliance Activities To Implement the Education for All Handicapped Children Act (Public Law 94-142)," unpublished report, April 1980.
78. Electronic Industries Foundation, Washington, D.C., "A Production and Marketing Strategy for Prototype Devices Developed Under the Rehabilitation Engineering Program," submitted to the Rehabilitation Services Administration, March 1978.
79. Ellis, D., "Methods of Assessment for Use With the Visually and Mentally Handicapped: A Selective Review," *Child: Care, Health and Development* 4:397, 1978.
80. Englehardt, H. T., "John Hughlings Jackson and the Mind Body Relationship," *Bull. Hist. Med.* 49:137, 1975.
81. Epilepsy Foundation of America, "Introduction to the Basic Statistics on the Epilepsies, 1978" (Washington, D.C.: Epilepsy Foundation of America, 1978).
82. Erlanger, H. S., et al., Institute for Research on Poverty, University of Wisconsin, Madison, Wis., "Disability Policy: The Parts and the Whole," unpublished paper, August 1979.
83. Fay, F., "Problems of the Severely and Multiply Handicapped," in *The White House Conference on Handicapped Individuals, Volume One: Awareness Papers* (Washington, D.C.: U.S. Government Printing Office, May 1977).
84. *Federal Register*, "Education of Handicapped Children: Implementation of Part B of the Education of the Handicapped Act," 47:42174, 1977.
85. _____, "State Vocational Rehabilitation and Independent Living Rehabilitation Programs: Final Regulations," 46:5522, 1981.

86. _____, "Vocational Rehabilitation Programs and Projects: Evaluation Standards," 40:58956, 1975.
87. Feinstein, A. R., *Clinical Judgement* (Baltimore: Williams & Wilkins, 1967).
88. Finkelstein, V., *Attitudes and Disabled People* (New York: World Rehabilitation Fund, 1980).
89. Galloway, J. R., et al., *Issues in the Pupil Referral/Evaluation Process* (Washington, D.C.: National Association of State Directors of Special Education, 1980).
90. Gannon, R., Director of Speech Pathology and Communications Assessment, Ontario Crippled Children's Center, Toronto, Ontario, personal communication, Jan. 8, 1981.
91. Gannon, R., Director of Speech Pathology and Communications Assessment, and McNaughton, S., Director, Bliss Symbolics Institute, Ontario Crippled Children's Center, Toronto, Ontario, personal communication, Jan. 8, 1981.
92. General Accounting Office, U.S. Congress, *Better Reevaluations of Handicapped Persons in Sheltered Workshops Could Increase Their Opportunities for Competitive Employment*, report No. HRD-80-34 (Washington, D.C.: U.S. Government Printing Office, Mar. 11, 1980).
93. _____, *Disparities Still Exist in Who Gets Special Education*, report No. IPE-81-1 (Washington, D.C.: U.S. Government Printing Office, 1981).
94. _____, *Medicare's Reimbursement Policies for Durable Medical Equipment Should Be Modified and Made More Consistent*, report No. HRD-81-140 (Washington, D.C.: U.S. Government Printing Office, 1981).
95. _____, *More Diligent Followup Needed To Weed Out Ineligible SSA Disability Beneficiaries*, report No. HRD-81-48 (Washington, D.C.: U.S. Government Printing Office, June 17, 1980).
96. _____, *Rehabilitating Blind and Disabled Supplemental Security Income Recipients: Federal Role Needs Assessing*, report No. HRD-79-5 (Washington, D.C.: U.S. Government Printing Office, June 6, 1979).
97. _____, "The Rehabilitation Services Administration's Research and Demonstration Grant Program and its Peer Review Relationship With the National Academy of Sciences and the National Institute of Handicapped Research Activities" (Washington, D.C.: GAO, Human Resources Division, July 1979).
98. _____, *Stronger Federal Efforts Needed for Providing Employment Opportunities and Enforcing Labor Standards in Sheltered Workshops*, report No. HRD-81-99 (Washington, D.C.: U.S. Government Printing Office, 1981).
99. _____, *Unanswered Questions on Educating Handicapped Children in Local Public Schools*, report No. HRD-81-43 (Washington, D.C.: U.S. Government Printing Office, 1981).
100. Gillespie, P. H., et al., "Legislative Definitions of Learning Disabilities: Roadblock to Effective Service," *J. Learning Disabilities* 8:660, 1975.
101. Gliedman, J., and Roth, W., *The Unexpected Minority: Handicapped Children in America* (New York: Harcourt Brace Jovanovich, 1980).
102. Graduate Medical Education National Advisory Committee, Health Resources Administration, Public Health Service, Department of Health, Education, and Welfare, *Interim Report of the Graduate Medical Education National Advisory Committee*, April 1979.
103. Gunby, P., "From 'Regeneration' to Prostheses: Research on Spinal Cord Injury," *J.A.M.A.* 245(13):1293, 1981.
104. Hammerman, S., and Maikowski, S., *The Economics of Disability: International Perspectives* (New York: Rehabilitation International, March 1981).
105. Havelock, R. G., *Planning for Innovation Through Dissemination and Utilization of Knowledge* (Ann Arbor, Mich.: Institute for Social Research, University of Michigan, 1971).
106. Health Insurance Association of America, *Compensation Systems Available to Disabled Persons in the United States*, 1979.
107. Health Insurance Institute, *1980-81 Source Book of Health Insurance Data*, 1981.
108. Hehir, H. J., Director, Provider and Medical Services Policy, Medicare Bureau, Baltimore, Md., personal communication to R. M. Smith, Everest & Jennings, Inc., Feb. 2, 1979.
109. Hobbs, N., *The Futures of Children: Categories, Labels and Their Consequences* (Nashville, Tenn.: Vanderbilt University, 1975).
110. Hobbs, N., et al., "Classifying Children: A Summary of the Final Report of the Project on Classification of Exceptional Children," *Children Today* 4(4):21, 1975.
111. Hoff, M. K., et al., "Notice and Consent: The School's Responsibility To Inform Parents," *J. School Psychol.* 16:265, 1978.
112. Howard, R., *Vocational Education of the Handicapped—State of the Art: An NASBE Report* (Washington, D.C.: National Association of State Boards of Education, 1979).
113. Hull, K., *The Rights of Physically Handicapped People* (New York: Avon Books, 1979).
114. Indices, Inc., *Functional Limitations: A State of the Art Review* (Falls Church, Va.: Indices, Inc., n.d.).

115. Janssen, T. J., *Reimbursement for Durable Medical Equipment: Volume I* (Final Report) (Washington, D.C.: Health Care Financing Administration, U.S. Department of Health, Education, and Welfare, March 1980).
116. Janssen, T. J., and Saffran, G., "Reimbursement for Durable Medical Equipment," *Health Care Financing Review* 2(3):85, 1981.
117. Juhr, G., et al., University Centers for International Rehabilitation, Michigan State University, East Lansing, Mich., "Barriers to the Development and Application of Technological Aids for Handicapped Persons," unpublished paper, March 1979.
118. Kakalik, J. S., et al., *Services for Handicapped Youth: A Program Overview* (Santa Monica, Calif.: Rand Corp., May 1973).
119. Katz, I., et al., "Effects of Task Difficulty, Race of Administrator and Instructions on Digit-Symbol Performance of Negroes," *J. Personality & Social Psychol.* 2:53, 1965.
120. Keogh, B., "Psychological Evaluation of Exceptional Children: Old Hangups and New Directions," *J. School Psychol.* 10:141, 1972.
121. Kleinfeld, S., *The Hidden Minority* (Boston: Little, Brown & Co., 1977).
122. Lansing, S., "Federal Support for the Handicapped Person," contract paper submitted to the Office of Technology Assessment, U.S. Congress, Washington, D.C., June 1981.
123. LaRocca, J., and Turem, J. S., *The Application of Technological Developments to Physically Disabled People* (Washington, D.C.: The Urban Institute, May 1978).
124. Lasch, C., *The Culture of Narcissism* (New York: W. W. Norton, 1978).
125. Lattin, D., "Doctors and Disabled People: Does Father Always Know Best?" *Disabled USA* 4(2):1, 1980.
126. LeClair, R., National Institute of Handicapped Research, Washington, D.C., "Science Information Exchange; Grants Awarded for FY 1979 for Handicapped Research by Federal Agencies," personal communication, Mar. 9, 1981.
127. Library of Congress, Congressional Research Service, "Cash and Non-Cash Benefits for Persons With Limited Income: Eligibility Rules, Recipient and Expenditure Data, FY 1977-79," report No. 81-44 EPW, Feb. 12, 1981.
128. _____, "Education of the Handicapped," Issue Brief No. IB78040, Feb. 25, 1981.
129. _____, "Social Security Disability Insurance: Reagan Budget Assumes Savings," Mini Brief No. MB81214, Mar. 23, 1981.
130. _____, "Social Security's Disability Programs: Amendments of 1980," Issue Brief No. IB79084, Feb. 25, 1981.
131. _____, "Technology To Aid Disabled Persons," paper prepared at request of the Committee on Science and Technology, U.S. House of Representatives, Mar. 31, 1981.
132. _____, "Vocational Education Act: Reauthorization in 1981," Issue Brief No. IB81007, Mar. 18, 1981.
133. Lifchez, R., and Winslow, B., *Design for Independent Living: The Environment and Physically Disabled People* (New York: Whitney Library of Design, 1979).
134. Lucyk, J. R., Broadcasting and Social Policy Branch, Department of Communications, Toronto, Ont., Canada, "Radio Reading Services for the Blind and Otherwise Print-Handicapped," unpublished paper, March 1980.
135. McCann, J., "Continent Ileostomy Reported Effective in 95%," *Medical Tribune*, Sept. 24, 1980, p. 13.
136. _____, "Swedish Surgeon is Adapting Pouch for Other Urinary Diversion Cases," *Medical Tribune*, Sept. 24, 1980, p. 13.
137. McCoy, S., and Glazzard, P., "Winning the Case But Losing the Child: Interdisciplinary Experiences With P.L. 94-142," *J. Clin. Child Psych.* 7(3):205, 1978.
138. McManus, L. A., "Evaluation of Disability Insurance Savings Due to Beneficiary Rehabilitation," *Soc. Sec. Bull.* 44(2):19, 1981.
139. *Medical World News*, "For Those Who Can't Speak," 22(4):32, Feb. 16, 1981.
140. _____, "Giving Autonomy to the Handicapped," 22(5):32, Mar. 2, 1981.
141. Medsger, B., "The Most Captive Consumers," *The Progressive*, March 1979, p. 34.
142. Mercer, J. R., *Labeling the Mentally Retarded: Clinical and Social Systems Perspectives on Mental Retardation* (Berkeley, Calif.: University of California Press, 1973).
143. Mittleman, M., "Insurance Rehabilitation Study Group—What Is It?" *J. Insurance Med.* 11(4):26, 1980.
144. _____, "Rehabilitation Issues From an Insurer's Viewpoint: Past, Present, Future," *Arch. Phys. Med. Rehabil.* 61:587, 1980.
145. Morrell, J., et al., *A Comprehensive Review and Evaluation of Individual Habilitation Plans: Design Specifications* (Falls Church, Va.: Rehabilitation Group, Inc., 1980).
146. Muller, L. S., "Receipt of Multiple Benefits by Disabled-Worker Beneficiaries," *Soc. Sec. Bull.* 43(11):3, 1980.
147. Muthard, J. E., "Putting Rehabilitation Knowl-

edge to Use," Rehabilitation Monograph No. 11 (Gainesville, Fla.: University of Florida, 1980).
148. Nagi, S. Z., "Definitions of Pathology, Impairment, Functional Limitations and Disability," in *Report of the First Mary E. Switzer Memorial Seminar*, E. G. Whitten (ed.) (Washington, D.C.: National Rehabilitation Association, 1975).
149. National Academy of Sciences, *Health Care for American Veterans*, prepared for the Committee on Veterans Affairs, U.S. House of Representatives, Committee Print No. 36 (Washington, D.C.: U.S. Government Printing Office, 1977).
150. National Academy of Sciences, National Research Council, *Science and Technology in the Service of the Physically Handicapped*, vol. I, (Springfield, Va.: National Technical Information Service, December 1976).
151. _____, *Science and Technology in the Service of the Physically Handicapped*, vol. II, 1976.
152. _____, Assembly of Life Sciences, *Final Report of the Committee on Prosthetics Research in the Veterans Administration*, 1976.
153. National Aeronautics and Space Administration, *Technologies for the Handicapped and the Aged* (Washington, D.C.: NASA Technology Transfer Division, 1979).
154. National Arthritis Advisory Board, National Institutes of Health, Public Health Service, Department of Health, Education, and Welfare, *Policy and Chronic Disease*, NIH publication No. 79-1896, May 1979).
155. National Association of Rehabilitation Facilities, *1980 Membership Directory*, July 1980.
156. National Commission on Social Security, *Social Security in America's Future* (Washington, D.C.: U.S. Government Printing Office, March 1981).
157. National Science Foundation, Division of Problem-Focused Research Applications, "Program Announcement; Science and Technology To Aid the Handicapped," 1978.
158. Navickis, B., "Robaids for the Disabled," *Stanford MD*, fall 1980.
159. Nemeth, C., and Ellis, S., *A Cost-Effectiveness Analysis of Vocational Education Programs for the Handicapped: Technical Report* (Richmond: Virginia State Department of Rehabilitation Services, June 1979).
160. *New York Times*, "New Library Device Reads to the Blind," Mar. 16, 1978.
161. Noble, J. H., "The Limits of Cost-Benefit Analysis as a Guide to Priority-Setting in Rehabilitation," *Eval. Q.* 1(3), 1977.
162. Noble, J. H., "Peer Review: Quality Control of Applied Social Research," *Science* 185(4155):916, 1974.
163. Office of Management and Budget, Executive Office of the President, *Special Analyses: Budget of the United States Government, FY 1979*, GPO stock No. 041-001-00157-3 (Washington, D.C.: U.S. Government Printing Office, 1978.
164. Office of Technology Assessment, U.S. Congress, *Assessing the Efficacy and Safety of Medical Technologies*, GPO stock No. 052-003-00593-0 (Washington, D.C.: U.S. Government Printing Office, September 1978).
165. _____, *Development of Medical Technologies*, GPO stock No. 052-003-00217-5 (Washington, D.C.: U.S. Government Printing Office, August 1976).
166. _____, *The Implications of Cost-Effectiveness Analysis of Medical Technology*, GPO stock No. 052-003-00765-7 (Washington, D.C.: U.S. Government Printing Office, August 1980).
167. _____, *The Implications of Cost-Effectiveness Analysis of Medical Technology/Background Paper #3: The Efficacy and Cost-Effectiveness of Psychotherapy*, GPO stock No. 052-003-00783-5 (Washington, D.C.: U.S. Government Printing Office, October 1980).
168. _____, *Strategies for Medical Technology Assessment*, in press, 1982.
169. Over, A. M., Jr., Williams College, Williamstown, Mass., personal communication, Dec. 9, 1980.
170. Over, A. M., Jr., et al., "A Model of the Demand for Durable Medical Equipment," submitted to the Health Care Financing Administration, Department of Health, Education, and Welfare, March 1980.
171. Ozer, M. N., "The Assessment/Evaluation Methodology in Use With Handicapped Persons," contract paper submitted to the Office of Technology Assessment, U.S. Congress, Washington, D.C., June 1981.
172. _____, "A Cybernetic Approach to Assessment: A Problem Solving Planning System," in *A Cybernetic Approach to the Assessment of Children: Toward a More Humane Use of Human Beings*, M. N. Ozer (ed.) (Boulder, Colo.: Westview Press, 1979).
173. _____, *Solving Learning and Behavior Problems of Children: A Planning System Integrating Assessment and Treatment* (San Francisco: Jossey-Bass Publishers, 1980).
174. Paine, R. S., et al., "A Study of Minimal Cerebral Dysfunction," *Develop. Med. & Child Neurol.* 10:505, 1968.
175. Parker, L., Kennedy Institute for Rehabilitation, Baltimore, Md., personal comunication, Dec. 1, 1980.

176. People-to-People Committee for the Handicapped, *Directory of Organizations Interested in the Handicapped, 1980-81 Edition* (Washington, D.C.: People-to-People Committee for the Handicapped, 1980).
177. Phonic Ear/Phonic Mirror, *Echo On* 2(4), Mill Valley, Calif., 1980.
178. _____, "Medicaid Funding for Electronic Communication Aids," June 1980.
179. Plourde, P. J., et al., *Comprehensive Management Information System for the State/Federal Vocational Rehabilitation Program: Final Systems Design* (Cambridge, Mass.: Abt Associates, Inc., July 1981).
180. President's Committee on Employment of the Handicapped, *Disabled USA* (published bimonthly until 1982; and quarterly thereafter).
181. _____, *National Health Care Policies for the Handicapped: A Report to the President by the National Health Care Policies for the Handicapped Working Group*, fall 1978.
182. Price, M., and Goodman, L., "Individualized Education Programs: A Cost Study," *Exceptional Child.* 36:446, 1980.
183. Purtilo, R., *Justice, Liberty, Compassion: Analysis of and Implications for "Humane" Health Care and Rehabilitation in the United States: Some Lessons From Sweden*, Monograph No. 8 (New York: World Rehabilitation Fund, Inc., 1981).
184. Queene, R., Administration on Developmental Disabilities, Office of Human Development Services, Department of Health and Human Services, Washington, D.C., personal communication, Jan. 15, 1982.
185. Randal, J., "What's New in Medicine," *New York Daily News*, Sunday Magazine, May 4, 1980, p. 48.
186. Reiss, J. B., Health Care Financing Administration, Washington, D.C., "Technology Assessment and Paying for Medical Services Provided Patients," first draft, unpublished paper, Apr. 6, 1981.
187. Rehabilitation Engineering Center, Children's Hospital at Stanford, *Team Assessment of Device Effectiveness*, 1980.
188. Research Triangle Institute, *National Survey of Individualized Education Programs (IEPs) for Handicapped Children*, 1980.
189. Reynolds, M., "The Production Engineering Process," *Communication Outlook* 2(4), 1980.
190. Ris, C., "Electronic Age Brings New Aids for the Disabled, But Economics Put Them Out of Reach of Many," *Wall Street Journal*, p. 52, Aug. 26, 1980.

191. Rucker, C. N., "Technical Language in the School Psychologist's Report," *Psychol. Schools* 4:145, 1967.
192. Ruggles, V., Associate Director of Patient and Community Services, Muscular Dystrophy Association, New York City, "Funding of Non-Vocal Communication Aids: Curent Issues and Strategies," unpublished paper, circa 1980 (date unknown).
193. Schecter, M., Expert Consultant, Office of Information, National Institute on Aging, Bethesda, Md., personal communication, Dec. 3, 1980.
194. Schipper, W., "Financial and Administrative Considerations," *J. School Health* 50(5):228, 1980.
195. Seitz, V., et al., "Effects of Place of Testing on the Peabody Picture Vocabulary Test Scores of Disadvantaged Head Start and Non-Head-Start Children," *Child Develop.* 46:481, 1975.
196. Sherwood, S., and Morris, J., *Executive Summary of a Study of the Effects of An Emergency Response System for the Aged: A Final Report* (Hyattsville, Md.: National Center for Health Services Research Report, Department of Health, Education, and Welfare, February 1980).
197. Sigelman, C., et. al., *Human Rehabilitation Techniques, A Technology Assessment*, vol. 2 (Washington, D.C.: National Science Foundation, 1977).
198. Slater, R., Medical Director, and Shala, B., Public Information Officer, The National Multiple Sclerosis Society, New York City, personal communication, Jan. 18, 1981.
199. Sontag, S., *Illness as Metaphor* (New York: Farrar, Straus & Giroux, 1978).
200. Spiegel, A., and Podair, S. (eds.), *Rehabilitating People With Disabilities Into the Mainstream of Society* (Park Ridge, N.J.: Noyes Medical Publications, 1981).
201. Stedman, D., "Service Delivery Systems," in *The White House Conference on Handicapped Individuals, Volume One: Awareness Papers* (Washington, D.C.: U.S. Government Printing Office, 1977).
202. Stoneman, Z., and Gibson, S., "Situational Influences on Assessment Performance," *Exceptional Child.* 45:166, 1978.
203. Tallent, N., and Reiss, W. J., "The Trouble With Psychological Reports," *J. Clin. Psych.* 15:444, 1959.
204. Thomas, S., et al., "Examiner Effect in IQ Testing of Puerto Rican Working Class Children," *Amer. J. Orthopsych.* 41:809, 1971.
205. Tobias, J., and Nevins, B., Center for Independent Living, Berkeley, Calif., "Rehabilitation Tech-

nology: Delivery System and Its Gaps," unpublished paper, December 1980.
206. Toms, L., et al., "Examples of Independent Living Services: Their Components, and Their Users, Working Paper" (Berkeley, Calif.: Berkeley Planning Associates, September 1979).
207. Tscos, P., and Bluestein, M., Lifeline Systems, Inc., Watertown, Mass., personal communication, January 1981.
208. Urban Institute, *Report of the Comprehensive Service Needs Study*, report submitted to the Rehabilitation Services Administration, Office of Human Development Services, U.S. Department of Health, Education, and Welfare, Washington, D.C., June 23, 1975.
209. U.S. House of Representatives, Committee on Education and Labor, Subcommittee on Select Education, *Oversight Hearings on Public Law 94-142* (Washington, D.C.: U.S. Government Printing Office, 1980).
210. U.S. House of Representatives, Committee on Science and Technology, *Report of the Panel on Research Programs To Aid the Handicapped* (Washington, D.C.: U.S. Government Printing Office, April 1977).
211. U.S. House of Representatives, Committee on Science and Technology; and U.S. Senate, Committee on Labor and Human Resources, *Application of Technology to Handicapped Individuals: Process, Problems, and Progress* (Washington, D.C.: U.S. Government Printing Office, Mar. 16, 1981).
212. U.S. House of Representatives, Committee on Ways and Means, Subcommittee on Social Security, *Status of the Disability Insurance Program* (Washington, D.C.: U.S. Government Printing Office, Mar. 16, 1981).
213. U.S. Senate, Committee on Finance, *Issues Related to Social Security Act Disability Programs* (Washington, D.C.: U.S. Government Printing Office, 1979).
214. U.S. Senate, Committee on Labor and Human Resources, Subcommittee on the Handicapped, *Rehabilitation, Comprehensive Services and Developmental Disabilities Legislation* (Washington, D.C.: U.S. Government Printing Office, August 1979).
215. U.S. Senate, Committee on Veterans' Affairs, *Veterans' Disability Compensation and Survivors' Benefit Amendments of 1980*, hearing June 17, 1980 (Washington, D.C.: U.S. Government Printing Office, 1980).
216. Utterback, J. M., "Innovation in Industry and the Diffusion of Technology," *Science* 183:620, 1974.
217. Verville, R. E., "The Disabled, Rehabilitation and Current Public Policy," in *Rehabilitating People With Disabilities Into the Mainstream of Society*, A. Spiegel and S. Posair (eds.) (Park Ridge, N.J.: Noyes Medical Publications, 1981).
218. Veterans Administration, *Annual Reports on the Exchange of Medical Information and Sharing Medical Resources, FY 1979*, prepared for the Committee on Veterans Affairs, U.S. House of Representatives, Committee Print No. 57 (Washington, D.C.: U.S. Government Printing Office, 1980).
219. _____, Department of Medicine and Surgery, Prosthetic Sensory Aids Service, *Bulletin of Prosthetics Research*, (published quarterly).
220. Weintraub, P., "Wired for Sound," *Discover* 1(3):50, 1980.
221. Wenchel, H. E., *A Profile of the Medical Technology Industry and Government Policies* (Washington, D.C.: Arthur Young & Co., 1981).
222. White, E., "P. L. 94-142's Touchiest Topics: Health Care, Discipline, Summer School," *Amer. Sch. Board J.* 168:19, 1981.
223. Whitehead, C., Policy Analyst, Office of the Secretary, Department of Health and Human Services, Washington, D.C., "Employment and Training of Handicapped Individuals," unpublished paper, Feb. 2, 1981.
224. _____, personal communication, Jan. 18, 1981.
225. _____, personal communication, Jan. 26, 1981.
226. *White House Conference on Handicapped Individuals, Volume One: Awareness Papers* (Washington, D.C.: U.S. Government Printing Office, May 1977).
227. Whitten, R. P., "Technology Transfer: NASA's Bioengineering-Applications Program," *Med. Dev. & Diagn. Ind. Monthly*, September 1980.
228. Williams, E., Nutritionist, Office of Technology Assessment, U.S. Congress, Washington, D.C., personal communication, Jan. 25, 1981.
229. Wood, P., *Impairment, Disability, Handicap: Toward the Development of a Functional Information System* (New York: World Rehabilitation Fund, in press).
230. Yoshida, R., et al., "Group Decision Making in the Planning Team Process: Myth or Reality?" *J. School Psych.* 16:237, 1978.
231. Ysseldyke, J., "Who's Calling the Plays in School Psychology?" *Psychol. Schools* 15:373, 1978.
232. Zigler, E., et al., "Motivational Factors in the Performance of Economically Disadvantaged Children on the Peabody Picture of Economically Disadvantaged Children on the Peabody Picture Vocabulary Test," *Child Develop.* 44:294, 1973.

Springer publishing company

Springer Series on REHABILITATION

Editor: Thomas E. Backer, Ph.D.
Human Interaction Research Institute, Los Angeles

Volume 1
THE PSYCHOLOGY OF DISABILITY

CAROLYN VASH, Ph.D. An incisive, insightful, and highly readable account of what it is like to be disabled and how health professionals can help individuals with disabilities cope constructively with their problems.

Part I describes the barriers disabled people face in performing everyday activities, their psychological reactions, and the resources that are available for overcoming these difficulties. Part II delineates various therapeutic strategies for helping disabled people, including both traditional services, such as psychotherapy and family counseling, and nontraditional approaches such as peer counseling and Eastern psychological approaches.
288 pages / 1981 / hardcover

Volume 2
DISABLED PEOPLE AS SECOND-CLASS CITIZENS

MYRON G. EISENBERG, Ph.D., CYNTHIA GRIGGINS, and RICHARD J. DUVAL, editors. This text looks at disability from a variety of perspectives — political, social, psychological, economic and educational. It details the prejudicial and discriminatory practices encountered by disabled people in their attempt to enter the mainstream of American society and presents methods that can be employed to remediate this situation.

Four areas are explored: societal attitudes toward the disabled; institutional and bureaucratic contributions to discriminatory practice; how the individual can cope psychologically with physical disability and discrimination; and how collective action can be directed against discrimination.
320 pages / 1981 / hardcover

Volume 3
BEHAVIORAL APPROACHES TO REHABILITATION

ELAINE GREIF, Ph.D. and RUTH G. MATARAZZO, Ph.D. A practical handbook for the application of behavioral strategies to the rehabilitation patient. The reader is afforded both an understanding of patients' psychological functioning in a variety of situations, and effective approaches and strategies in working with patients and their families during rehabilitation.
176 pages / 1981 / hardcover

Order from your bookdealer or directly from publisher.

Springer Publishing Co. 200 Park Ave. South, New York, NY 10003

Springer publishing company

"An excellent resource for those interested in the broader scope of rehabilitation." —Physical Therapy

ANNUAL REVIEW OF REHABILITATION

Elizabeth L. Pan, Ph.D., Thomas E. Backer, Ph.D., and Carolyn L. Vash, Ph.D., Editors

"The 20 contributing authors are administrators and psychologists and these professionals have presented comprehensive and well-written articles. The editors have made an effort to provide a balance of topics relevant to practitioners, administrators and researchers."—Physical Therapy (on Vol. 1)

Volume 3 • Contents (partial):

M.G. Eisenberg and M.A. Jansen, Rehabilitation Psychology: The State of the Art • S.G. Fey and W.E. Fordyce, Behavioral Rehabilitation of the Chronic Pain Patient • M. Brown, W.A. Gordon and L. Diller, Functional Assessment and Outcome Measurement: An Integrative Review • R.G. Hadley and P.A. Hadley, Rehabilitation of People with Alcohol Problems • F.M. Bucks and G.W. Hohmann, Parental Disability and Children's Adjustment • G.G. March, G.W. Ellison and C. Strite, Psychosocial and Vocational Approaches to Multiple Sclerosis

352pp, 1983

Volume 2 • Contents (partial)

C.A. Peck, T. Apolloni and T.P. Cook, Rehabilitation Services for Americans with Mental Retardation • M. Berkowitz, Disincentives and the Rehabilitation of Disabled Persons • D.J. Dunn, Current Placement Trends • R.T. Fraser, Epilepsy • J.F. Jonas, Cerebral Palsy • B.J. Kemp, Case Management Model of Human Service Delivery

320pp, 1981

Volume 1 • Contents (partial)

Howard Rusk, M.D., Foreword • R. Humphreys, Disability in America: 1980 and Beyond • C. Vash, Sheltered Industrial Employment • J.E. Bitter, Continuing Education in Rehabilitation • L. Barrett/S. Shea, Developing Evaluation Standards for Vocational Rehabilitation • T.E. Backer, New Directions in Rehabilitation Outcome Measurement • G.S. Brody/M. Johnson, Rehabilitation Following Severe Burns

416pp, 1980

Order from your bookdealer or directly from publisher.

Springer Publishing Co. 200 Park Ave. South, New York, NY 10003